MW01518967

Chrys Miranda
54 De Alwis Place
Dehiwela

Economic Change and Political Conflict in Developing Countries with Special Reference to Sri Lanka

Sirimal Abeyratne

VU University Press
Amsterdam 1998

Dedicated to
Sirimalie, Chathu and Anju

The series Sri Lanka Studies in the Humanities and the Social Sciences was established in order to provide a quick avenue for publishing the results of original research on Sri Lanka. It is a monographs series. These monographs are exclusively in English but all volumes will contain brief summaries in Sinhala and in Tamil. An international board of editors guarantees the quality of the series.

EDITORIAL BOARD
Leslie Gunawardana (University of Peradeniya, Sri Lanka)
Peter Kloos (Vrije Universiteit Amsterdam, The Netherlands)
Eric Meyer (Centre d'Etudes de l'Inde et de l'Asie du Sud, Paris, France)
Gananath Obeyesekere (University of Princeton, USA)
Jonathan Spencer (University of Edinburgh, Great Britain)

EDITOR IN CHARGE
Peter Kloos

OTHER VOLUMES IN THE SERIES

No. 1   Sirimal Abeyratne – *Anti-Export Bias in the 'Export-Oriented' Economy of Sri Lanka*, 1993

No. 2   Josine van der Horst – *'Who Is He, What Is He Doing'. Religious Rhetoric and Perfomances in Sri Lanka during R. Premadasa's Presidency (1989-1993)*, 1995

No. 3   Birgitte Refslund Sørensen – *Relocated Lives: Displacement and Resettlement within the Mahaweli Project, Sri Lanka*, 1996

No. 4   Jagath P. Senaratne – *Political Violence in Sri Lanka, 1977–1990. Riots, Insurrections, Counter-insurgencies, Foreign Intervention*, 1997

No. 5   Marianne Nürnberger – *Dance is the Languange of the Gods; The Chitrasena School and the Traditional Roots of Sri Lankan Stage-dance*, 1998

VU University Press is an imprint of:
VU Boekhandel/Uitgeverij bv
De Boelelaan 1105
1081 HV Amsterdam
The Netherlands

tel.   +31 (0)20 6444355
fax   +31 (0)20 6462719

isbn   90-5383-606-3

layout by Sjoukje Rienks, Amsterdam
cover photo: Members of the armed forces inspecting the bomb blast of 17 October 1997 at the World Trade Centre, courtesy Associated Press/Gemunu Amarashinghe
cover design by Auke Bender, Amsterdam

© S. Abeyratne, Amsterdam 1998
All rights reserved. No part of this book may be reproduced, stored in a retrieval system, or transmitted, in any form of by any means, electronic, mechanical, photocopying, recording, or otherwise, without the prior written permission of the holder of the copyright.

Table of Contents

Acknowledgements

I was able to develop new insights into development economics from a multi-disciplinary perspective largely because of the teaching and intellectual inspiration of my promotors Professor Dr Peter Kloos and Professor Dr W.D. Lakshman. I express my sincere gratitude to them for their valuable guidance. The valuable contributions and assistance of many scholars in Sri Lanka as well as in the Netherlands at various stages of this study are also highly appreciated. I owe thanks to Mr Sarath Vidanagama, Head of the Department of Economics of the University of Colombo for his support. I extend my gratitude to Howard Nicholas not only for his assistance, which enabled me to carry out this study, but also for his guidance, which inspired me to understand the real world of economics. I received invaluable comments from my colleagues at the PhD research group of the Vrije Universiteit of Amsterdam. I am grateful particularly to Josine van der Horst, Therese Onderdenwijngaard, Piyal de Silva, Jagath Senaratne and all those who commented at various seminars on earlier drafts of the chapters of the study. I owe a special word of thanks to Mr Bandula Samarasinghe and the late Ms P. Thilakaratne for their personal contribution to my studies in the Netherlands.

I am grateful to the University of Colombo (Sri Lanka)—Institute of Social Studies (the Netherlands) Co-operation Project for sponsoring this study in the Netherlands, and to the Institute of Social Studies for providing study facilities during my stay in the Netherlands. I thank especially Ms Els Mulder, Head of the Project, and the Project staff at the Institute of Social Studies and at the University of Colombo, as well as the staff of the Institute of Social Studies, for their assistance and co-operation. I extend my thanks to the officials of the Central Bank, the Department of Census and Statistics, the University Grants Commission and various other institutions in Sri Lanka for their friendly assistance in collecting data for the study. My thanks are due to L.H. Tilakaratne and H.B.V. Susantha for their assistance in collecting data. I am grateful to E.C. Vasanthan for translating the summary of the study into Tamil, to Jacqueline de Vries, for editing, and to Sjoukje Rienks for formatting the text.

I wish to thank Ranjith Kaluthanthiri, Ben White, Ratna Saptari, K.L. Chandratilleke, Jacque van der Bos, Gonny van der Bos, Athula Ranasinghe, Margerita van Oel, Jaseentha D'Silva, K. Rabindran, and many other friends who made my stay in the Netherlands pleasant. I am grateful to all those who were not mentioned here, but helped me in bringing this work to completion. Finally, my special thanks are due to my wife Sirimalie and my two little daughters Chathu and Anju, for being with me as well as for being without me, patiently, during the course of the study. It is to my wife and two daughters that I dedicate this work.

Sirimal Abeyratne
Vrije Universiteit Amsterdam
January 1998

List of Tables and Charts

Tables

Chapter II

Charts

Chapter IV

Chapter V

Chapter VI

Chapter VII

Acronyms and Abbreviations

AKUF	Arbeitsgemeinschaft Kriegsursachenforschung, Hamburg University, Germany
CBSL	Central Bank of Sri Lanka
CFSs	Consumer Finance Surveys of Sri Lanka
CP	Communist Party
DCS	Department of Census and Statistics of Sri Lanka
ECLA	Economic Commission for Latin America
FP	Federal Party
GCE (AL)	General Certificate of Education (Advanced Level) – replacement of HSC
GCE (OL)	General Certificate of Education (Ordinary Level) – replacement of SSC
HDI	Human Development Index
HDR	Human Development Report
HSC	High School Certificate - replaced by GCE (AL)
IBRD	International Bank for Reconstruction and Development
ILO	International Labour Organization (Office), Geneva
IMF	International Monetary Fund
IPKF	Indian Peace Keeping Force
JVP	Janatha Vimukthi Peramuna (People's Liberation Front)
LSSP	Lanka Sama Samaja Party (Lanka Equal Society Party)
LTTE	Liberation Tigers of Tamil Eelam
MEHE	Ministry of Education and Higher Education, Sri Lanka
MEP	Mahajana Eksath Peramuna (People's United Front)
MPE	Ministry of Planning and Employment, Sri Lanka
NICs	Newly Industrialized Countries
NPC	National Planning Council, Sri Lanka
OECD	Organization for Economic Cooperation and Development
PCY	Presidential Commission on Youth
PIOOM	Programma Interdisciplinair Onderzoek naar Oorzaken van Mensenrechtenschendingen, Leiden University, The Netherlands
PPP	Purchasing Power Parity
PQLI	Physical Quality of Life Index
ROE	Review of the Economy/Annual Report of the Economy, CBSL
SIPRI	Stockholm International Peace Research Institute, Stockholm, Sweden

SLFP	Sri Lanka Freedom Party
SLRs	Sri Lanka Rupees
SSA	Social Scientists' Association, Sri Lanka
SSC	Senior School Certificate - replaced by GCE (OL)
TULF	Tamil United Liberation Front
UGC	University Grants Commission, Sri Lanka
UNDP	United Nations Development Programme
UNHCR	United Nations High Commissioner for Refugees
UNP	United National Party
UNRISD	United Nations Research Institute for Social Development
UTHR	University Teachers for Human Rights (Jaffna), Sri Lanka
WDR	World Development Report

Introduction

I

The purpose of this study is to provide a framework for understanding the economic dimensions of political conflicts in developing countries, and to use that framework to examine the Sri Lankan experience. In particular, I attempt to develop a conceptual framework to explain the emergence of political conflicts in the context of local and global economic transformation. This conceptual framework makes use of existing ideas, concepts and theoretical guidelines, which were not necessarily developed for the purpose of analysing political conflicts, to study political conflicts in Sri Lanka.

This study is relevant to developing countries in general. In the decades following the Second World War, political conflicts and the resultant organized armed struggles appear to have been concentrated largely in the so-called 'developing' region of the world: developing countries are much more exposed to political conflicts than developed countries are. Moreover, the great majority of these conflicts has been *intrastate*, even though they exhibited features of external relations and external involvement. These modern political conflicts seem to have been organized on either territorial bases, in futile attempts to equate 'nation' with 'state', or political power bases within the state, in attempts to bring about changes in the existing political system.

The nature of modern political conflicts and their geographical location gives rise to two questions: why have political conflicts been concentrated in developing countries, and can the issue be tackled by a generalized approach? There is little doubt that the specificity of political conflicts in the modern world challenges universalist and static theoretical approaches. A theoretical framework free from the problem of over-generalization is called for.

Aside from Marxism, there is no economic theory dedicated to the explanation of political conflict. Yet modern political conflicts are not the class conflict treated in Marxism. They occur more in underdeveloped than in developed capitalist societies, they are rooted more in the peasantry than in the industrial working class, and they are motivated more by nationalism than by class solidarity (Moore 1993). At least in the case of developing countries, a Marxist approach which views a particular form of political conflict as the driving force of social change tends to over-generalize. Neo-Marxist theorists have provided a good deal of theoretical insight into the problem of political conflicts in developing countries (Amin 1976, Emmanuel 1972, Wallerstein 1979). But the theoretical bases of the neo-Marxist paradigm inevitably lead to the pessimistic conclusion that 'underdeveloped' economies in the capitalist world are subject to an increasing 'peripheralization', which leads to political conflicts. These theories are reductionist in their emphasis on the centre-periphery relationship.

The economic aspects of political conflict are analysed in modernization theory. Modernization theory does not refer to a unified approach: everything related to 'modernity' can be incorporated into the term (Harrison 1988). In contrast to the neo-Marxist notion of the inevitable deepening of the centre-periphery divide, the more optimistic modernization view holds that there is a single path to development, a path available to all societies (Davies 1962, Eisenstadt 1966, Huntington 1968, Moore 1964, Smelser 1963a). Until recently, the modernization approaches, which view political conflicts as an 'intermediate phase' in the linear modernization process, could not be considered free of over-generalization. Generally speaking, modernization theory does not primarily aim to explain political conflict: political conflict is implicit rather than explicit.

Unlike the older notion that conflicts are a by-product of the modernization process, a more recently developed notion is more sceptical of the development project, and shares some fundamental features with the neo-Marxist paradigm. These approaches to modernization and development (Alvares 1992, Apter 1987, Marglin & Marglin 1990, Sachs 1992, Schrijvers 1993) opine that the Western capitalist form of development cannot be reproduced, as is evidenced by the civil conflict, environmental destruction and other social calamities of the past decades. I argue that economic change in developing countries is influenced by both local and global forces and is not linear, either towards 'peripheralization' or 'development', as there are wide variations in economic performance in different countries.

There is also a separate body of theories of conflict, violence and revolution which has been discussed and debated widely in recent sociological and psychological literature (Aya 1990, Gurr 1993, Rule 1988). At an analytical level, however, the usefulness of theories such as *rising expectation* (Smelser 1963b), *relative deprivation* (Gurr 1970) and *political calculation* (Tilly 1978) is confined to the sociological and psychological mechanisms of political conflict. They prove to be of limited use when it comes to analysing economic, cultural, or political problems. The focus of these theories is on a particular aspect or a stage of a multi-faceted complex process of political conflicts evolving from various forms of social tensions to collective violence or war. Nor do these theories distinguish 'developing' countries. The present study focuses not on the mechanisms of collective violence or war, but on the economic reality underlying the emergence of political conflicts in developing countries. Therefore, the study strives to provide an economic analysis which will complement the social science literature on political conflicts.

The importance of the study of political conflict in Sri Lanka is readily apparent from even a glance at the recent history of the country. During the last three decades or so, Sri Lanka has experienced a twin political conflict in the Southern and Northern parts of the country, at a cost of some 100,000 human lives, the displacement of people, the destruction of physical property and economic activity, and impediments to economic growth.

Sri Lanka has often been described as an exceptional case in the Third World in terms of its human development record (e.g. Bhalla 1988, Isenman 1980, Lal & Rajapathirana 1989) and democratic political liberalism (e.g. Jupp 1978, Kearney 1973, Wilson 1979). But the country's economic prosperity did not last for more than a decade after Independence in 1948. The extensive welfare system was continued, although its continuation became increasingly onerous in the face of declining economic capacity. Along with its economic performance, the country's democratic political system and territorial unity came under increasing threat. In 1971, there was a youth insurrection aimed at capturing state power, among the Sinhala community, the ethnic group which accounted for nearly three-fourths of the population. The 1980s were marked by a twin escalation of armed conflict among the Sinhala and Tamil youth. Due to the operations of the youth movements, coupled with the state-sponsored violence, political violence became a regular feature of day-to-day life in Sri Lanka (Chandraprema 1991, Gunaratna 1990, Manor 1984, O'Ballance 1989, Piyadasa 1984, Ram 1989, UTHR 1994). The Sinhala youth insurrection, which erupted in the late 1980s for the second time, was repressed mercilessly but temporarily. As repressive military measures do not provide a solution to the problems underlying political conflicts, it remains to be seen whether political violence will erupt again in the future. While the Sinhala youth were active in the Southern provinces, youth movements of the Tamil community—the country's second largest ethnic group, which accounted for about one-eighth of the population—gradually developed into a guerrilla struggling for a separate Tamil state in the Northern and Eastern provinces.

The economic dimension of political conflict in Sri Lanka has been largely ignored in social science studies. This is because the issue of political conflict has been studied overwhelmingly from sociological, anthropological and political science perspectives. These studies provide little scope to analyse the economic dimensions of the country's political conflict. In the rare instances that the economic dimensions have been brought into the picture, analysis has been impeded by reductionist and voluntarist arguments resulting from the absence of a rigorous conceptual formulation.

The Tamil separatist movement has been widely studied, through the perspectives on ethno-nationalism (Hennayake 1992, 1993, Kumaraswamy 1987, Silva 1986, Spencer 1990, Tambiah 1986, SSA 1985), political change, ethnocentric politics and political discrimination (Hubbell 1990, Ponnambalam 1983, Silva 1986, Silva 1995, Sivanandan 1984, Tambiah 1992, Wilson 1988), changing class and communal relationships (Jayawardena 1984, 1985, 1987, Rogers 1994) as well as the dismantling of democracy (Manor 1984, Moore 1992). Not surprisingly, some of the discussions on the Tamil movement have been clouded by ideological and dogmatic positions.

The available studies on the Sinhala youth insurrection have focused on the frustration and disappointment of the Sinhala youth, resulting from socio-economic change and modernization in Sri Lanka (Hettige 1992, Ivan 1989, Moore 1993, Obeyesekere 1974). However, the analysts from various perspectives seem to have been interested more in the Tamil problem than the Sinhala problem. The two facets of the country's political conflict, i.e. the Tamil separatist movement and the Sinhala youth insurrection, have been discussed as analytically separate issues, because they seem to exhibit certain distinct traits. Oberst (1991) and Kloos (1993) are among the few who have seen the Sinhala and Tamil political problems as sharing common ground. The former explored the distribution of certain scarce economic resources as a source of frustration, while the latter discussed the issue as a challenge faced by the modern state in the processes of globalization and localization.

A few studies have elaborated on the significance of some economic factors to the evolution of the Tamil separatist movement (Gunasinghe 1984, Nithiyanandan 1987, Oberst 1986, 1991) and Sinhala youth insurrection (Dharmasena & Karunaratne 1993, Ivan 1989, Lakshman 1992). Gunasinghe (1984) analysed the impact of both regulatory and liberal Sri Lankan regimes on ethnic relations, while Nithiyanandan (1987) and Oberst (1986) focused on discriminative state policies affecting the economic gains of Tamils. The economic studies on the Sinhala youth insurrection analysed the impact of economic policy on the distribution of gains among the rural youth. Apart from these studies, however, coherent economic analyses of the evolution of Sri Lanka's political conflict are hardly available.

The country's political conflict appears to be an issue of topical interest in the economic discipline. In economic development studies, the problems in the country's economic history have been widely discussed. Yet the emergence of political conflict appears to have been regarded as an issue with which economists have nothing to do, and which is better left to other social scientists. However, the available evidence suggests that the economic and sociological perspectives are not mutually exclusive and that the discussion of the issue of political conflicts cannot be carried out fruitfully within the confines of strict disciplinary boundaries.

The argument which I develop in this study is to be understood in the context of the economic 'development'—or, to use a more accurate term, in my view, economic 'transformation'—in developing societies. The problem of development in a developing economy is a creation of the process of development itself. The basic development problem faced by developing countries has been to generate economic resources and opportunities to meet the rising demand for socio-economic advancement in the context of local and global economic transformation. I use the term 'socio-economic advancement' to indicate individual and collective upward social mobility, in terms of both ascribed and perceived status derived from material possessions, consumption, income, education, career prospects and other such things.

The rising social aspirations can be analysed in two ways, in relation (a) to globalization—the formation of a world society—and (b) to development achievement itself. In developing economies which have been integrating with the global economy and which have been becoming exposed to global technological change, the rising aspirations for socio-economic advancement are increasingly governed by forces beyond the control of the people or the state. The achievements of development aspirations and the provision of basic needs solve the problems at one level, and create more problems at higher levels of socio-economic advancement. However, development achievements are rationalized as desirable and interdependent in the development and modernization theories. But development results in an increasing scarcity of economic resources and opportunities in relation to rising social expectations and increasing limits on the generation and distribution of resources. Consequently, development creates a 'development paradox' in developing countries, as it raises expectations, increases scarcity and limits possibilities. The development paradox results in a growing 'social exclusion' that triggers off a process of localization—a formation of relatively smaller social groups.

In the Sri Lankan case, I contend that the economic dimension of political conflicts should take into account the salient characteristics of the economic transformation of the country, where the domestic economy is a sub-system of a global economy. The economies in the modern world are no longer viewed as analytically separate systems, as they have become increasingly integrated with the global economy through global technological transformation and the institutionalization of a market system. Many of the empirical studies on the economic dimensions of political conflicts in different countries have viewed internal economic discrimination or distribution as the economic sources of political conflicts (Lewis 1985, Samarasinghe & Coughlan 1991, Wyzan 1990). Internal factors are not unimportant, but they are not analytically separate issues which might be dealt with simply by rectifying domestic policy. From an economic point of view, the distributive implications of economic resources play a major role in the evolution of political conflicts, but they need to be approached from a wider perspective, incorporating both local and global economic dynamics.

Thus, I perceive internal and external dimensions in the economic analysis of Sri Lanka's political conflict. Internally, the welfare state, the liberal democratic system, economic policy and demographic trends, along with the country's economic transformation should receive due consideration. Externally, the effects of global technological and institutional transformations on the relative scarcity and the distribution of domestic economic resources as well as on the development of people's aspirations for socio-economic advancement should receive due consideration.

The scope

The term 'political conflicts' is used generally to explain either *active* or *potential* use of collective violence to achieve a specified political objective. The use of collective violence is the manifestation of political conflicts and the means of achieving the pre-determined objectives, when the achievement is not possible using non-violent means. However, for analytical purposes, data on the *actual* manifestation of political conflicts must be used, as the potential use of collective violence is implicit rather than explicit. The actual use of collective violence means the deliberate destruction of persons or property by people acting together (Rule 1988: 11). However, it is true that the demand for a comprehensive and useful definition of a social phenomenon such as 'political conflicts' is often a source of controversy (Popper 1952, Aya 1990). It is not my purpose to become involved in this study in this controversy on terms and definitions.

In my analysis, I do not pay much attention to the mechanisms of the actual use of collective violence, as my major concern is with the historical formation of political conflict in Sri Lanka. Thus, the study basically analyses not the 'mechanism' of collective violence, but *economic* change under which people can be mobilized to make use of collective violence in the last stage of the formation of political conflicts. I limit the empirical investigation to major areas of economic transformation, which I consider the most important aspects of an economic analysis. The empirical analysis of the Sri Lankan case is confined to the post-independence period, from 1948 to the 1980s, which is the period of the formation of the present political conflict of the country and its eruption into armed struggle. However, in many cases the parameters of the present political conflict were already set out in the British colonial period. Thus, where it is necessary, I undertake investigations into the period before independence as well.

The use of data

The empirical analysis of the study is based on socio-economic data for Sri Lanka from a macro perspective. It basically deals with the historical patterns of the generation and distribution of the economic resources required to meet the society's expectations of socio-economic advancement, and their implications on the intensification of social exclusion and the formation of political conflicts. The data required for the analysis have been primarily obtained from secondary sources.

Regarding patterns and historical trends of socio-economic and demographic variables, two types of survey data, one from the Consumer Finance Surveys (CFSs) of the Central Bank of Sri Lanka (CBSL) and the other from the population census data of the Department of Census and Statistics (DCS) of Sri Lanka, provide useful information. For the international comparison of armed conflict, data from publications of the UNDP, UNHCR, SIPRI and some other research institutes have been used. National accounts data from the CBSL for Sri Lanka and from the World Bank for international comparisons have been used. In addition, data compiled at the University Grants Commission (UGC) provide information on higher education.

It is not surprising that aggregate data present a generalized picture. This typical limitation is unavoidable in macro analyses, but I attempt to discuss the variations that exist within macro variables. CFSs in Sri Lanka were carried out for 1953, 1963, 1971, 1978/79, 1981/82 and 1986/89. In the last CFS of 1986/87, the Northern and Eastern provinces were not included, due to difficulties in conducting the surveys under the conditions of a civil war. However, this is not regarded as a limitation of the study, because by definition the most important period of time that I should take into account is from independence to the early 1980s. The same problem arises in the population census. The practice of taking population censuses commenced in Sri Lanka in the late eighteenth century, but for the purpose of the study I use census data from 1946, 1953, 1963, 1971 and 1981. Due to the war in the Northern and Eastern provinces, censuses have not been carried out since then.

An important limitation of an historical analysis based on survey data is the comparability of data, due to the changes in classifications, particularly with respect to CFSs and population census data. In many cases, I have reclassified data, for the sake of both comparability and simplicity. In certain cases, however, I have had to resort to using the same classifications used in the surveys. In these cases, I have made reference to the problem of comparability.

Organization

The study comprises eight chapters. In Chapter 2, I focus on a statistical analysis of the regional distribution of political conflicts in the world during the decades following the Second World War. In terms of the 'intensity' of political conflicts, I argue that the developing countries have been exposed more to political conflicts than developed countries, while a large share of these political conflicts has been intrastate in character. With a brief discussion of the distinctive economic characteristics of developing countries in contrast to developed countries, I formulate the groundwork for a conceptual framework to address political conflicts in developing countries. Against this background, in Chapter 3 I undertake a critical evaluation of traditional economic approaches to political conflicts. My focus in this discussion is on three dominant theoretical perspectives: classical Marxism, the neo-Marxist paradigm and liberal modernization theory. I argue that none of these theories is appropriate to understand political conflicts in developing countries.

I attempt to conceptualize an economic analytical framework in Chapter 4 to address the case of intrastate political conflicts in developing countries. Having admitted that there are variations in economic transformation in the context of local and global forces of economic change, I argue that political conflicts in developing countries are associated strongly with the problem of development. The basic development problem is not the provision of 'basic needs' but the ability and the commitment of the state and the society in individual developing countries to generate economic resources and opportunities to meet the rising expectations of society. The development process can result in a growing 'social exclusion', as opposed to the 'social inclusion' which is expected from development. Social exclusion, compounded by many other factors outside the economic arena, constitutes a fertile ground for political conflicts.

The next three chapters are devoted to the analysis of the Sri Lankan case of political conflicts. Chapter 5 provides an overview of the formation of political conflict in Sri Lanka against the development of the country's economic crisis. I argue that the formation of a competitive society and its consumer-orientation at the expense of economic growth coupled with political and demographic trends has played a major role in the formation of political conflict. In relation to rising expectations, the economy has made little progress. This has led to an increase in the scarcity of economic resources and opportunities, and acute social exclusion particularly among the younger generation. In Chapter 6 I discuss the distributive implications of the country's economic crisis and the development of expectations for socio-economic advancement. To address the issue, I select a set of key economic resources and opportunities in terms of income, consumption, education and employment underlying the expectations and achievements of socio-economic advancement. In the discussion, I attempt to highlight that large segments of the population have experienced social exclusion. These segments consist of educated youths with high aspirations but few opportunities. In Chapter 7 I consider some important aspects of communal and regional competition for socio-economic advancement in Sri Lankan society against the growing scarcity of economic resources and opportunities. I discuss the problem of regional and communal competition in terms of employment and education. In concluding the study, in Chapter 8, I first summarize the basic elements of the conceptual framework and empirical findings of the study. Then I address the question of how social exclusion resulting from the development paradox can be an economic source of political conflict.

Developing Countries and Political Conflicts: A New Phenomenon

II

By investigating modern political conflicts in the world, I intend in this chapter to demonstrate the importance of, and to lay the groundwork for, an economic perspective on intrastate political conflicts in developing countries. By political conflicts I mean conflicts characterized by the *actual* or *potential* use of collective violence. A statistical analysis will necessarily be based on the actual manifestation of violence of political conflicts, as the available macro data hardly indicate the potential for political conflicts. On the basis of published statistical data, I will investigate political conflicts in the modern world as they appear in the form of organized armed struggles during the decades following the Second World War.

First, I investigate political conflicts in the modern world in terms of their characteristics. Second, I explore the statistical evidence on the location and the intensity of political conflict. Third, I outline the intensity of militarization in the world with specific reference to the economic and political connections between developed and developing countries. In terms of the intensity of political conflicts and of militarization, I will show that modern political conflicts have been concentrated mainly in the 'developing' regions, while they are also strongly linked to the rest of the world. Finally, in a brief discussion of developing countries, I will outline the distinctive economic features of the developing region.

Postwar trends in political conflicts

Both violent and non-violent forms of action are available to human beings to pursue their goals. When non-violent action does not guarantee the fulfilment of these goals, people might resort to violence. Collective violence is one form of resolution to political conflicts as well as a manifestation of the way in which oppressed groups disrupt law and order.

The demand for comprehensive and useful definitions in social science for a complex phenomenon such as 'political conflicts' constitutes a source of controversy (Aya 1990, Popper 1952). Acknowledging the existence of this controversy, I consider the actual use of collective violence as the 'deliberate destruction of persons or property by people acting together' (Rule 1988: 11). Generally, political conflicts last a long time. They are, moreover, guided by broad political objectives. If they escalate into collective violence, they can threaten the existing political, social and economic system.

The issue of political conflicts has never before drawn as much attention in the media, in international policy and political discussions, as well as in academic debates. These concerns focus on various forms of destruction, international mass population movements due to political conflicts, and the militarization of states and of anti-state forces. Certainly, violent conflict between states and between organized groups including states has been a feature of much of human history (Holsti 1991, Tilly 1993). Nevertheless, the widespread current concern about the issue leads one to hypothesize that there may have been a significant increase in political conflict in the world, whether as a whole or regionally.

Is our world characterized by increasing political conflicts? In my view, there is no clear answer to this question. It is true that people today hear more about political conflicts than they did in the past. This is because people are better informed about political conflicts in all corners of the world than ever before. With the rapid development and expansion of media technology during the last few decades, at least part of the answer to the question of 'increasing violence' pertains to the effects of modern mass media (Kloos 1993: 10). Moreover, the effects of political conflict quickly spread, affecting both economic and political conditions throughout the world, because individual economies and societies have been integrating in terms of communication, transportation and transaction. A global network of information is required, and people need to be better informed.

Arms technology and the volume of the international armaments trade have increased. Conflicting parties are better-equipped today than ever before. The opening up of international links to those who engage in collective violence has become crucial to sustaining political conflicts. Further, in most political conflicts, and in the domestic political arena in most developing countries, the involvement of other countries and international bodies has become more important. The effects of increased international involvement in individual conflicts can be seen both in terms of conflict resolution and the continuation of conflict. It is, however, difficult to determine the net effects of international involvement in domestic political conflicts, which might vary from case to case. Cooper and Berdal (1993) address the short-term and long-term political strategic goals of foreign military interventions in political conflicts, and the broader implications of the role of military intervention of international bodies such as UN forces in domestic conflicts. According to PIOOM[1] data, there are now 20 countries, all in the developing regions, under UN peace-keeping military operations. Ayoob (1991), Gourevitch (1978) and Hill (1978) also analyse current international relations of internal security and politics. Gourevitch (1978: 911) concludes that the current international situation is both an outcome and a cause of domestic politics; thus, international economic relations and military

---

1 *Programma Interdisciplinair Onderzoek naar Oorzaken van Mensenrechtenschendingen* (Programme of Interdisciplinary Research into Causes of Breaches of Human Rights), Leiden University.

pressures influence a wide range of domestic behaviour, from policy decisions to political organization.

The majority of political conflicts since the mid-twentieth century exhibit two characteristics. First, they have been concentrated in the so-called *developing* or *underdeveloped* regions of the world. Second, most have been *intrastate*. Observing the ongoing armed conflict in 1991, Heldt et al. (1992: 420) noted that most armed conflicts were within rather than between states, while only one interstate major armed conflict was recorded, namely the Gulf War. Even though armed conflicts have taken the form of interstate conflicts, according to Heldt et al.(1992) they exhibit intrastate characteristics.

The role of industrialized countries in political conflicts located in other parts of the world in creating or sustaining the conflicts and possibly becoming one of the major conflicting parties should not be underestimated. According to Holsti (1991: 274-78), between 1945 and 1989, there were 58 major armed conflicts in the world, of which 56 were in developing countries. The direct involvement of industrialized countries has been a striking feature in many of these conflicts. According to Singer's estimates, there were 79 civil wars between 1946 and 1992, but none occurred in industrialized countries, while 16 became 'internationalized' due to foreign intervention (1994: 5-6).

The intrastate nature of political conflict in developing countries can be attributed to the artificial creation of modern states, with territorial boundaries defined by colonial rulers. The boundaries of the European nation-states were formed by both natural and cultural phenomena, while 'boundaries between Third World states ... are usually the result of colonialism and of European competition, that is, of extra-continental rivalries' (Kloos 1993: 8). Legitimate and centralized power was extended within these boundaries by the new states, and exercised over people with distinct characteristics.

The problem is that there has been no effective union between the *state* and the *nation* in many new states. In the view of Connor (1972), theories of nation building have tended either to ignore the question of ethnic diversity or to treat ethnicity superficially, as a matter of minor importance in the process of effective state integration. Modern political conflicts are directly linked to the domination of Western Europe during the last few centuries. The conceptualization by modernization and neo-Marxist theories of the Western role in economic change in developing countries and in their political conflicts are addressed in the next chapter.

Evidence on the concentration of armed conflicts

Recent empirical studies and data on armed conflicts demonstrate the concentration of political conflict in developing countries (Goor 1994, Heldt et al. 1992, Jongman & Schmid 1994, Schlichte 1994, Singer 1994). In this section, I discuss the available evidence, and discuss to what extent statistical data on armed conflicts could indicate the *intensity* of political conflicts, so that different regions in the world can be classified according to the level of political conflicts.

The intensity of political conflict could be measured by the socio-economic and human costs involved. However, the intensity concept can also be extended beyond these measures. The ability of societies to cope with political conflicts, an ability largely determined by economic and political conditions, reduces the intensity of political conflicts in two ways. The economic and political clout of the state can directly limit the potential for the emergence of large-scale collective violence. Indirectly, it can act as a counter force, neutralizing the effects of other factors leading to political conflicts. The omission of the 'ability' can thus distort the picture of political conflicts, especially at the level of cross-country evaluations.

Measuring political conflict

According to a PIOOM world map of political conflicts, entitled Wars and Armed Conflict in 1993, ongoing 'wars' and 'lower-intensity armed conflicts' in the world are scattered throughout developing regions. The 'wars' are defined as major armed conflicts with more than 1000 deaths per year, while the 'lower-intensity conflicts' are understood as armed conflicts with less than 1000 deaths per year. According to the map, the majority of the conflicts, both wars and lower-intensity conflicts, are concentrated outside the 'developed' regions, mainly in Eastern Europe, Africa and Asia. The East Asian region has no wars, but lower-intensity conflicts. Latin America and the Middle East, which are also usually classified as part of the developing world, appear to have a relatively small number of conflicts. No country in the developed world is engaged in a war, while Great Britain and Spain are the only two countries in this region with lower-intensity conflicts. North America and Australia are completely free of wars and lower-intensity conflicts.

Such a classification of countries according to political conflicts relies entirely on arbitrary criteria. No country has escaped political conflicts, though the complexity and degree will vary. The inclusion or exclusion of a country in a conflict-free category is often the result of the criteria employed to define conflicts. However, classification is necessary in a cross-country assessment of political conflicts. Although this cannot be avoided, it results in the analytical exclusion of a wide range of political conflicts, simply because they do not satisfy the criteria adopted.

Classifications typically make use of class ranges, defined by arbitrary criteria. In such classifications, the extreme values in the upper and lower ends of a class range will receive equal weight. Further, values which are very close to each other can fall easily into different classes. They are weighted differently. Variations in criteria also lead to different classifications of the same events in different studies. For example, conflicts in Northern Ireland and some other countries are classified as 'wars' in Schlichte (1994), but as 'low-intensity conflicts' in Jongman and Schmid (1994). In contrast, the conflict in Burundi has been treated as a 'war' in the latter and as an 'other armed conflict' in the former, as it does not satisfy the 'war' criteria. Moreover, changes in classifications cause the events to move between categories over time.

Table 2.1 *Regional distribution of current major armed conflicts*

Region[a]	Number of armed conflicts		
	1991 SIPRI data[b]	1992 PIOOM data[c]	1993 AKUF data[d]
Europe	6	21	4
Western Europe[e]	1	–	1
Other Europe[f]	5	–	3
Central and South America	9	15	5
Africa	31	48	19
Middle East	6	12	6
Asia	20	31	18
Former USSR	–	33	6
Total	72	160	58

a. There is no uniformity among the data sources in terms of regional classifications. The regional classification system in this table can also be different from that of the sources. For example, Turkey is included in Other Europe; Afghanistan in Asia; and Armenia, Georgia, Russia and Tadjikistan in the former USSR, which is not the case in some of the data sources.
b. SIPRI data include wars which meet the criteria of prolonged combat between the military forces of two or more governments or of one government and at least one organized armed group, involving the use of weapons and causing battle-related deaths of at least 1000 per year (Heldt et al. 1992).
c. PIOOM data include (i) wars that caused more than 1000 battle-related deaths per year under the SIPRI war definition, (ii) low-intensity conflict that recorded less than 1000 battle-related deaths per year and, (iii) serious disputes in the range between the lower level of low-intensity conflict and the upper level of political tensions (Goor 1994, Jongman & Schmid 1994).
d. AKUF data include (i) wars which meet criteria of government involvement, organization of fighting and a degree of continuity and, (ii) other armed conflicts which do not satisfy the war criteria (Schlichte 1994).
e. The only reported country in Western Europe is Northern Ireland.
f. The category 'Other Europe' includes armed conflict in former Yugoslavia and Turkey.
Sources: SIPRI data from Heldt et al. (1992); PIOOM data from Jongman & Schmid (1994); AKUF data from Schlichte (1994).

In addition to problems arising from classification criteria, relatively significant events can be excluded, and relatively insignificant events included, in such typologies. A world map of conflicts recently published by the *New York Times* marked 48 countries as involved in serious internal conflict, apparently omitting a number of countries with such conflicts (Kloos 1993: 5-6). Due to the strict criterion of 'more than 1000 deaths per year' to define a 'war'—a criterion used both by SIPRI[2] and PIOOM—armed conflicts which erupted in Azerbaijan and Georgia in 1991, continuing conflicts in Burundi, Djibouti, Mali and Spain in 1991, and some other armed conflicts which existed but were not active in 1991, have escaped classification (Heldt et al. 1992: 418). Depending on differences in classification criteria, therefore, wide variations occur in information given in different data sources. No approach can be considered perfect. In fact, there is no adequate solution to the classification problem. But adverse effects on con-clusions based on these classifications adopted can be minimized, if the criteria used are flexible. This means the application of criteria which include a num-ber of elements, rather than a single strict criterion or a few of them.

Problems associated with an investigation into political conflict are not restric-ted to classification problems. Political conflicts are investigated only at the level of their manifestation. Yet the issue of political conflicts encompasses not only those which have manifested a certain level of violence, but also those with a potential for violence. In the long term, the formation of political con-flicts is more important than the short-term factors which trigger civil violence. At the empirical level, however, conflicts with a potential for outbreak of vio-lence easily escape attention, as empirical data do not generally measure 'potential'. Hence, investigations into political conflicts are inevitably confined to conflicts which have become manifest.

Even then, the data on the distribution of political conflicts are based on indi-rect information. Direct access to data is restricted by the conflict environment itself. This imposes a major limitation on empirical studies of political conflicts. Investigators are compelled to proceed with incomplete information, which re-sults in a high degree of approximation. Available indicators for the intensity of political conflicts are, therefore, not satisfactory. Statistical indices show the quantity and not the quality of conflict, while differences in population densi-ty, geographical area and economic conditions often distort the picture.

A cross-country study of political conflicts must, then, use multiple indicators. Even then, one must be aware of the limits imposed on the investigation by qualitative differences in political systems, culture, religion and traditions.

The regional distribution of armed conflicts

Simple statistical indicators regarding the regional distribution of ongoing major armed conflicts, both national and international, and of civil wars during the period 1946–92 are presented in Tables 2.1 and 2.2, respectively. The former does not distinguish between interstate and intrastate armed conflict. However, of the ongoing conflicts at the end of 1993, only the war between Croatia and

2 Stockholm International Peace Research Institute, Stockholm.

Serbia is regarded as an interstate war (Schlichte 1994: 9). Even these two coun-tries became separate states only after 1991, so the war between Croatia and Serbia started as an intrastate conflict. Regardless of the differences in the area and populations of each of the regions, the fact is that most conflicts of the last few decades have occurred outside Western Europe and North America. As Table 2.1 shows, in the early 1990s there were 72 ongoing armed conflicts ac-cording to SIPRI data, 160 according to PIOOM data, and 58 according to AKUF[3] data. Despite variations among the figures owing to the differences in classifi-cation criteria, they are consistent in the ranking of regions with regard to armed conflicts.

Table 2.2   *Regional distribution of civil wars, 1946-92*[a]

Region	Wars		Battle deaths	
	Number (in 1000s)	Share of total (%)	Number (in 1000s)	Share of total (%)
Eastern Europe (including Turkey)	7	8.9	166	2.5
Central and South America	16	20.2	596	9.0
Africa	23	29.1	2202	33.3
Middle East	10	12.7	323	4.9
Asia (excluding Middle East)	23	29.1	3329	50.3
Total	79	100	6616	100

a. Figures include 20 civil wars that were internationalized by foreign military inter-ventions, and 16 ongoing civil wars.
Source: Singer (1994).

According to these data, Western Europe has only one armed conflict, i.e. the conflict in Northern Ireland, while there were no such armed conflicts in North America. Africa and Asia occupy first and second place respectively as regions exposed to armed conflict. Central and South America and the Middle East have a relatively small number of conflicts.

The uneven distribution of political conflict between the Northern and the Southern parts of the world and within different regions of the latter is further confirmed by the regional distribution of civil wars during the last few decades. According to Table 2.2, there have been 79 civil wars in the world during the period 1946-92, with over 6 million deaths in battle. Western Europe and North America are reported to have had no civil wars, while Eastern Europe has suf-fered the lowest number of civil wars and deaths. It should be noted that in the

3 *Arbeitsgemeinschaft Kriegsursachenforschung* (Working Group for Research on the Causes of War), University of Hamburg.

post-war period, Eastern Europe began to have civil wars only after the late 1980s, with the break-up of the socialist states. Over 90 per cent of the post-war civil wars occurred in the rest of the world. Africa and Asia accounted for 46 of the 79 civil wars in this period. Their shares were equal. Over 50 per cent of world's civil war deaths were in Asia alone, while Africa recorded over 33 per cent. In the regional distribution of civil wars and related deaths since 1946, Central and South America and the Middle East regions have had fewer wars and war-related deaths than Asia and Africa.

Table 2.3   *Regional distribution of human costs of political conflicts[a], 1992–93*

Region	Deaths[b]		Displaced in the home country		Refugees in other countries	
	Number (000s)	Share of total (%)	Number (000s)	Share of total (%)	Number (000s)	Share of total (%)
Western Europe[c]	4	0.0	–	–	–	–
Eastern Europe[d]	292	2.2	1448	6.5	2233	15.3
Central and South America	413	3.2	1104	5.0	105	0.7
Africa	9356	71.6	17395	78.4	5723	39.3
Middle East	412	3.2	800	3.6	1157	7.9
Asia	2590	19.8	1445	6.5	5355	36.7
Total	13067	100	22192	100	14573	100

a. Armed political conflicts include wars causing over 1000 deaths per year, and low-intensity conflicts.
b. Figures refer in the original source to minimum cumulative deaths.
c. The reported countries are Northern Ireland and Spain.
d. Turkey is also included.
Source: Jongman & Schmid (1994).

Data on the regional distribution of conflict effects in terms of deaths and population displacements are summarized in Table 2.3. Data on North America show no conflict at all in these terms: it is the only region in the world which, according to these classification criteria, was free of political conflicts. The data for Western Europe, which show political conflicts only in Northern Ireland and Spain, report no displaced or refugee figures. There have been at least 4000 deaths in Western Europe, but this figure is negligible relative to the figures for conflict-related deaths in other regions.

The highest human costs in terms of deaths, displacements and refugees are reported for Africa. Of over 13 million conflict-related cumulative deaths in the world, Africa alone accounts for 71.6 per cent. In addition, 78.4 per cent of over 22 million displaced people are in Africa. Asia accounts for 19.8 per cent of the conflict-related deaths. In terms of refugee flows, Africa accounts for 39.3 per cent, a low figure relative to the high number of deaths and displaced people. The main conclusion emerging from these data is that developing countries, including Eastern Europe, have been the most affected by political conflicts.

There are, however, variations among individual states and among different regions in the world in terms of armed conflicts. The fact that North America and Western Europe—a large part of the industrialized world—appear in these data as free from political conflicts is at least partly a result of the criteria employed. Under different criteria, some of these countries or perhaps all of them would be included among the countries with political conflicts. In addition to Northern Ireland and Spain, which are occasionally reported in the data, Quebec and Belgium are involved in political conflicts. Moreover, Western democratic states, including Japan, are 'at risk', as discrimination against minority groups causes significant ethnic or racial tensions. According to Gurr (1993: 11), 93 countries in the world, with 233 minority groups accounting for 17.3 per cent of the world population, are at risk. Gurr defines minorities as *politicized communal groups* which meet two criteria: they experience economic or political discrimination, and they have taken action in support of their collective interests (1993: 5-6). Racial conflict has long been a part of North American and Western European history, perhaps the longest conflict in modern history. It is implied that these conflicts are either less violent than those in the rest of the world, or cannot be labelled violent by the usual criteria. Rather, they fall into the 'individual' or 'small-scale' categories, because much of the racial conflict in the developed world is covert. These conflicts were scattered geographically and over a long period of time, and did not have enduring, large-scale institutional bases. Hence, while this racial conflict could qualify as long-term conflict with a potential for violence, specific characteristic have prevented it from being classified as armed political conflict.

Minority conflict between 1945 and 1989 shows significant regional variation (Gurr 1993: 101-107). According to Gurr's classification, Asia, North Africa and the Middle East, and Africa South of the Sahara show an increase in minority conflicts. The level of violent protest and rebellion in these regions is higher than in other regions. In Latin America and the Caribbean, minority conflicts increased substantially since the 1960s, but their non-violent manifestation is more pronounced than violent protest and rebellion. Western democracies and Japan are examples.

Refugee flows: regions of origin and destination

Refugee flows refers to people who escape the threat of political conflicts by seeking refuge under the right of asylum. The refugee flows in the world have been increasing in absolute terms more than ever before before. According to UNHCR estimates (1993: 1), at the beginning of 1993, 18.2 million people in the world had been forced to leave their home countries for fear of persecution and violence. An important issue in question is 'from where to where'.

Refugee flows can be useful indirect indicators of political conflicts, bearing in mind several reservations. Misunderstandings can arise, for refugee statistics indicate only the number of *actual* refugees crossing the borders of their home countries. Obviously, the number of *potential* refugees—those who want to leave but cannot—are more telling than the number of actual refugees. Large-scale displacement of people *within* the same country is also a result of political conflicts, but the available indicators poorly represent 'internal' refugees.

Table 2.4   *Regional distribution of world refugee population, 1992*

Region[a]	Region of Asylum of Refugees		Region of Origin of Refugees			
			Same Region		Other regions[b]	
	Number (000s)	Share of total (%)	Number (000s)	Share of total (%)	Number (000s)	Share of total (%)
Europe	4379.1	23.0	563.1	5.5	3816.0	43.4
Western Europe	1653.4	8.7	–	–	1653.4	18.8
Other Europe	2725.7	14.3	563.1	5.5	2162.6	24.6
North America	1041.2	5.5	–	–	1041.2	11.8
Latin America	885.5	4.7	153.2	1.5	731.6	8.3
Africa	5393.2	28.4	5342.9	52.3	50.6	0.6
Middle East	4471.0	23.5	1408.4	13.8	3068.4	34.9
Asia (excl. Middle East)	2769.1	14.6	2740.2	26.8	28.7	0.3
Oceania	59.6	0.3	–	–	59.6	0.7
Total	18998.7[c]	100	10207.8[d]	100	8796.1[d]	100

a. The regional classification here follows that of the source data; hence, note that some of the countries in Europe (Turkey) and the former USSR (Tadjikistan) are included in the Asian region, unlike in other tables in this chapter.
b. Refugee flows originating in 'Other Regions' include 'various' and 'not identified' refugee categories, as given in the data source, and 'identified' refugees who originate from a different region. Re. the latter category of 'identified', note that refugee flows from a particular country to a neighbouring country are also classified under the heading 'Other Regions' if the neighbouring country belongs to a different region due to regional classification.
c. Grand total figure, which is different from the column total, is from the data source.
d. Column total.
Source: UNHCR (1993: 149-53).

Further, actual refugee flows may not be an accurate indicator of political conflict because not all people seeking political asylum are political refugees: some seek asylum for other (mainly economic) reasons. An important factor which has been overlooked in the interpretation of economically motivated refugee flows is that in most cases there is also political conflict in the home country: no receiving country will grant asylum on economic grounds.

Table 2.4 shows the regional distribution of the world refugee population according to the region of asylum and the region of origin. The limits of these indicators should be kept in mind, and the insufficiency of information taken into account. These indicators are also distorted by national and regional differences in land area and population size. If we accept the statistics regarding the regional origin of refugee flows as a proxy of the regional distribution of political conflict, a few noteworthy conclusions emerge. North America, Western Europe and Oceania have not been the origins of refugee flows, but developing countries in Africa, Asia, the Middle East and Latin America have. Over half of world refugee flows originates in Africa, while Asia produces over one-fourth. The balance, less than one-fourth, emanated from other developing countries and other European countries, mainly Eastern Europe.

As developing countries have often been the origin of mass refugee flows[4], there has been some controversy regarding the relationship between refugee flows and 'poverty'. However, the suggestion that poverty produces refugee flows is misleading, as it implies that where there is the poverty, there must also be refugee flows (Zolberg et al. 1989). There is no direct relationship between the two. The question is whether poverty itself produces refugee flows.

What is more important, not only the origin but also the destination of refugee flows should receive due consideration. Statistical analysis at a macro level supports the argument that refugee flows in the world have moved largely from 'poor' countries in the developing region to the same region, and not from developing to developed regions. The developing regions together still absorb over 85 per cent of refugee flows originating in developing countries (Table 2.4). Some 28.4 per cent of the world's refugee population is absorbed by African countries, while 23.5 per cent goes to the Middle East and 14.6 per cent to Asia. Evidently, the developing part of the world itself appears to have granted asylum on a large scale, despite political, social and economic pressures. Western Europe and North America host a relatively small proportion of world refugees.

The concentration of the majority of refugee flows in the developing regions in terms of both refugee origins and destinations is logical. Reasonably accurate data on populations displaced due to political conflicts within their home countries are not available. The majority of international refugees leave their countries as part of mass outflows, and find refuge in neighbouring countries. This is 'the most common pattern in developing countries, where the pressures exerted by large refugee populations are taxing the hospitality of even the most generous countries' (UNHCR 1993: 31). This explains why Asia and Africa have been the regions of both *origin* and *asylum* for the largest refugee populations. The point appears to be true even for Western Europe. On the one hand, a high proportion of its asylum applicants originates from neighbouring countries, particularly in Eastern Europe. On the other hand, there has been a sharp increase

---

4 Before the emergence of mass refugee flows from Eastern Europe especially after the late 1980s.

in the number of refugees since the outbreak of political conflicts in Eastern Europe (UNHCR 1993). Those who travel long distances in search of asylum, beyond the neighbouring countries, are individuals rather than a mass refugee outflow.

World militarization and its regional distribution

The extent of militarization can sometimes be used as an indirect measure of political conflicts, because in principle the two phenomena are positively correlated. This is not always the case, however. The most militarized states in the world, in terms of arms production, military establishments and military expenditures, have not been more exposed to political conflict than other states. There is no single explanation for variations in the level of militarization among individual countries (Hill 1978: 52). Many factors pertaining to individual countries as well as regions intervene. For this reason, general explanations of militarization exhibit wide variations in their conclusions (Hill 1978, Mintz 1986, Rosh 1987, Terrel 1971, Zimmerman & Palmer 1983). The important question, which has not yet been answered adequately, is why poor countries are prepared to sustain economically heavy military burdens.

Table 2.5 *Indicators of militarization in industrialized and developing countries*

Indicator	Industrialized Countries[a]	Developing Countries[a]	World Total
Military expenditure,			
as % of GDP, 1989	4.9	4.4	4.8
as % of health & education			
expenditure, 1990/88	28.0	169.0	42.0
Official development assistance,			
as % of military expenditure,			
1990	11.5[b]	0.6[b]	–
Real GDP per capita			
(adjusted to PPPs),			
as % of USA level, 1989	71.6	10.9	22.0
GNP per capita,			
as % of USA level, 1989	81.4	3.7	18.3
Size of armed forces,			
as % of teachers, 1987	97.0	64.0	71.0
as % of physicians, 1987	300.0	1800.0	1500.0

a. Classification of countries in industrialized and developing categories is as in the source (1992: 213).
b. Granted in the case of industrialized and received in the case of developing countries.
Source: UNDP (HDR 1992: 166-67; 186; 200).

The militarization of industrialized countries is determined by economic factors as well as by external political interests. The USA and the former USSR, and many of the Western industrialized countries in general, have the greatest military capabilities. By economic factors, I mean the high incomes of industrialized states, that enable them to maintain high military expenditure and military establishments. Moreover, an important economic cause of the militarization of industrialized countries, as I discuss below, is the production and sale of arms. By political interests outside the territory, I mean the direct and indirect involvement of industrialized states in the politics of other regions. The Cold War, and the accompanying conflicts fought in developing regions, was the cause of much of the arms build-up (UNDP HDR 1992: 86). Socio-economic conditions in newly independent states left much potential for communist revolutions (e.g. China in 1949) and socialism. In response to this perceived threat, capitalist countries showed an increased interest in the developing countries.

The Cold War is virtually over, yet military spending in the USA, the former USSR and in European NATO countries has decreased only slightly. The second half of the 1980s showed a reduction of military spending in many parts of the world, including the developing regions. Since 1983, according to Goldblat 'the military expenditures of the developing world, combined, have been falling, except for countries involved in armed conflict' (1987: 1). However, a decrease of only 3 per cent in world military spending was recorded for the period 1987-90; in 1990 world military spending was more than twice its 1960 level (UNDP HDR 1992: 85).

Table 2.5 presents vital aggregate indicators related to military expenditures in industrialized and developing countries. It should be noted that, apart from the wide variation in factors affecting military spending, its disparities across countries highly distort the averages given in the table. When military expenditure figures in the two regions are taken as the measures of militarization, both absolute and relative figures show a substantial distortion. Military expenditure in industrialized countries was 4.9 per cent of GDP in 1989, while in developing countries it was 4.4 per cent. Yet the real GDP per capita (adjusted to purchasing power parities, PPPs) of developing countries is 10.9 per cent of the USA level, and that of industrialized countries is 71.6 per cent of the USA level. In absolute terms, military expenditure is high in the industrialized regions, and income levels there would enable these countries to maintain military expenditure at that level at less cost to their welfare status than is the case in developing regions. For developing countries, the maintenance of comparable relative military expenditure is a heavy burden when the costs in terms of welfare are considered.

The heavy burden of military expenditure in developing countries is illustrated by an analysis of the resources spent on, for example, health and education. In industrialized countries, military expenditures amount to 28 per cent of sums spent on health care and education. The military expenditure of developing countries amounts to 169 per cent of the sum devoted to health care and education. According to UNDP estimates, in 1989 the total debt of all developing countries amounted to 43 per cent of their GNP, varying from 11 per cent in China to 427 per cent in Mozambique (*HDR* 1992: 164-65). The average debt service ratio for all developing countries, as a percentage of exports of goods and services, increased from 13.3 to 23.2 per cent during the period 1970-89. With developing countries heavily in debt to industrialized countries, military spending in developing countries has been largely financed by their external debt, while at the end of 1970s one-fourth of their debt accumulation was due to arms imports (Brozoska 1983: 275).

Table 2.6 *Regional distribution of world arms trade 1982–91*
(percentage of total values at 1990 constant prices)

	Exports		Imports	
Region[a]	1982-86	1987-91	1982-86	1987-91
Industrialized Countries	93.0	92.3	32.9	38.7
North America[b]	30.3	34.7	2.6	2.3
European Community	23.0	18.1	8.9	12.3
OECD Countries	54.4	54.3	20.1	27.7
Developing Countries[c]	7.0	7.7	67.1	61.3
Least Developed Countries	0.0	0.0	3.0	6.3
Middle East	1.8	1.3	31.7	24.7

a. Regional classification as in the source.
b. North America includes Mexico, which is not an industrialized country.
c. Developing countries include newly industrialized countries in East Asia and high-income oil-exporting countries in the Middle East.
Source: SIPRI (1992: 308-09).

Table 2.6 shows the distribution of exports and imports of arms in industrialized and developing countries during the period 1982-91. The largest exporters are the industrialized countries, while the largest importers are the developing countries. More than 90 per cent of total arms exports in the world have been carried out by industrialized countries. According to SIPRI estimates, 88 of the world's 100 largest arms-producing companies are owned by the USA and Western European countries of the Organization for Economic Co-operation and Development (OECD), while the USA alone had 47 companies in 1990 (1992: 363). Over 80 per cent of armaments in the world are sold by the USA, the former USSR, France and the United Kingdom; the USA and the former USSR accounted for almost 70 per cent (SIPRI 1992: 314). The shrinking defence requirements of industrialized countries, according to the UNDP, have led arms producers to find markets in developing countries (*HDR* 1992: 86). Developing countries, faced with increasing political conflicts, constitute the largest arms market. Thus, arms production is a significant source of income for industrialized countries, and a significant source of expenditure for developing countries.

Moreover, in the recent past, countries in the developing regions have become enthusiastic about producing arms themselves. In 1945 only 4 developing countries produced arms, but by 1982 this figure was over 50. Countries which play a comparatively advanced role in the world economy and which at one time or another have suffered from an arms embargo are very likely to produce relatively large amounts of military weaponry (Rosh 1990).

The *least* developed countries, having contributed 3 per cent world arms imports in 1982–86, doubled their share during the period 1987–91 (UNDP *HDR* 1992). The share of developing countries in world arms imports was 67.1 per cent during 1982–86 and has dropped slightly, to 61.3 per cent in 1987–91, largely due to the fall of the share of arms imports in the Middle East. The political conflicts of developing countries are not the sole determinant of the levels of arms imports and militarization. One cannot assume a positive relationship between the two variables. Nevertheless, as Rosh (1987) argued on the basis of a regression analysis, countries which are characterized by ethnic cleavage allocate a larger percentage of their resources to military expenditures in order to maintain control over ethnically diverse and fragmented populations.

Hill (1978: 53) found that military commitments of poorer nations are influenced strongly by domestic political instability, while the military commitments of wealthier nations are a response to international relationships and to one domestic condition of regime coerciveness. High income levels also determine military spending levels, as is revealed by the high share of arms imports of the high-income oil exporting countries (Table 2.6). As I have already pointed out, their level of exposure to political conflict was relatively low. The high degree of militarization in the Middle East countries was seen by Mintz (1986) as 'an action-reaction process' among the neighbouring countries. Rosh (1987) has also argued that states such as those in the Middle East, located close to potential antagonists, tend to become highly militarized. This argument could be extended beyond the strict concept of 'geographical neighbourhood', because, as Zimmerman and Palmer note (1983), the weapon build-up in the super power states (i.e. the USA and the former USSR) was also an 'action-reaction' process.

The extent of militarization in developing countries is directly linked to the military capabilities of industrialized countries. Among other things, the military-related economic activities of industrialized countries strengthen their economic bases. They also establish the institutional framework to control the political environment outside their territories.

Mullins notes an important difference between Western European states and new states in the Third World in terms of the development of military capacity. In the European model, 'there is a feedback relationship between development and military power, with the need for military power driving development, while development itself provides the wherewithal for the creation of military power' (1987: 104). The militarization in the European states is a result of the economic development and formation of the nation-states over the last few centuries. Military conditions related to the creation of modern nation-states in Europe have been studied (Tilly 1975, 1990). Territorial, commercial and navigation issues were the sources of the majority of European wars after the Middle Ages (Holsti 1991). The model demonstrating the correlation between militarization and development in the formation of modern European nation-states is not applicable to the militarization of new states in the developing regions. According to Mullins, 'the strength of the GNP-military capability relationship does not go up with either the size, wealth, or military power of a state or with its growth rate in wealth or military capability' (1987: 105). Unlike the states in the European model, the new states that do best either in terms of development or in terms of military capacity do not necessarily demonstrate a strong relationship between these two variables.

Obviously, the military capability of developing countries is smaller than that of industrialized countries in terms of its monetary values. Yet the maintenance of modern military capacity is a heavy burden on these nations because of their low income levels and poor welfare status. When 70 per cent of population in least developed countries with the lowest human development record fall below the poverty line (1980-89), it is difficult to rationalize the economic burden caused by the doubling of military spending in the period 1960-89 (UNDP *HDR* 1992: 161, 167). When the heavy economic burden of military spending is taken into account, the intensity of militarization in developing countries can be considered to have been much higher than that in industrialized countries.

Economic features of the developing region

Asian, African and Latin American countries, where economic conditions and living standards are poorer than in developed countries, are conventionally termed *developing, less developed, underdeveloped* or *Third World*. The term 'less developed' denotes a *static* economic gap between the two groups of countries. In contrast, the term 'developing' may imply an ongoing process closing this economic gap, through economic advancement in these countries. A similarly static connotation appears in the tern 'underdeveloped', the oldest label, though the connotations of this term changed with the development of the neo-Marxist paradigm (see Chapter III). The term 'Third World' implies, in addition to economic disparity, differences in the characteristics in political systems between the 'first', the 'second', and the 'third' worlds.

The economic problems of developing countries have been discussed widely. These countries share a number of characteristics such as poverty, low productivity, high population, unemployment and underemployment and low standards of living. Table 2.6 shows some aggregate statistics on vital economic differences between these two groups of countries. The East European socialist economies have not been taken into account in the table, because comparable economic data were hardly available. The population of developing countries, at 3682 million, is almost five times that of the 737 million in the developed region. Yet the average per capita GNP (US $610) in developing countries is only about 5 per cent of that in the developed region (US $11810). Developing countries' per capita export earnings—US$ 118—and external reserves—US$ 43 —compare to US$ 1478 and US$ 686 respectively in developed countries. Unlike the developed countries, they are internationally indebted. Moreover, nutritional and health standards are very low, compared with those of developed countries.

Keynes' *The General Theory of Employment, Interest and Money* (1936) laid the groundwork for the development of a methodology for the empirical valuation of national income and related concepts. The invention of the national accounting methodology by economists such as Hicks (1940), Kuznets (1948a, 1951), Little (1949) and Nutter (1957), later coupled with various other human development indicators (Todaro 1985, UNDP *HDR* 1992), provided a statistical yardstick for the evaluation of the material progress of societies. The contemporary empirical evaluation of national income levels and other related indicators and of their cross-country applications (Abraham 1948, Kuznets 1948b, 1953) provided a criterion for the classification of nations as 'developed' or 'underdeveloped'. As Samuelson put it, 'an underdeveloped nation is simply one with real per capita income that is low relative to the present-day per capita incomes of such nations as Canada, the United States, Great Britain, France and Western Europe generally' (1976: 847).

Another important incident was the initiation of the concern of industrialized societies with the development programmes of developing countries (Esteva 1992: 6). Although many were optimistic that development assistance was the solution to underdevelopment, this concern can also be considered a political aspect of the Cold War, as I have shown earlier. In addition, the 'new' programme legitimized the fact that underdeveloped countries are actually 'underdeveloped'. A consciousness of underdevelopment developed, which dominates all varieties of development and modernization thinking, and rationalized Western development.

A set of Western development theories emerged to explain the causes of underdevelopment and to evaluate the possibilities to upgrade the economic conditions in developing countries. These Western development theories, which legitimized the expansion of capitalist nuclei in developing countries, justified both the need for material progress in developing countries and Western development assistance (Hunt 1989). Western development assistance was formulated in terms of financial aid, technology transfer, policy advocacy and intellectual support. In all respects, the economic advancement achieved by developed countries provided the 'model' of development. However, as I will discuss in Chapter IV, the problem of development is the creation of a particular historical process embodied in global technological and institutional transformation, while the concept of development is normative and deterministic.

At one level of analysis, it is not difficult to see some developed countries as having political conflicts, and some developing countries as having no such conflicts. Yet, at a macro level, an outstanding feature of the regional distribution of political conflicts is that developed countries are less exposed to political conflict than developing countries. This provides a fair rationale to argue that relative economic advancement is of great importance in countering politi-

Table 2.7   *Socio-economic indicators of developing and developed countries, 1985*

Indicators	Developed countries[a]	Developing countries[a]			
		All countries	Low inome economics	Middle income economies	Upper income economies
Population (millions)	737	3682	2439	1242	567
Per capita GNP (US$)	11810	610	270	1290	1850
Per capita exports (US$)	1478	118	22	306	509
Per capita international reserves (US$)	686	43	13	100	156
Per capita external public debt (US$)	–	171	38	431	587
Per capita daily calorie supply	3417	2470	2339	2731	2987
Life expectancy at birth (years)	76	61	60	62	66
Fertility rate	1.8	4.0	3.9	4.3	3.7
Infant mortality rate (per 1000)	9	71	72	68	52

a. 'Developed countries' refers to industrial market economies in the data source. Data for socialist economies are not reported.
Source: World Bank (WDR 1987).

cal conflict. Potential political conflicts in developed countries are not supported by the economic conditions which could otherwise cause them to develop into threats to the existing social order and the stability of the state.

Despite a few exceptions regarding the existence of industrialized countries such as Japan and Australia in the Asian region, and of one or two industrialized countries undergoing political conflicts, the evidence that I explored revealed that political conflicts are unevenly concentrated in the developing region of the world. The developing region itself has become the destination for a vast majority of refugees threatened by political conflicts. In terms of the social and economic opportunity costs, militarization in developing countries has far surpassed the point that could be expected in terms of economic conditions. The fact that developing countries have been exposed more to political conflicts than developed countries raises an important question regarding the relationship between political conflicts and the distinctive economic features which are attributed to the term 'developing'.

The fact that modern political conflicts occur primarily in developing societies casts doubts on the validity of theoretical generalizations. Generally, political conflicts are not confined to a particular part of the world or to a particular period in history. As other forms of social interactions, every society may have undergone conflicts and they continue to do so. Yet, within this universal phenomenon, political conflicts develop under different circumstances. Universal and a-historical theoretical frameworks cannot explain the circumstances under which human societies in particular contexts experience political conflicts. In this regard, the preceding investigation presents an important issue to be addressed in social science studies. As the research on modern political conflict indicates a significant relationship with economic features of developing countries, there is a need for an economic perspective at both theoretical and empirical levels.

Summary

In the preceding discussion, I have shown some important characteristics and trends of political conflicts in the modern world during the period after the Second World War. The political conflicts were defined broadly as *actual* or *potential* use of collective violence. Yet for analytical purposes the political conflicts were treated here as organized and large-scale 'armed struggles', i.e. *actual* use of violence, particularly as the *potential* for violence is difficult to assess using statistical indicators. It was acknowledged that the international concern about political conflicts has increased due to their international repercussions, the increased international involvement in local political arenas, the rapid development of information technology, arms production and global trade in arms, as well as increases in the international connections of conflicting parties. I have argued that political conflicts in the modern world have been concentrated in the so-called *developing* regions of the world, though they are closely connected to economic and political developments in the industrialized world. In addition, modern political conflicts have been *intrastate* in character, even with the close involvement of other countries.

It is true there have been political conflicts in some developed countries, while some developing countries have not gone through political conflicts. At a macro level of analysis, however, it cannot be denied that the developing regions have been exposed to more civil political conflict than developed regions have. A large part of the armed struggles has taken place in Asian, African and Latin American regions. These regions have become the *origins* as well as the *destinations* of most of the world's refugee flows which have emerged in response to (the threat of) political conflicts.

An analysis of the militarization of developing and developed regions in the world, based on simple quantitative measures and military capacity shows that, on average, the latter regions are more militarized than the former. However, if the economic burden of militarization, its opportunity costs, and the role of militarization in the domestic political atmosphere are taken into account, the 'intensity' of militarization in developing countries appears to have surpassed the point that they could be expected to reach in terms of economic conditions. Economic and political roots of high levels of militarization in some of the developed countries have been directly and indirectly associated with, among other things, the political instability of the developing region. The world arms trade is largely trade between developed and developing countries. The developed region is the largest arms producer in the world; the developing region is the largest arms buyer.

The high concentration of political conflict in the developing region of the world presents an important research issue. It casts doubts on the validity of over-generalized theoretical approaches to political conflicts. It calls for the attention of development economists to non-economic social phenomena. Whatever the validity of the connotations of terms typically used to designate 'developing' countries, all of these terms point to the economic weakness of these countries. The perception of part of the world as 'underdeveloped' is a result of development thinking. By Western economic standards, developing countries suffer from low levels of income, low productivity, unemployment, and poor living conditions. The issue in question is how 'underdevelopment' or its inherent socio-economic characteristics can help to explain modern political conflicts, which remain concentrated in developing countries. To what extent can existing economic approaches to political conflicts explain the phenomenon? In the next chapter, I will address this question.

The Economics of Political Conflicts: A Critique of Traditional Approaches

III

My purpose in this chapter is to evaluate traditional major theoretical approaches in which economic factors are considered a significant component of social change and political conflict. There are three of these approaches: classical Marxist theory, neo-Marxist theory and liberal modernization theory. My point of departure is that, as I have argued in the previous chapter, the developing region of the world has been exposed increasingly to intrastate political conflicts, compared to the decreasing prevalence of such conflicts in the developed region. My critical evaluation assesses the appropriateness of these approaches as an analytical tool for the case of developing countries.

No theory of political conflicts has been developed within the mainstream economic tradition. Evidently, individuals or social groups interact in the market on the basis of different and even conflicting economic interests. Therefore, economics are of fundamental importance in the emergence of antagonism between individuals or social groups. Mainstream economic theory, however, which leans heavily on the idea of 'equilibrium', contemplates mainly the harmony of economic interests and assumes the absence of antagonism in economic interactions. The assumption is that economic interaction among individuals or social groups acting in their own interests will eventually maximize everyone's benefits. Therefore, an economic analysis of political conflicts emerged not in mainstream economic theory but in the Marxist, neo-Marxist and modernization theories.

In the first section of this chapter, I focus on classical Marxism and its relevance to political conflicts in developing countries. Classical Marxism is concerned with class antagonism regarding the generation and distribution of production. Contradictions within 'modes of production' and hence 'relations of production' lead to social change. Second, I deal with political conflict in neo-Marxist theories. Neo-Marxist theorists, who believed that their conceptualization was based on Marxist theory, focus on international exploitative relationships in the world capitalist system. Increasing 'peripheralization' and 'dependency' are associated in this approach with political destabilization in underdeveloped countries. Third, I discuss the modernization theory which was developed as an alternative to Marxist views on social change. The liberal modernization theory, though not a theory of political conflict, focuses on the destabilizing effects of modernization in underdeveloped societies. Modernization theories consider the forward movement of societies, from a simple primitive stage to a differentiated, modern, 'developed' society, to lead to political stabilization. This chapter reveals that important aspects of the link between economic change and political conflicts are already established in the traditional theories. However, classical Marxism hardly describes the case of developing countries, while the theoretical boundaries of the two other alternative paradigms are too strict, and raise questions regarding the disparity of economic change and political conflict in developing countries.

Political conflicts in classical Marxism

The Marxist school of political economy took the transformation of society through the generation of surplus production and its relation to political conflicts to be the motor of social change (Marx 1954). In placing society, rather than individuals, at the centre of the economic system, Marxism posited that economics is the study of class relations:

> Economics deals not with things but with relations between persons, and, in the last resort, between classes; these relations are, however, always *attached to things* and *appear as things* (Marx & Engels 1950: 339).

In the Marxist view, political conflict is the driving force behind the transition from one mode of production to another. In every class society, surplus production is appropriated from the workers or direct producers by the dominant class. Unlike in pre-capitalist modes of production, which are devoid of technological change and economic growth, and where the object is to produce use values, in capitalist modes of production the object is to produce exchange values for surplus creation, leading to technological change and economic growth. Observing the industrialization of Western Europe in his time, Marx perceived the development of antagonistic relationships between capital and labour which would eventually lead to the working class putting an end to capitalism.

Class struggle and political conflicts

Marx focused on political conflicts in the form of *class struggle*, which he saw as arising from internal contradictions in capitalism. How do the types of political conflict that we are dealing with fit into a Marxist analysis? The Marxist approach to political conflict is problematic, because political conflicts in developing countries are not of the same type as those dealt with in Marxist thought. It is also difficult to maintain that Marx was concerned with a particular form of political conflict, namely class struggle, for Marxist theory posits that all forms of political conflict are the expression of class conflict:

> ... all historical struggles, whether they proceed in the political, religious, philosophical or some other ideological domain, are in fact only the more

or less clear expression of struggles of social classes (Marx & Engels 1950: 223-224).

Class struggle would eventually and inevitably bring about social revolution, transforming the social system from one 'mode of production' to another. Since the disintegration of tribal societies, which—in the Marxist view—have the basic characteristics of a 'communist' society, all societies were divided into classes, the ruling classes being the appropriators of the surplus produced by direct producers. 'The history of all hitherto existing society is the history of class struggle', said Marx and Engels (1950: 33), referring to the conflict between the direct producers of the surplus and the owners of the means of production. Whenever a part of society has a monopoly on the ownership of the means of production, workers must contribute labour for their own subsistence and further for the subsistence of the owner of the means of production (Marx 1976: 344). Surplus production is the surplus value generated by labour, which can produce a 'value' exceeding what is needed for subsistence. The owners of the means of production extract the greatest amount of surplus labour and thus the relationship between the two classes is necessarily antagonistic, in all class societies.

> Freeman and slave, patrician and plebeian, lord and serf, guild-master and journeyman, in a word, oppressor and oppressed, stood in constant opposition to one another, carried on an uninterrupted, now hidden, now open fight, a fight that each time ended, either in a revolutionary re-constitution of society at large, or in the common ruin of the contending classes. (Marx & Engels 1950: 33)

A straightforward empirical implication of Marx's conflict theory, as Rule pointed out, would be 'high levels of civil violence throughout entire social systems during periods of transition from one form of class rule to another' (1988: 57). No ruling class relinquishes its special power based on the *state* apparatus without a struggle. The state is an instrument or an organ of the dominant class, because, in the Marxist view, 'political power ... is merely the organized power of one class for oppressing another' (Marx & Engels 1950: 51).[1] But empirical reality does not match this prediction. Political violence may indeed lead to a transition from one form of class rule to another. Although class antagonism and social revolution *can* lead to this transition, it would be wrong to believe that class struggle *always* does. The struggles between masters and slaves, between landlords and sharecroppers, and between capitalists and workers did not transform all societies from one particular stage to another. Social evolution has

---

1 The definition of the state has been the subject of much debate, even within the Marxist tradition. See *International Social Science Journal* (1980) 32 (4) for differing perspectives on the state. There are also non-Marxist definitions of the state, while Weber's definition includes the legitimate power of the state to control coercion. See for instance Finer (1975: 85-86), Tilly (1975: 70) and Tilly (1990: 68-70).

been more a 'process' of transformation than a 'revolutionary change' between stages.

Class conflict, as the 'prime mover' resulting in civil violence and eventually social revolution is an over-emphasized concept. In Marxism, it is assumed that 'in class society everyone lives as a member of a particular class, and every kind of thinking, without exception, is stamped with the brand of a class' (Tsetung 1971: 66). Yet those who refer to a variety of struggles note that their idea of class conflict is open to the objection that the people involved in these struggles did not cast their actions in terms of class, were not truly aware of their class interests, and did not even define their enemies in class terms (Tilly & Tilly 1981: 17). The only possibility is that the underlying reality in conflicts is class antagonism, whether those involved in these struggles are aware of this or not.

In Marxist thought, all forms of conflict are the response to the appropriation of surplus value at the point of production. It may be true that all forms of political struggles exhibit class elements in varying degrees, covertly or openly. But the focus on the exploitation of workers by employers is too narrow, and tends to ignore a wide range of complex political issues by reducing all forms of political conflict to struggles between producers and exploiters (Miliband 1991). Political conflicts are much more complex than classical Marxism assumes. Groups that engaged in political struggles in different societies have not necessarily been the class of people 'exploited at the point of production'. They may have been members of the working class but not direct producers, e.g. student and unemployed groups. It could be that they are not members of the industrial working class at all, such as peasants. Even the idea that class conflict, endemic in every complex society, produces active collective struggle is open to criticism. As Rule argues, the only reasonable assumption is its opposite: 'In most settings, most of the time, class conflicts are neither conspicuous in most people's social perceptions nor objectively responsible for militant action' (1988: 64). The fact is that members of the exploiting and the exploited classes collaborate routinely on a daily basis. The Marxist phenomenon of the appropriation of surplus value from the direct producers is universally valid, but it is not the basis of collective action to the same extent.

The two hostile camps: capitalists and workers

Marxism sees society clearly divided into two antagonistic classes: the *bourgeoisie* and the *proletariat*[2] (Marx & Engels 1950: 33-34). Capitalism is seen as the highest stage of the evolution of class societies, and all forms of technological innovation and the formation of capitalist institutions are seen to occur for

---

2 Marx and Engels (1950: 33) define *bourgeoisie* and *proletariat* as follows: 'By bourgeoisie is meant the class of modern capitalists, owners of the means of social production and employers of wage-labour. By proletariat, the class of modern wage-labourers who, having no means of production of their own, are reduced to selling their labour-power in order to live.'

the maximization of capitalist profits through the maximization of labour productivity. Therefore, coercion, in one form or another, is seen as intrinsic in the capitalist system. In reality, although the extraction of surplus is maximized, it is not so that capitalism is necessarily more oppressive than earlier systems of exploitation. But because workers under capitalism are formally free agents, and part of a different system of industrial organization, they are better able to struggle against employers than was the case previously.

In a society with various and complex class strata *within* and *between* the capitalist and working classes, it is difficult to see the class dividing line in a Marxist sense. With capitalist industrial expansion a wage-labour force is formed by the mobilization of all social strata. Yet, even with the establishment of capitalism, the peasantry persists and continues to play an important economic role. In a Marxist sense, the peasantry does not fit the definition of the working class. Even with the recruitment of labour from all classes of the population, it has not so far been proved that the wage-labour force, as a whole, sinks below the conditions of existence of the working class, as Marx predicted (Marx & Engels 1950: 43). In Western Europe, the working class, rather than being pauperized through capitalist development, has risen well above the painful conditions which existed during the period of its industrial take-off. New middle class strata, consisting of various occupations resulting from capitalist development, have emerged from the working class itself and have been able to grasp a substantial share of surplus production. Capitalism, with its 'free' wage-labour system, has opened up various routes for mobility among various social strata. Social mobility has become a major preoccupation, and this means that class consciousness has decreased. When a social system offers opportunities to loosen the bonds of social class, individuals' efforts may not be to present themselves as a group, but, more rationally, as individuals. Although Marx viewed social class as the engine of revolutionary change, Olson (1963: 531) argues that those whose class ties are the weakest are the most apt to take part in revolutionary change, while those who are most class conscious are least likely to do so. In any case, the formation of new social strata, the weakening of old class ties and the strengthening of new class ties, all within the capitalist system, have produced obstacles to revolutionary change. The emergence of the middle class has eroded the potential for class struggle. For this reason, in practice, the great majority of wage earners has refused to play the role in class struggle or revolution that Marx assigned to them. The significance of class struggle has declined along with the advancement of capitalism.

Revolutionary potential within the two worlds

Regarding political conflicts in various parts of the modern world, viewed as an outcome of the contradictions within capitalist modes of production, we must distinguish between developing and developed countries. In terms of the stage of capitalism at which these two groups of countries are found, whatever the criteria used, developed countries must be viewed as at a higher stage of capitalism than developing countries.[3] As a result, if we take a Marxist line of argument, the capitalist institutions in developed societies should not have a considerable lifetime ahead relative to those in developing countries (Rule 1988: 58). If this is the case, there should be more political conflicts in developed countries, destabilizing their capitalist institutions, than in developing countries. Even though class relations in these developed societies are antagonistic, organized collective action is not challenging the established social and political order, as Marx envisaged. On the contrary, such tendencies exist in developing countries, even though they are at lower stages of capitalism. Marxism does not provide a plausible answer to the question why economically backward societies have been more exposed to political conflicts than developed capitalist societies have.

Capitalism appears to be sustained by its inherent dynamics in abating the potential growth of class antagonisms and in extending the lifetime of capitalist institutions. Implicit assumptions in Marx's account of capitalist crisis are that new technology is developed and that labour is specialized in industry to produce the *same* commodity that will lead to a continuous decline of its price. Yet in the modern world there is a *differentiation* of commodities, and new commodities are *created*. These developments eventually prevent profit shares from declining. Benefits of economic growth trickle down to workers, and wages rise. Government intervention has made an important contribution in this regard. Furthermore, industrial capitalism in the integrated world system is still heavily monopolized by a few nations. Whatever the degree of technological developments and labour specialization in industry, a large part of the world still generates a substantial demand for commodities produced in industrialized countries. This means that the co-existence of various stages of capitalist development in different parts of the world will weaken the potential for capitalist crisis.

The position of classical Marxist political economy was that political conflicts through the generation of surplus production should be treated in a general economic theoretical discourse that does not distinguish between developed and developing countries. In fact, 'it is now commonly recognized that neither Marx nor Engels had much to say about the underdeveloped' (Harrison 1988: 63).[4] Marxism was based on the historical formation of the capitalist mar-

---

3 Also it is important to note Lenin's (1975) declaration that imperialism is the ultimate stage of capitalism, a stage which, in Lenin's definition, Western capitalist economies were already reaching at the end of the 19th century: 'Imperialism is capitalism in that stage of development in which the dominance of monopolies and finance capital has established itself; in which the export of capital has acquired pronounced importance; in which the division of the world among the international trusts has begun; in which the division of all territories of the globe among the biggest capitalist powers has been completed' (1975: 106).
4 At least there were two opposite notions explicit in the classical Marxism regarding underdevelopment in the underdeveloped countries (Svensson 1991: 11-12). One was that underdevelopment, especially in the Asian part of the world, had endogenous causes related to the specific 'Asian mode of production' that retarded capitalist development. For analyses of Marx's view on Asian societies see Banerjee (1985), Krader (1975), Melotti (1977), Pryor (1990) and Shiozawa (1990). The other notion was that, in Lenin's (1975) view, imperialism, a direct consequence of the development of

ket economy in Western society. Witnessing the economically progressive but socially regressive changes in Western countries in the eighteenth and nineteenth centuries, Marx's political economic discourse captured the reality of the industrial revolution, which was the reality of his time. The question is whether this reality can be applied to the rest of the world as well. Classical Marxist theory postulated that all societies would go through 'identical stages' leading to capitalism, whether the guiding forces were internal or external: 'the country that is more developed industrially only shows, to the less developed, the image of its own future' (Marx 1954: 19). And the less developed countries were expected to reach the same status of industrialized countries through the global expansion of capitalism.

In all forms of political conflicts in every society, the economic aspect is important, just as any other aspect, as an initiating or sustaining force. But these dimensions cannot be reduced to one of the appropriation of surplus value. The scope in classical Marxism is too narrow as well as too general for the analysis of political conflict in developing countries. An important part of the question at issue is left untouched in Marxist analysis, though Marxism has provided a theory of economic conflicts. Nevertheless, classical Marxism provides considerable insight into how technology and industrialization divide societies into differentially developed parts, rather than generating development in society as a whole.

Political conflicts in neo-Marxist theory

The neo-Marxist perspective is a paradigm rather than a 'single' theory. There are differences of opinion among neo-Marxist theorists, but they share a common basic analytical framework (Hunt 1989). The leading neo-Marxist theorists are Baran (1957), Frank (1969, 1978), Emmanuel (1972), Amin (1976, 1977) and Wallerstein (1979). Assuming a uniform pattern of capitalist development in all societies in the world, Marx anticipated capitalist development in underdeveloped countries through colonialism. But neo-Marxists observed that capitalist development in underdeveloped countries has been blocked by the exploitative relationships between developed (centre) and underdeveloped (periphery) countries. Therefore, neo-Marxists internationalized the Marxist concept of class struggle, conceptualizing a centre-periphery exploitative relationship.

The concept: class struggle internationalized

An outstanding feature of neo-Marxist theory is its approach to the issue of development or underdevelopment in the context of international exchange relations. Neo-Marxists adopted an historical perspective on the development

Western capitalism, prevented capitalist development in the underdeveloped world. The latter was the point of departure for neo-Marxist analyses, as I discuss later.

of international exchange relations, but viewed these relations in terms of surplus extraction, from the periphery by the centre. Thus, development in the centre and the underdevelopment in the periphery co-exist, and are a result of the same international surplus exploitation. Development in underdeveloped regions is considered possible only through radical political change: the revolution of the working class in underdeveloped countries.

Neo-Marxist writers consider their theories to expand on Marxist analysis, but there is a fundamental contradiction between Marxist and neo-Marxist analyses. Neo-Marxist writers pleaded for working class revolutions in pre-capitalist societies in the underdeveloped world. Classical Marxism, being a theory of evolution, considers social change to result universally from class struggle, but never pleaded for any changes in the process of social evolution. Moreover, as I have already discussed, the class struggle in capitalist society evolves into the revolution of the working class only at the highest stage of capitalist development.

The conceptualization of political conflicts within the neo-Marxist analytical framework draws attention to *world system theory* (Wallerstein 1979) and *dependency theory* (Amin 1976, Frank 1978). These theories share common ground, because generally neo-Marxist analyses are based on the assumption that there is a single world system dominated by capitalist development in the centre.

The world system and political conflict

In world system theory, the notion of 'national development' in underdeveloped countries is rejected, as there is said to be only one capitalist world economic system. There have been isolated economic sub-systems in history, but these have become parts of a single world system through colonialism and Western capitalism.

> And the only totalities that exist or have historically existed are minisystems and world-systems, and in the nineteenth and twentieth centuries there has been only one world-system in existence, the capitalist world economy (Wallerstein 1979: 4-5).

The mini-systems, defined as entities marked by a complete division of labour and a single cultural framework, no longer exist. Therefore, today we have only a world system, which is defined as 'a unit with a single division of labour and multiple cultural systems' (Wallerstein 1979: 5). A division of labour is an interdependent 'grid' for the satisfaction of its essential needs. In the world system, the needs of economic actors are satisfied by a combination of their productive activities and exchange, constituting the division of labour (Wallerstein 1979: 14). In Europe, markets and trade were highly developed and helped Europe acquire economic dominance. In explaining the relationship between capitalism and the world system, Wallerstein (1979: 6) points out that 'we are merely defining the same invisible phenomenon by different characteristics'. Core states inhibit national development in underdeveloped countries, as the dependence of the latter on the former has increased. This results in more and more 'peripheralization' of the underdeveloped countries within the international division of labour.

In the system of exchange in the capitalist world economy, the exchange of surplus value is a zero-sum game: only one partner gains, and the other loses. Who acquires the maximum profit depends on the structural positions in the world economy. According to Wallerstein, 'the interests of various local groups converged in Northwest Europe, leading to the development of strong state mechanisms, and diverged sharply in the peripheral areas, leading to very weak ones' (1979: 18). The strong core states in the centre imposed *unequal exchange* on the weak states in the periphery (Emmanuel 1972). Thus, in the capitalist world system, the capitalist appropriates the surplus value of the labourer, while in the same way, the core states in the centre appropriate the surplus value of the weak states in the periphery. The core areas in the modern world economy, according to Wallerstein (1979: 185), are characterized by a complex range of occupational activities, multiple social strata, a strong state machinery and a relatively high overall standard of living. In contrast, the underdeveloped areas in the periphery are characterized by a relatively narrow range of economic activities, few social strata, a weak state machinery and a low standard of living. However, there is a thin upper stratum in the periphery, as well as a thin lower stratum in the core.

In world system theory, all social groupings, such as classes, ethnic groups, status groups and ethno-nations are aspects of the world economy, rather than of the economies of nation-states. According to Wallerstein (1979: 24),

> 'much of the confusion that has surrounded the concrete analysis of their functioning can be attributed quite simply to the fact that they have been analysed as though they existed within the nation-states of this world economy, instead of within the world-economy as a whole'.

Because of the disproportionate concentration of industrial activity in the core areas of the world system, a proletariat of the kind which developed in industrialized countries does not exist in underdeveloped countries.

This idea of a world system, as I have pointed out earlier, conflicts with that of classical Marxism, which anticipates a clear division of society into two hostile camps. Instead, neo-Marxist theory perceives different categories of social strata and social groupings in underdeveloped countries. In contrast to the predictions of classical Marxism, when social conflicts become more acute, social groups become more conscious about the classes to which they belong. Therefore, according to Wallerstein (1979: 181), social groups approach class distinctions asymptotically. World system theory considers the social groups in the peripheral states 'classes', so that political conflict is the 'class conflict'.

Wallerstein (1979) analysed social conflict in the post-colonial states. Europeans enjoy the highest status in colonial and many post-colonial states. In addition, politically dominant local elite groups seek upward mobility in the world system. As the 'proletarian states' in the periphery are exploited by the core states, the world system prevents them from retaining surplus and does not provide sufficient job outlets at the national level. Due to the appropriation of surplus by the centre, underdeveloped countries, which have no capital accumulation to enable national development, experience scarcity of resources and opportunities. This compels the dominant elite groups, which appropriate the domestic surplus, to use ethnic, religious, racial or other criteria, or a combination of these, to acquire advantages over others. Therefore, underdevelopment increases, and domestic political conflicts escalate in the peripheral countries, as long as these countries are bound up with the world capitalist system. The world system approach to political conflicts in the *periphery* concludes that the political conflict in the underdeveloped areas is an expression of the contradiction between the centre and the periphery, rather than a contradiction within the periphery.

Dependency and political conflict

Dependency theory consists of not only a neo-Marxist version, but also a structuralist version (Hunt 1989). The neo-Marxist version fits into the neo-Marxist paradigm, sharing basic features with world system theory as well. The principle argument in dependency theory is that within the single world capitalist system, economic structures in underdeveloped areas are dependent on the centre. Initially, access to markets in the periphery for low-cost inputs for industrialization and for the sale of manufactured products led to economic expansion in the centre. Since the late nineteenth century, the periphery has been dependent on the autonomous centre:

> Since the last decades of the nineteenth century, however, real wages at the centre have increased at a faster rate, and this has caused the expansionism of the capitalist mode to assume new forms (imperialism and the export of capital) and has also given the periphery new functions to perform (Amin 1976: 76).

The importance of the imperialism of the centre and of the export of capital to the periphery is not that the centre is dependent on the periphery. This counteracts the falling rate of profits in the centre. In contrast, these new forms of the capitalist mode have rendered the periphery dependent, restricting the growth of incomes and the expansion of domestic markets. Consequently, the dependency relations of the periphery have decreased their potential for autonomous capitalist development. Thus, dependency involves the marginalization of the masses in the periphery, which continues to be expropriated of its surplus by the centre in the form of profit repatriation and unequal exchange. Neo-Marxist dependency analysts advocate social revolution and the withdrawal of the periphery from the world capitalist system.

In the structuralist version of dependency, two interdependent development structures in the centre and the periphery are seen as parts of a whole. The centre is characterized by an autonomous development structure due to its endogenous growth capacity, while the periphery is characterized by an underdeveloped structure. The periphery depends on the centre at several levels, in terms of consumption (which reflects the demand of the domestic elite) and in terms of production (which requires imported inputs, machinery and technology) (Furtado 1970). This pattern of consumption and production results in a slower growth of employment, increasing income inequality and mass marginalization. These disparities are further aggravated by capital-intensive foreign investment and its links with the national governments.

Dependency analysis can provide concepts, regarding the external dependence of developing countries and their relations to domestic inequalities, which are useful in the conceptualization of economic change and political conflicts in these countries. Further, the empirical studies on conflict and coercion in dependent states have confirmed that external connections can play a major role in the formation of domestic political conflicts (Moaddel 1994, Jackson et al. 1978) Yet there are limitations of the conventional dependency analyses that should be considered. Structuralist dependency theory has not advocated social revolution in the periphery. Rather, it takes a pessimistic view about development in the periphery, and confines the analysis to the problem (Hunt 1989). However, the industrialization strategies derived from structuralist dependency analysis aim to de-link trade between the centre and the periphery, through structural changes and industrialization (ECLA 1950, Prebisch 1959). Both neo-Marxist and structuralist versions agree that the dependency of the periphery perpetuates underdevelopment. But the rise of certain dependent states during the post-war period, particularly the so-called newly industrialized countries (NICs), and the growth of other Asian economies during the past two decades presents a major challenge to the dependency analysis. This has led dependency analysts to acknowledge that some development in the periphery is possible, but from their point of view this is 'dependent development' (Wallerstein 1979). Moreover, the development that can take place in the periphery could be 'partial and distorted' (Hunt 1989: 221). Actually, every economy in the world is dependent on the rest of the world some degree. There are advantages and, as the dependency theorists suggest, disadvantages in this dependency. But it cannot be concluded that the periphery as a whole faces *only* disadvantages, and that economic change in developing countries is governed *only* by their dependency relations.

Two basic features of the neo-Marxist paradigm are analytically interrelated. One is the rejection of a 'universal' path of development towards capitalist development. In the words of Wallerstein, 'neither Great Britain nor the United States nor the Soviet Union is a model for anyone's future'(1979: 133). The other feature is the treatment of developing countries as sub-systems within the global economy. Yet both features are too rigid, and inevitably ignore any phenomena outside these boundaries, or reduce them to fit the given boundaries. As I will discuss in Chapter IV, the case of developing countries is different from that of the developed countries. And for the same reason, individual economies in the modern world are no longer analytically separate isolated systems. But the neo-Marxist paradigm substantially limits the scope to explore the internal forces of development such as state policy, economy, and culture, as it views every change in developing countries as a result of the centre-periphery relationship. Also, there is no other international relationship between the centre and the periphery in neo-Marxist terms, because all relations are assumed to be only exploitative.

The centre-periphery concept has established the mechanism of the increasing 'peripheralization' of developing countries. Increasing development in the centre, and increasing underdevelopment in the periphery are the result. Therefore, domestic political conflicts emerge and persist in peripheral countries as an expression of contradictions inherent in the capitalist world system. However, it should be noted that there have been significant variations in the development of different countries in the developing region, which can hardly be fitted into a neo-Marxist approach. The consequence of the increasing 'peripheralization' is increasing political conflict, which was also seen as international class struggle. The pessimistic conclusion of the neo-Marxist paradigm is that there is no scope for development in developing countries as long as they are part of the world system. The practical validity of advocating the isolation of underdeveloped countries is questionable, however, in an increasingly integrated global economy.

Political conflict in modernization theory

With the emergence of new independent states in the underdeveloped world, their social, political, cultural and economic evolution has received much attention in studies of modernization. There is no single approach to modernization. Modernization is a broad label for a variety of sociological, anthropological and economic perspectives on social transformation. The theme of modernization theory is the transformation of human societies from a simple 'primitive' to differentiated and complex 'modern' stages. The transformation of societies occurs when traditional values, norms and institutions are replaced by modern ones, and with the enlargement of the range of choices (Apter 1987, Marglin 1990, Sen 1988). A dominant theme in modernization theory is the comparison of modernization in developing countries to Western growth:

> Historically, modernization is the process of change toward those types of social, economic, and political systems that have developed in Western Europe and North America from the seventeenth century to the nineteenth. (Eisenstadt 1966: 1)

For many modernization theorists, modernization is Westernization, even though this may not necessarily be the case in reality. Banuri (1990a) points out that equating Third World modernization with 'Westernization' has been so successful that social progress has become defined in terms of the modernization project. Modernization and development often appear to be closely linked, as they share many features of the transformation of human societies (Apter 1987, Marglin 1990, Harrison 1988). As I explain in Chapter IV, the terms 'development' and 'underdevelopment' are related to modern technological and institutional transformation. Human societies transform or modernize along varying routes. Whether this transformation can be designated 'development' is a separate issue, which necessarily involves normative and deterministic value judgements.

Evolution of the concept

Studies of modernization originated in the nineteenth century in the work of researchers such as Durkheim (1964) and Weber (1946), who analysed the forces and nature of social change, particularly in Western countries. Early modernization theory is based on evolutionism and diffusionism, which developed as alternative approaches to each other. While the concern of evolutionists was the evolution of culture *over time*, diffusionists focused on its transmission *in space*, through social interaction. In both evolutionist and diffusionist perspectives, social change is a smooth, gradual and inevitable progressive transformation of human societies from the primitive to the modern stage. A unilinear evolutionary path is 'given' for all human societies. The idea that the evolution of societies along this path is natural and inevitable was at the core of evolutionist thinking. In the diffusionist view, common cultural patterns, or cultural artefacts, originate from a single source and diffuse among societies because innovations are likely to occur only once and are not repeated at different points of time in different places.

Colonization and the emergence of development assistance from industrially developed countries and international organizations demonstrated the importance of diffusion of economic and technological complexities. Against this background, a large body of studies emerged on the modernization of underdeveloped countries in response to the Western influence on their social change. These studies, which have been classified as neo-evolutionary, generally agreed with that all societies are normative and adaptive systems, and that both innovation and diffusion are important sources of modernization (Bellah 1964, Eisenstadt 1964a, 1964b, Moore 1964, Parsons 1964, 1966, 1971, Sahlins & Service 1960). Thus, the core issue addressed by neo-evolutionist was the adaptive capacity of human societies to social innovations and diffusions that cause their 'social advancement'. According to Parsons (1964), societies can expedite evolution through the diffusion of innovations and practices from societies at higher evolutionary stages to those at lower stages. Diffusion can occur without the whole set of prerequisite conditions necessary for innovation, and thus, as

Harrison put it, 'it is easier to pass on the message than to originate it' (1988: 37). According to Parsons (1964: 341), two distinctions must be made in the concepts of innovation and diffusion. Regarding innovation, a distinction must be made between the impact of its introduction and of its continuation. Regarding diffusion, a distinction must be made between the conditions under which an adaptive advantage can develop for the first time and those favouring its adoption from a source in which it is already established. Thus, in Parsons' view (1971) and that of other neo-evolutionists, modern Western societies have a greater general adaptive capacity than other societies, and modernity was disseminated throughout the rest of the world 'only by colonization'. A partial exception to this generalization was made regarding Japan, because, according to Parsons (1971: 2), although it was relatively autonomous and 'diffusion' did not follow colonization, even in Japan the Western influence was evident.

Within the neo-evolutionary school, social evolution was considered a process of differentiation, meaning the increasing autonomy of social structures and the emergence of new forms of integration. Differentiation, according to neo-evolutionists, provides the tools for the analysis of successive stages of the evolutionary process (Eisenstadt 1964b: 376). Unlike the old evolutionary perspective, neo-evolutionism permitted the incorporation of various intermediate stages of modernization (Eisenstadt 1964a). Furthermore, social evolution, according to Eisenstadt, need not give rise to changes in overall institutional systems everywhere, though there might be potential for such systematic changes (Eisenstadt 1964b: 385).

In recognizing a process of diffusion (specific evolution) apart from the general evolutionary process, neo-evolutionists actually pinpointed the Western link to social change in underdeveloped countries process. The assumption appears to have been that the Western influence was beneficial to underdeveloped countries, which could take 'short cuts' to higher stages of modernization through this Western link. As Hoogvelt (1976: 15) pointed out, written language that encouraged the emergence of a separate class of literate, administrative bureaucrats that institutionalized authority in office, and money that facilitated the free mobility of resources are important benefits of diffusion. Also they serve as sources of heterogeneity. The idea of specific evolution through diffusion is creative as well as self-limiting, in the sense that it inevitably involves specialization, and hence 'uneven' social change.

Parsons (1951) developed the approach known as structural functionalism, for modernization studies in general. The formal subject of modernization theories was social change in developing societies that brings these societies to a 'more' developed stage, based on the Western model. All developing societies, without exception, are assumed to strive for economic development of the type achieved by Western societies, and thus one structural component of the system is 'given'. Because of the principle of 'structural compatibility' modernization theories tend to list other components as compatible with economic development. According to Hoogvelt (1976: 53), modernization theories in general adopted the structural functionalist premises, first in viewing developing societies as social systems undergoing social change as a result of the introduction, the impact or the superimposition of Western institutions and, second, in pre-conceiving the direction of this change on the basis of the principle of compatibility. The major issue addressed in contemporary development and modernization studies is the transmission of Western economic and technological complexities in facilitating modernization in developing countries. Methodologically, this implies that the economic and technological complex contains the reproductive cells of the remaining non-economic, yet compatible, structural elements of Western societies.

The pattern variables constructed by Parsons provided the methodology to contrast advanced with less advanced societies, or advanced with less advanced phases in a society. Pattern variables were basic dichotomies in role orientations. Parson claimed that advanced social systems, characterized by a high degree of occupational specialization and rationality, favour roles which are functionally specific, achievement-oriented, universalist and affectively neutral. In contrast, roles in relatively undifferentiated traditional social structures are functionally diffuse, ascriptive, particularistic and affectively rewarding (1951: 177). The empirical validity of Parsons' classification of social structures according to pattern variables was challenged by Frank (1969). The normative argument, presented by those who employed the pattern variable approach (e.g. Hoselitz 1960), was that underdeveloped countries should eliminate the pattern variables of underdevelopment and adopt those of development in order to become industrialized. It legitimized the necessity of internally consistent action patterns of modern economic and technological institutions which were imposed upon underdeveloped countries, and were welcomed by them.

Classical Marxism and modernization theory, though they emerged as alternative approaches to social change, are compatible in at least one respect. Both doctrines see Westernization as the only way to development. Marxism considered the capitalist form of development in Western society as a global force, and assumed that sooner or later all societies would go through the same stages. Modernization theory assumed that social change in the West is the universal model for development. The two approaches differ in the sense that modernization theory's analysis does not stretch beyond the differentiated 'modern' stage (the stage at which advanced societies now are), while Marxism also analysed the crisis in capitalism, socialist revolution and communism.

Political conflicts: an intermediate phase of modernization

Liberal modernization theory, unlike Marxism, is not a 'conflict' theory. Hence, modernization approaches do not lead exclusively to political conflicts, but to a wide range of social phenomena. Nonetheless, development was logically certain and inevitable in early modernization theories assuming 'smooth' social transformation. For this reason, a direct link between political conflicts and social transformation did not emerge in early modernization theory.

In the 1960s, discontinuities and inequalities of modernization were recognized, and political conflict and revolutionary potentials, among other things, entered the theoretical framework of modernization (Eisenstadt 1966, Heilbroner 1963, Huntington 1968, Moore 1964, Olson 1963, Smelser 1963a). Just as Marxism, however, modernization theory did not recognize the specificity of the underdeveloped region. Political conflict was seen by modernization theorists as part of the adjustment to, or as a by-product of, modernization. Therefore, destabilizing forces were expected to play a role in modernizing societies until they reached a higher stage, comparable to that of advanced Western countries.

Under certain circumstances, the differentiation in social structure may lead to regression, stagnation, and attempts to break down the social order. The neo-evolutionary perspective allows for some evolutionary uncertainty. According to Parsons, 'a very critical point is the capacity to cope with unstable relations between system and environment, and hence with *certainty*' (1964: 340). Moore (1964) adopts a similar line of argument, recognizing discontinuity in social change, in contrast to early modernization. Moore's point of view was that social change is 'irregular in magnitude, rate and direction, along with more orderly progressions'(1964: 331). This is because it is characterized by reversals (cycles and swings, completion of processes), the partial restoration of former structural features, polarization, resistance to changes and revolutionary potentials.

Outlining the potentialities of group conditions, Smelser (1963a: 43-44) pointed out a 'three-way tug-of-war' among the forces of tradition, forces of differentiation and new forces of integration. Structural changes associated with modernization are disruptive to the established social order, according to Smelser (1963a), for three reasons. First, differentiation is often in conflict with the traditional social order. Second, structural change is uneven modernization, creating *anomie* in the classical sense (it generates disharmony between life experiences and the normative framework which regulates them). Third, *anomie* is partially relieved by new integrative devices which are again in conflict with older, undifferentiated systems of solidarity.

Thus, Smelser's view is that 'discontinuities' in modernizing societies are the expression of opposition to modernization. Responses to modernization in the form of anxiety, hostility and fantasy become 'collective behaviour' (1963a). Eventually they become social movements—peaceful agitation, political violence, millenarianism, nationalism, revolution, and underground subversion (Smelser 1963a: 44). Smelser furthermore posited that the people most readily drawn into such movements are those who suffer most severely from the displacements caused by structural change. In his work on collective behaviour, Smelser theorized that political conflict resulted from 'disequilibrium' of the four structural components of social action—values, norms, mobilization of motivation, and situational facilities (1963b). When any of these components comes under strain, malcontents may collectively act to reconstitute the equilibrium.

Colonialism was the major impetus of modernization in underdeveloped countries. Modernization in colonial states is associated with increased protest movements which became an important part of national politics. Increasing differentiation, structural specialization, and interdependence among social groups brought various groups together in a single framework of interaction. Due to the disorganization of modernization, protest movements become inherent in all modernizing societies (1966: 37). If this was the case, there was nothing new in the types of political conflicts that contemporary underdeveloped countries were undergoing. This was a stage of political conflict that Western countries had already gone through.

In Eisenstadt's view, colonialism was beneficial to underdeveloped countries. He blamed, therefore, not colonialism itself, but the 'unevenness' and the imbalance of the modernization process caused by colonialism (Eisenstadt 1966: 111). Most importantly, heavy, large-scale and state-dependent industrialization in underdeveloped countries

'lagged behind the development of political and ideological demands and aspirations of small, intensive closed groups of intellectuals, but it came before the broader strata started to become modernized in the cultural or political field' (Eisenstadt 1966: 72).

Thus, colonialism failed to change economic, cultural and political fields evenly, and therefore unbalanced modernization was created in underdeveloped economies by colonial rulers, increasing the likelihood of protests. The message is that colonialism granted a good thing to the people in underdeveloped countries, but colonial rulers were unable to distribute it equally. Political conflicts in colonial states were the result.

The idea that the speed of achievements lags behind rising aspirations has been a dominant theme in modernization and development studies on the disorganized nature of social change. Heilbroner, describing development as a 'revolution of rising expectations', pointed out that social transformation is apt to be marked not only by rising expectations, but also by a loss of traditional expectations, due to the growing awareness of deprivation (1963:132). From a neo-Marxist point of view, as I discussed earlier, Frank argued that the revolutionary potential in underdeveloped countries is an outcome of 'not the rising expectations but the falling consumption' (1969: 129). People in underdeveloped countries revolt not against tradition or non-capitalist institutions, but against the capitalist system. However, the idea of rising expectations and awareness of relative deprivation was shared by Smelser (1963a) and many others. According to Smelser, 'different social groups and strata became more and more aware of each other's standing in terms of power, prestige, and wealth, and began to measure themselves and other groups in terms of relatively similar values and standards'(1963a: 11). The speed of rising aspirations and increasing awareness coupled with the relative slowness of economic improvements forms 'the probability of revolution' in modernizing societies (Moore 1964: 338).

Furthermore, as psychological theories of revolutions (Davies 1962, Gurr 1970) explain, it creates a 'revolutionary state of mind'. The J-curve theory of revolution formulated by Davies (1962) is closely associated with the neo-evolutionist idea of discontinuities in modernization. The theory argues that the revolutionary state of mind is created by the increasing gap between expectations and gratification. Davies attempted to fit some of the great historical revolutions into a J-curve. It may be debated whether it is possible to represent social complexities in a linear curve: the simplicity of the J-curve theory made it questionable.

The notion of relative deprivation dominates Gurr's general theory of collective violence (1970). He distinguished stages in the development of collective violence (and attempted to support this theory with empirical findings (Gurr 1970, Gurr & Duvall 1973). These psychological theories of violence have been criticized heavily due to their emphasis on the 'revolutionary state of mind' as the single factor underlying the eruption of large-scale organized armed conflicts (Aya 1990, Rule 1988).

Social disorganization and resulting political conflicts are often associated with the 'dislocation' of people due to modernization. Lerner (1958) found that a large group of people in modernizing societies did not belong to either 'traditional' or 'modern' categories, and were actually in a transitional phase between the two categories. They were prone to discontentment and extremism, especially if their progress was blocked by a lack of suitable political institutions. Studies in this school of thought postulate that people dislocated from traditional ties, for instance, by differentiation (Smelser 1963a) and by rapid growth (Olson 1963, Terhal 1992), without at the same time being integrated into the modern social order, are the social groups most likely to be engaged in political upheavals. Some argued that there is no reliable and regular sense in which modernization directly breeds political conflicts (e.g. Tilly 1973).

The implicit assumption of modernization theory has been, therefore, that political conflicts are inevitable by-products of modernization, and will dwindle once modernization is 'completed'. This idea implies that people in modernizing societies will have to live with political conflicts until modernization is completed. This legitimation of political conflict precludes any appeal to minimize or forgo such conflicts. In addition, the notion that a particular end of transformation will be reached, in stages, has featured widely in the modernization literature. In fact, societies do not go through identical stages, nor is there a static and universal 'end'. Moreover, modernization theory attributes the difficulties in modernization to developing countries, and reduces political issues there to domestic circumstances. Modernization theory can thus be seen to have failed to position modernization and contingent domestic political issues in a global framework. When external factors such as the Western model of modernization and the influence of colonization were brought into the picture, they were treated as altruistic forces which operate in favour of modernization and development in underdeveloped countries.

Marxism considered political conflicts, narrowly defined, as the driving force of social transformation from one mode of production to another. In contrast, modernization theory referred to them as a temporary phenomenon driven by social evolution. Modernization theory appears to have transcended classical Marxism. Modernization theory observed the development of complex social strata, as part of social transformation, rather than the two antagonistic camps observed in Marxism. The importance of accommodating this social complexity is that, unlike Marxism, modernization theory helps to grasp the variety of factors leading to different forms of conflict. A Marxist approach lacks this possibility, and thus can grasp only the class elements in conflict or search for ways to interpret all varieties of conflict as class conflict. However, at the same time, modernization theory, due to its broad focus—not only on political conflicts but on all aspects of social change—suffers from a lack of coherence and lacks a systematic theoretical representation of political conflict.

As I discussed in the previous chapter, political conflicts have been concentrated largely in developing countries, the states designated by neo-Marxists as the 'periphery'. If this fact provides a fair rationale to argue that the increasing 'peripheralization' in developing countries is the cause of political conflicts, then it also provides a rationale for the alternative modernization approaches, which explain an inverted U-curve relationship between political conflicts and modernization. There is no consistency in the conclusions of various empirical studies based on either neo-Marxist or modernization approaches (Jackson et al. 1978, Moaddel 1994). Moaddel (1994), in his cross-national analysis on political conflicts, found that both 'peripheralization' and 'modernization' appear to have been associated with political conflict, through effects on domestic economic conditions, social stratification and state structure. The major controversy regarding an analytical framework combining world system theory with modernization theory is that the two approaches are based on contradictory fundamentals. Otherwise, ingredients in both neo-Marxist and modernization theories, as well as in classical Marxism provide valuable information for the conceptualization of an economic perspective on political conflicts in developing countries.

Summary

In the preceding analysis, I investigated the appropriateness of traditional economic theories for the analysis of political conflicts in developing countries. Mainstream economic theory does not provide an adequate economic framework for the analysis of political conflicts, as it assumes a harmony of interests, and non-antagonistic relations among, economic agents and activities, in a sense that society aims for a state of equilibrium. I have, therefore, examined the ability of classical Marxist, neo-Marxist and modernization perspectives to analyse political conflicts. The link between economic change and political conflicts appears to be important in each of these theories. The major traditional theories that were evaluated were based on different concepts of social evolution. The usefulness of the theories pertains to of the information they provide. As single approaches, their usefulness can be debated, particularly in an analysis of political conflict in developing countries.

Only Marxist analyses focused primarily on political conflict. In classical Marxism, political conflict inherent in all class-based societies is the driving force of social change. At the highest stage of industrial capitalism, the class struggle leads to the revolution of the working class, putting an end to class-based modes of production. In contrast to what Marx anticipated, today political conflict is widespread not in the highly developed industrial capitalist countries, but in underdeveloped societies. These conflicts do not necessarily stem from antagonism between the 'proletariat' and the 'bourgeoisie', but occur largely in agrarian societies among various social groups due to a wide range of complex economic, political, social and cultural factors.

Studies in modernization theory focused on the transformation of underdeveloped societies towards the modern stage of 'development' reached by Western industrialized countries. Societies of either 'developed' or 'developing' countries are indeed being transformed. Whether this transformation is 'development' is a different issue. No society in the world has reached an ideal 'end' stage of transformation. For modernization theorists, generally, the effect of colonization was benevolent for underdeveloped countries, as it facilitated modernization by enabling developing countries to skip innovative steps. As does classical Marxism, modernization theory assumes a universal and unilinear evolutionary path. Modernization theory is, however, not a theory of political conflicts but of social transformation. Nevertheless, political conflicts are a by-product of modernization in every society.

Neo-Marxist theorists, in contrast, shift the focus of analysis away from internal towards external forces underlying political conflict in underdeveloped countries. Both modernization and neo-Marxist theories, in contrast to classical Marxism, pay attention to the case of underdeveloped countries. Yet, they contradict each other. For modernization theory, developing countries are modernizing or developing. For neo-Marxists, capitalist development in dependent underdeveloped countries is restricted by the exploitative centre-periphery relationship in the capitalist world system. This mechanism was established by colonialism and capitalist development in the centre. States in the centre became politically stabilized through the extraction of surplus from the periphery, while the increasing 'peripheralization' of underdeveloped countries exacerbated political conflict. The neo-Marxist perspective considered political conflict in underdeveloped countries an expression of the contradictions inherent in their relations with the 'centre'. The extent of political conflicts in underdeveloped countries will increase, with the deepening of 'peripheralization', unless these countries withdraw from the capitalist world system. Generally, social change in developing countries is seen as uniform and unilinear, in both neo-Marxist and modernization approaches, but in opposite directions. For modernization theorists, it an upward movement, and, for neo-Marxists it is a downward movement. The theoretical boundaries in both modernization and neo-Marxist approaches to political conflicts in developing countries are quite strict, in the sense that variations in both global and local economic changes and their relation to domestic political stability cannot be addressed directly in either perspective. Otherwise, both approaches offer useful ingredients for the conceptualization of the distinctive case of developing countries from an economic perspective.

Political Conflicts in Developing Countries: A Paradox of Development

IV

The analysis in this chapter links the preceding chapters with the forthcoming empirical investigation into the economic dimensions of civil political conflict. In this chapter I argue that intrastate political conflicts in developing countries are significantly associated with the 'problem of development'. Generally, developing countries are faced with the problem of *generating economic resources to meet rising social aspirations*, rather than providing a set of pre-defined 'basic needs'. All developing societies are late in the development process, compared to Western Europe, and their economic transformation is taking place in a global economic environment in the last decades of the twentieth century. The development problem of developing societies is thus conditioned not only by local factors, but also by forces resulting from globalization. Economic transformation does not, however, occur in a uniform or a unilinear pattern in all developing countries, leading to either failure or success in the achievement of the development goals through wealth creation, as was anticipated by neo-Marxist theories or modernization theories.

The development paradigm rationalizes achievements and rising social aspirations. A contradiction embodied in economic transformation is, however, that development itself contributes to a decline of economic resources and opportunities required to satisfy social aspirations. I use the term development paradox to describe this contradictory process. As a consequence of the *development paradox*, which is not anticipated by development theorists and planners, large segments of society experience social exclusion and frustration. Therefore, I argue that from an economic point of view, the possibilities for the emergence of political conflict are higher in developing than in developed countries. I am, however, aware that the emergence of political conflicts encompasses a wide range of issues not exhausted by a discussion within the disciplinary boundaries of economics.

Briefly introducing the concept of development, I first raise some controversial issues regarding the conventional meaning of the term development, and change known as 'development' in developing countries. I reject the unilinear notions of economic change and the benevolent nature of aggregate changes in the development process. Second, I conceptualize some contradictions in economic change in terms of global commoditization, which creates both *wealth* and *scarcity* at the same time. The contradiction between globalization and localization as a determinant of the development problem is explored, as a contradiction which leads to income and consumption inequalities in developing countries. Third, I analyse the contradictions in the 'basic needs' approach in development thinking. I argue that the provision of basic needs solves but at the same time creates problems at different levels of the development process. Finally, I argue that in a globalizing socio-economic environment, economic change implies a 'paradox of development'. Social exclusion in the context of the development paradox causes the formation of frustrated and localized social groups, which are incorporated into global society, and thereby contributes to the emergence of political conflicts in developing societies.

Development and its rationality

All kinds of development studies are implicitly based on the notion that, by nature, human societies are initially 'underdeveloped'. According to the neo-Marxist paradigm, they were first 'undeveloped' but later became 'underdeveloped' because their surplus was appropriated for the 'development' of Western capitalist countries. However, the 'developed' countries have become developed, achieving conditions which are desirable and rational for societies of underdeveloped countries, too. As discussed in the previous chapter, a similar idea prevails in modernization theory. Underdeveloped countries initially consist of 'traditional' societies. They should and will reach the ultimate stage of 'modernization', again a condition already achieved by developed societies. The transition of human societies from their traditional to modern stage involves the adoption and adaptation of social, economic and political systems developed in Western industrialized societies. Just as modernization theory distinguishes between traditional and modernized societies, development theory distinguishes between underdeveloped and developed societies.

Interpretation of development

In economic literature, the term 'economic development' was initially synonymous with economic growth. In the early post-war period, many developing countries were able to achieve pre-determined growth targets, but the living standards of the masses remained largely unchanged (ILO 1978, Seers 1972, World Bank WDR 1990). This was believed to be due basically to the lack of mechanisms for the distribution of the benefits of growth and for the satisfaction of basic needs of the poor. Therefore, it was widely recognized that an increase in output or income does not translate automatically into an improvement of people's well-being. This recognition caused a shift in development thinking, from 'growth maximization' to approaches based on the concepts of 'growth plus distribution' or 'basic needs'. The meaning of the term 'development' was widely discussed in this context (e.g. Chenery et al. 1974, Griffin & Khan 1992, ILO 1978, Seers 1972, Sen 1983, UNDP *HDR* 1990). In the 1970s, economic development was redefined as the reduction or elimination of poverty, inequality and unemployment in a growing economy (Seers 1972).

Along with the notion of growth plus distribution, the provision of basic needs received much attention in development policy and planning. According to the ILO (1978), basic needs consist of minimum requirements for personal consumption (such as food, shelter, clothing), access to essential services (such as sanitation, transport, health, education), the availability of adequately remunerated employment opportunities, and the satisfaction of qualitative needs (e.g. a healthy, humane and satisfying environment, popular participation in decisions affecting livelihood and freedom). The UNDP describes 'human development' as a process of enlarging people's choices:

> The most critical of these wide-ranging choices are to live a long and healthy life, to be educated and to have access to resources needed for a decent standard of living. Additional choices include political freedom, guaranteed human rights and personal self-respect. (UNDP *HDR* 1990: 1).

As the term development describes an ideal state, incorporating both quantitative and qualitative improvements, a set of indicators (per capita income, life expectancy, mortality, literacy and school enrolment) is typically used to assess the degree of development.[1] Two commonly used composite indicators are the Physical Quality of Life Index (PQLI) developed by Morris (1979) and the UNDP Human Development Index (HDI). The former is based on life expectancy, infant mortality and literacy, while the latter is based on life expectancy, literacy and GDP per capita adjusted for purchasing power parity (PPP).

Strictly speaking, the term 'development' says nothing about copying the Western development experience. Yet Western development is the model of development for developing countries, as well as the yardstick for assessing development performance. Therefore, Western capitalism has been the point of departure for development theory ever since Adam Smith published his *Wealth of Nations* in 1776 (Smith 1910). Development thinking has been Eurocentric nature. Economic development is seen as a process during which developing countries become similar to developed countries. Development policies were implemented with the financial, technological and intellectual assistance of developed countries with the intention of copying the economies of the latter, to become more productive according to Western standards. The successful implementation of this programme is considered the key to enabling developing societies to create wealth so that they can become developed according to the Western model.

As the meaning ascribed to the term development is highly restricting, it should be carefully considered. Growth-related indicators such as per capita income do not consider the negative *externalities* of the development process, but do see some negative activities as positive elements in the development process. I use the term *externalities* to indicate either positive or negative ef-

---

1 In addition, a number of authors and institutions have published lists of alternative measures for the assessment of development in terms of structural changes and human welfare. For a summary of these indicators, see Todaro (1985).

fects which are external to the economic activities. Although per capita income does not show the distributive aspects of economic development, it is an aggregate measure widely used to indicate the *potential* of an economy to maintain *living standards*. By definition, indicators of national income do not consider factors such as deforestation, negative externalities of development. On the contrary, processes such as deforestation and phenomena such as civil wars can increase *value added* in national accounting methods, increasing economic growth and national income statistically. Growth-related development indicators are based on monetary values, and the negative externalities of growth are difficult to quantify in monetary values, hence they are not easily incorporated in growth-related indicators. Moreover, the positive impact of negative externalities on economic growth multiply over time. The problems arising from growth-induced negative externalities, such as environmental pollution, ecological disasters and diseases, must be solved by the development programmes themselves. The very nature of the national income method means that these programmes, designed to solve the problems arising from economic growth, in turn multiply the increase in economic growth rates.

The economic transformation of developing countries is obviously a controversial matter. The basis for the controversy is disagreement about what should be *included* in and what should be *excluded* from analyses of economic 'development'. Even in developed countries, economic development becomes a controversial issue if the net contribution of Western development to their own societies and to the rest of the world is assessed. Indeed, all economies and societies are transforming. Whether this transformation is development or not depends on what the term 'development' is taken to mean.

Development or transformation?

A basic question arising from the development paradigm is whether developing countries are 'developing' as the term implies. Liberal modernization theories viewed economic change in developing countries as 'positive', towards modernization, while neo-Marxist theories viewed that it as 'negative', towards peripheralization. Recent studies discussing development and modernization (Alvares 1992, Apter 1987, Buarque 1993, Marglin & Marglin 1990, Sachs 1992, 1993)are sceptical about the potential for 'development' in developing countries according to Western standards. This pessimistic scepticism shares with liberal modernization and neo-Marxist paradigms the idea of the unilinear direction of economic change. The point made in these studies is that the development project, implemented in underdeveloped countries since the mid-twentieth century, has not achieved its goals, but has increasingly created constraints on the accomplishment of the project.

The development project has resulted in an uneven record of development socially and regionally, environmental pollution and ecological disasters have resulted, and so have higher levels of civil conflict (Banuri 1990b). One could argue that the growth of Western economies occurred despite such negative externalities arising from their economic transformation. But the issue is whether the world can tolerate the negative externalities arising from economic development in the 'whole world'. In contrast, one could show that in the course of global technological transformation, development itself innovates solutions to deal with the negative externalities of the development project.

Owing to differences in methodology, definitions and classifications, empirical studies have interpreted economic change in developing countries differently. According to some studies on economic change, there are no signs that the income gap between developing and developed countries will narrow (Griffin & Khan 1992, UNDP *HDR* 1992). According to Mehmet (1995), conditions in many developing countries are worse today than they were in the 1970s. The World Bank (*WDR* 1995: 53) shows that the ratio of GDP per capita in the richest countries to that of the poorest countries increased from 11 in 1870 to 38 in 1960 and to 52 in 1985. Nonetheless, according to another World Bank document, 'developing countries are advancing much faster than today's developed countries did at a comparable stage', in terms of income and consumption and social indicators (WDR 1990: 1). The UNDP shares this idea: 'developing countries have made significant progress towards human development in the last three decades' (*HDR* 1990: 2). This claim is, however, based on the *average* progress achieved by developing countries, despite the significant variations among individual countries and regions.

Economic change in developing countries is not unilinear. Developing countries as a whole are neither heading towards the status of developed countries, nor are they moving towards increasing peripheralization. There are wide variations in the growth performance in individual developing countries. Some countries have actually closed the income gap between them and developed countries. Moreover, the growth performance of some countries in East Asia and the Pacific region has been higher than that of high-income developed countries. In contrast, for many countries the income gap between them and developed countries has increased.

Economic transformation is not simply a movement from one stage to another. We can speak of stages of development or modernization only if there are starting points and finishes. Although it has become customary to designate industrialized countries as 'developed', no nation is 'developed' in the sense of having reached any 'end' (Klein 1988). Similarly, the so-called developing countries are not undeveloped or underdeveloped in the sense of *not* having reached any 'development end'. As a whole, these countries are not 'developing' either, contrary to what the term implies, in the sense of experiencing a uniform process of economic transformation leading to a given development end.

Rationalizing development

The necessity and the desirability of economic development are implied even in the normative concept of 'development'. The term implies that it is ideal to be 'developed'. The term development and its measurement posit that the living standards of society at this ideal stage are higher than those at an underdeveloped stage, or comparable with those of developed industrial economies. When development is considered desirable, change towards development becomes rational. Development is rationalized by modernization and development theories on the basis of its *intrinsic* and *instrumental* desirability:

> The expansion of choice is intrinsically desirable if valued for its own sake independently of the choices actually made, and it is instrumentally desirable if valued because it allows the attainment of preferred positions hitherto beyond the individual's reach (Marglin 1990: 4).

It cannot be denied that income generation is of prime importance, since all other achievements related to basic needs are subservient to material progress. According to Lewis (1955), the advantage of economic growth is not that wealth increases happiness, but that it increases the range of choices available to society. Therefore, the idea of 'development' is fundamentally based on nations' ability to expand the range of choices available to them.

The provision of basic needs is rationalized on the basis of the desirability of developmental achievements in two respects, namely *equity* and *efficiency*. First, even though economic growth is a condition for development, it is not a sufficient condition. The benefits of economic growth must be delivered to society if economic development can be said to have taken place (Seers 1972, UNDP *HDR* 1990). In fact, social groups which lack the minimum resources to maintain living standards have the 'right' to access to basic needs (World Bank *WDR* 1990). Second, the provision of basic needs is rationalized on the basis of the interdependence of development achievements leading to efficiency. Social services such as education, health and nutrition reinforce each other, while the improvements in these qualitative factors accelerate economic growth (World Bank *WDR* 1990). The basic needs paradigm implies that a development strategy based on the concept of 'basic needs first' will provide an effective foundation for sustained long-term economic growth. Modernization and development theories consider a healthy and educated population, urbanization, and political participation to be preconditions for industrialization and economic development (Webster 1984). Improvements in education, health and nutrition are seen as the formation of human capital which will increase productivity (World Bank *WDR* 1990). On both equity and efficiency grounds, the provision of basic needs is desirable and rational.

Contradictions in economic change

Development can produce a paradox due to inherent contradictions. The contradiction in development is that development generates social aspirations on the one hand, and restrict the fulfilment of those aspirations on the other hand. Development is a process of making things *more and more* available to the masses, i.e. the concept of *abundance*. Yet at the same time, and as a result of the same process, development makes things *less and less* available to the masses, i.e. the concept of *scarcity*. This production of both abundance and scarcity should be understood in relation to social expectations of developmental achievements.

An important component missing in development discourse is the perception, by individuals or social groups, of their own development, in terms of what they expect to achieve. Development theorists have conceptualized and planners have decided 'what people want', on the basis of dogmatic and static standards. As Webster (1984: 19) argued, there is a simple assumption underlying the basic needs paradigm, leading to a determination of basic needs merely through an assessment of the biological and physiological demands of the human body for food, warmth and shelter. The assumption underlying the definition of basic needs raises a few fundamental questions: whether human needs are only biological and physiological; if so, whether resources available in developing countries are inadequate to satisfy the basic needs of their own societies; and whether the fulfilment of these pre-defined basic needs solves the 'development problem'.

Human 'needs' were originally biological and physiological, for human beings must satisfy their biological needs to survive. If these are the kinds of human needs we are talking about, the scarcity of resources may not be as important as it is considered to be. Yet *scarcity* is the central issue in economics and continues to be so because of the lack of resources and opportunities to satisfy not biological or physiological needs, but social needs as well. Marxists, institutional economists, sociologists and anthropologists are aware that human wants are socially determined (Appadurai 1986, Miller 1995, Preteceille & Terrail 1985, Veblen 1992). That is why human wants are unlimited, and correspondingly, resources limited.

Development in underdeveloped states is not merely an internal problem of these societies. On the one hand, the development problem has resulted from the fact that economic transformation in developing countries occurs later than in Western Europe. On the other hand, that economic transformation takes place in a global economic environment. Thus, development in developing countries has been conditioned by the economic transformation of Western Europe and by globalization. In a broader perspective, 'globalization stands for the formation of a world economy, world polity, and a world culture, in short, for the emergence of a world society' (Kloos 1993: 6). Moreover, globalization has been dominated by the economic transformation of Western Europe, though the process started with human evolution. The very unequal economic transformation in Western Europe and the globalization of its effects during the last few centuries have created the 'need for development' and introduced 'goals of development' for so-called developing societies. Nevertheless, the same processes of economic transformation, connected to the problem of development, continue to restrict the economic resources and opportunities in developing countries, producing scarcity in its present meaning.

Commoditization: a source of scarcity

A process known as 'commoditization' (Appadurai 1986) is the source of economic growth. I use the term commoditization for the complex process of *producing more and new exchangeable commodities in less time*, in other words an increase in production and productivity. Commoditization, according to Kopytoff (1986: 73), takes place in two ways: it is an expansion with respect (a) to each thing, by making it exchangeable for more and more things, and, (b) to the system as a whole, by making more and more different things more widely exchangeable. Because commoditization is the source of economic growth, it also has a strong relationship with 'development'. The improvement of economic conditions is dependent on economic growth. Thus commoditization is rationalized explicitly or implicitly in the development paradigm.

Just as commoditization is the source of *economic growth*, by definition it is also the source of *resource scarcity*. By transforming more and more use values into exchange values or exchangeable commodities in a given period of time, commoditization continues to convert almost everything into commodities. The fact that more and new things become commodities in less time means that scarcity becomes more acute. Commoditization should be considered not in a local but in a global context. The expansion of the range of commodities is a process initiated in and hence dominated by industrialized countries. Yet all economies have become integrated through globalization. In this context, commoditization has resulted in a corresponding expansion of 'social needs' rather than 'human needs' on a global scale. The expansion of social needs on a global scale is, indeed, part of the creation of a global society.

All forms of development literature are based on the premise that underdeveloped societies are poor because they lack the resources to fulfil the needs of society. In liberal modernization and development theories, which take the 'nation-state' as the unit of analysis, poverty in underdeveloped countries is merely a domestic problem. In the face of commoditization and globalization, the validity of this assumption is questionable. When economic problems of underdevelopment are analysed in the context of a global economic system, poverty in developing countries is understood as a social consequence of commoditization and globalization. Thus, an increasing homogeneity of global tastes and aspirations has resulted. The gap between *wants* and *scarcity* in individual societies was created and defined by these on-going processes of commoditization and globalization.

The key microeconomic assumption of individuals' rationality for utility maximization is therefore an oversimplification of the complex behaviour of consumers (e.g. Baxter 1988, Block 1990, James 1993, Miller 1995, Sen 1977). Consumption behaviour is influenced and determined by social and cultural factors, and is often irrational. Consumption fulfils a wide range of personal and social functions. According to Campbell, 'consumption serves to satisfy needs, or indulge in wants and desires, to compensate the individual for feelings of inferiority, insecurity or loss, and to symbolize achievement, success or power' (1995: 111). Consumption is also as a way of communication, expressing attitudes, reflecting commitments and emotions, and constructing personal identity.

Modern consumption patterns must be analysed in relation to commoditization and globalization; likewise, consumption demand is not simply a request of rational individuals for certain things within a constant range of choices, subject to prices and incomes. Demand is determined by social and economic forces, and it can manipulate, within limits, these forces (Appadurai 1986: 31). In the historical formation of demand, these two aspects of demand affect each other. On the one hand, demand is a *message-sending force*. It sets parameters for both consumption (taste) and production (profit) within its relevant sphere of influence, signalling others to consume and produce more. On the other hand, it is a *message-receiving* force. One's demand is determined exogenously as a result of others' consumption and production, among other things. Thus, consumption and production are determined by each other, thereby accelerating commoditization on a global scale.

The range of commodities expands enormously on a global scale, wherever commoditization takes place. The comparison of countries' incomes enables the assessment of national capacities to meet their own demand. On the basis of national income statistics, developing countries are considered to be poor, compared to developed countries, because their income is inadequate to meet the demand for the expanding range of commodities. Developing societies, faced with the challenges of commoditization, experience an increasing scarcity of resources. In turn, the problem of scarcity is supposed to be solved by commoditization itself, which is economic growth.

Commoditization: a source of inequality

A basic contradiction in global commoditization is the exclusion of societies with consumer aspirations from material consumption, through the interaction between globalizing prices and localizing incomes. Before the integration of countries in a single global market, commodities within a limited range of choices were more or less non-tradable. With the continuous production and expansion of new commodities and larger volumes of existing commodities, the range of commodities has expanded, due to technological transformation in industrialized countries. Therefore, the fruits of uneven global technological transformation could be enjoyed in almost all developing countries even without modern technology, local income levels permitting.

While consumption aspirations are governed by global forces, their achievement is subject to local income levels. The implications of global commoditization for developing countries with a low level of per capita income are increasing resource scarcity and consumption inequality. In the absence of price discrimination, government intervention, and transport costs, prices of internationalized commodities tend to equalize across national borders. In the globalizing world, however, the time and costs of transportation, transaction and communication decline. The world market tends towards an 'international commodity price equalization' in a single global market. Even if prices vary among countries (as the case may be with a relaxation of the above assumptions), there is no reason for the price differences to be proportionate to the income disparity between developing and industrialized countries.

The globalization of commodities and their prices rationalizes the need for an international equalization of income.[2] But globalization has not equalized incomes internationally. International income inequality is a theme in all development and underdevelopment theories concerned with the economic growth of developing countries (Hunt 1989). For Western development theories which see underdevelopment as a domestic problem of the states involved, income disparity is a matter of international differences in production and productivity. Neo-Marxist approaches to underdevelopment focus on centre-periphery relations based on unequal exchange in both commodity and factor markets as the sources of income inequality. No single factor can explain global income disparity. It has various institutional and historical causes which call for an extensive, multi-disciplinary analysis.

However, one important question should be raised regarding international income disparity. If there is no reason to expect that income in different societies should be equal, why should income disparities between countries be a matter of such concern in development thinking? It is the impact of commoditization. According to Polanyi (1957: 41), the social catastrophe concomitant to modern society is not due to 'industrialism', but to industrialism as instituted via market capitalism. Therefore, income disparities acquired their validity as development issues because of the commoditization resulting from industrialization and because of the integration of different economies in a globalized market.

The globalization of commodities and their prices along with localization of incomes constitutes the fundamental economic reality explaining the difference between development and underdevelopment. This phenomenon justifies income generation in underdeveloped countries through commoditization itself, as it increases the national economic capacity required to cope with global commoditization. Thus, the resource scarcity in developing countries, or 'underdevelopment', is a construction of global commoditization. The economic change which is required to overcome the problem of resource scarcity, is economic growth, or in other words, commoditization itself in the domestic economy. By raising national income, economic growth increases the economic capacity to cope with the global commoditization. Therefore, economic growth is the requirement and becomes a prime objective of development policy in developing countries.

---

2 Conventional trade theory also concludes that, under strict assumptions relating to free trade, there is a mechanism of equalization of *relative factor incomes*. When labour-abundant (developing) countries specialize in the production and sale of labour-intensive commodities, and capital-abundant (industrialized) countries in capital-intensive commodities, the *relative* factor price (wage-profit ratio) increases in the labour-abundant and decreases in the capital-abundant country.

Chart 4.1 *International consumption inequality:*
developing economies in a commoditizing world

Local per capita income	Ability to meet commoditization	Global commoditization	International consumer inequality
declining	declining fast	continuing	growing fast
stagnant or growing slowly	declining	continuing	growing
growing	growing	continuing	stagnant or declining

Chart 4.1 shows alternatives that any developing country can experience under different circumstances, and their possible impact on the country's exclusion from global material consumption. Unless developing countries are able to maintain a fast rate of income generation, their international consumption inequality can grow. *International* consumption inequality has an important impact on *internal* consumption inequality, because the former can result in consumption by some social segments through the exclusion of others. This phenomenon explains a large part of growing income and consumption inequalities in underdeveloped areas. If the relatively low per capita income of developing countries does not permit socially perceived global material consumption standards at national levels, consumption by affluent social groups can only be sustained by aggravating income inequality. This means that unless resources are generated adequately, commoditization and its globalization lead to a greater concentration of income and hence also to the concentration of material consumption among higher social classes.

There is, however, another important factor which determines distribution, namely state policy. Depending on development policies affecting distribution, income and consumption inequality within society can grow, remain constant, or decline. In relation to the present discussion of contradictions in global commoditization, it is important to question whether effective distributive policies can solve the development problem in underdeveloped societies, if income generation is insufficient to meet global commoditization.

Let us take as an example a developing economy with stagnant economic conditions, facing global commoditization. Because this economy is part of the global economy, consumer behaviour patterns are conditioned by commoditization. Society faces an increasing range of choices, and increasing costs of consumption (James 1993, Miller 1995). Given its stagnant income, society would deal with commoditization by restricting the consumer choices available to lower social classes. Due to the contraction of the range of choices, the poverty of lower social classes will increase in two ways. On the one hand, in light of the expanding consumer choices, the lower social classes feel that their purchasing power has declined. On the other hand, the higher social classes benefit from expanding consumer choices, and will absorb an increasing share of national income, causing a further decline in the potential income of lower social classes. Affluent minorities will enhance their *entitlement* or *capability*, in Sen's terms (1983,1988), at the expense of the lower social classes. This results in an increasing consumption inequality. Consumer inequality will be further exacerbated in an economy with declining economic growth.

When faced with stagnant or declining economic growth, the state can intervene to achieve distributive equality. A political atmosphere is required which will enable the elimination of globalization forces of international transaction, transportation and communication. History has shown that the idea of the complete isolation of an economy from global integration is far from realistic, as such economies were not viable economically and politically. Any distributive equality, achieved deliberately in any developing economy with stagnant or declining incomes, makes no sense, as the society's ability to cope with global commoditization is declining. Internal distributive equality would be meaningless if the country's distributive inequality is worsening internationally.

Even with some degree of economic growth, commoditization can aggravate consumption inequality. The well-known inverted U-curve hypothesis (Kuznets 1955), which has much in common with liberal modernization theory, states that inequality increases at early stages, and declines at later stages of economic growth. The Kuznets hypothesis deals with inequality as an internal problem and generalizes inequality as an intermediate phenomenon in economic growth in any society. Studies have confirmed that there is no uniform pattern in the relationship between income inequality and economic growth (Hunt 1989: 261). Moreover, different patterns and degrees of state commitment and capability can influence the relationship between distribution and growth, as I will discuss later.

Basic needs and social expectations

Development creates problems that must be solved by further development. Development is the enlargement of the range of choices (UNDP *HDR* 1990), when the 'choices' are defined loosely in aggregate terms. Development can also entail a contraction of the range of choices available to societies which are faced with a scarcity of resources and opportunities, in light of expectations. The range of choices will diminish if the old or traditional choices are eliminated or undervalued socially. From generation to generation, societies in developing countries expect higher levels of achievement socio-economic advancement. By socio-economic advancement, I mean upward social mobility of individuals or social groups. The sources of rising expectations in developing societies can be approached in relation to the global and social context in which development takes place, and in relation to the development achievement itself.

The fulfilment of basic needs by conventional standards and specifications is often considered to solve the 'development problem' in developing countries, but the concept of basic needs becomes meaningless when what the people expect to achieve does not fit the specifications of basic needs as defined by conventional development thinking.

Basic needs: a source of solutions and problems

Absolute poverty exists, in the sense of the lack of means for subsistence: 'a situation in which people are barely existing, where the next meal may literally be a matter of life or death as the cumulative effects of malnutrition and starvation enfeeble' (Webster 1984: 16) However, it is questionable whether curing the problem of absolute poverty will satisfy the poor. People who escape from absolute poverty suffer from *relative deprivation*, in economies which lack the resources and opportunities to match expectations. People expect not just food, clothing and shelter, but certain kinds of food, clothing, and shelter. Furthermore, many other things are expected to improve the 'quality of lifestyle'.

By definition, different quantitative and qualitative aspects of socio-economic advancement are interdependent, and hence develop as consequences of each other. Therefore, the notion of the desirability and rationality of various aspects of economic change on efficiency and equity grounds continues to dominate development thinking. However, the question is whether improvements in the quality of life in developing countries did solve problems, or, rather, gave rise to social expectations that could not possibly be met. Different aspects of achievements rationalized in the context of development make people not developed, but *qualified* or *free* to generate expectations for further achievements.

The World Bank states that 'efforts to reduce poverty are unlikely to succeed in the long run unless there is greater investment in the human capital of the poor' in terms of social services (*WDR* 1990: 74). Improvements in education, health and nutrition directly address the worst consequence of being poor. According to Webster, the welfare strategy of modern governments in developing countries 'would serve primarily to relieve some *symptoms* of poverty rather than its cause' (1984: 21). However, welfare systems are rationalized by the basic needs approach to development, and compels modern nation-states to expand their welfare roles by delivering social services (Blaug 1974, Webster 1984, World Bank *WDR* 1990, UNDP *HDR* 1990). Development, in other words, increases people's freedom by expanding the range of choices and minimizing external constraints in the pursuit of social goals (Todaro 1985: 87). Even though the expansion of social services increases the freedom to choose and minimizes the constraints, the question is whether it improves accessibility.

The strong positive relationship between education, employment and income has been studied extensively in both economic and sociological literature (Becker 1974, Blaug 1974, Hall 1994, Polachek & Seibert 1993). As far as the generation of social expectations is concerned, education performs a twin task in development. On the one hand, it increases people's awareness of their changing environment and the potential standards of living. On the other hand, it provides a basic qualification for new generations to move away from a 'traditional' towards a 'modern' socio-economic environment. For these reasons, as Wallerstein mentioned, in traditional agricultural economies, 'major contemporary demand has been for more educational facilities for their children, seeing the educational system quite correctly as the only likely route of social mobility' (1979: 185). Consequently, younger generations in post-war developing societies generally have a higher level of education, and consequently of awareness and social aspirations, than their parents.

Education primarily serves to free new generations in the traditional rural sector from their traditional social ties and to grant them the basic qualifications required for access to the modern sectors. Thus, the expansion of education also narrows the range of choices for educated people, for they no longer expect to remain in their traditional economic systems. Education in developing countries promotes the flight of youth from the traditional peasantry to urban-based modern occupational categories which are socially valued and financially rewarded. Taking into account the coexistence of traditional and modern sectors in developing countries, Western development theorists such as Lewis (1958) rationalized the labour flight from the former to the latter as a prerequisite of economic development. This rationalization was based on the fact that the marginal productivity of labour is low (perhaps even less than zero) in the traditional rural agricultural sector, reflecting disguised unemployment. However, labour flight also occurs in traditional developing societies which lack the urban industrial capacity to absorb the rural population. Consequently, in many developing countries labour flight from peasant to modern sectors converted disguised traditional unemployment into open modern unemployment (Blaug 1974).

Other areas of concern have been health care and nutrition. The basic needs approach rationalized the state's responsibility as a provider of these social services. Disease, malnutrition, high infant mortality and low life expectancy are basic characteristics of underdevelopment. As the technology to deal with these problems of underdevelopment is accessible, with or without economic growth, it is rational to provide social services to the population. This also accelerates economic growth by increasing productivity. People have the 'right' to these social services, and the modern state has the responsibility to provide them. Yet the basic question is whether the implementation of such welfare systems can solve the problem of development. The welfare system solves the problem at one level by removing some important symptoms of underdevelopment, but contributes to other development problems at the same time.

Welfare systems can improve the capacity of the masses to participate in economic development, but only if the developmental process can absorb the masses. Population increases, both quantitatively, due to population growth, and qualitatively, due to increased welfare. High population growth is considered to be a typical characteristic of underdevelopment. Population growth in many developing countries has been rapid during the past few decades because of the improvement in social services such as modern health care and nutrition. The welfare state inevitably contributes to the emergence of a healthy and educated population with higher social aspirations, which is a qualitative population increase. If economic resources and opportunities are lacking, the population will feel excluded from socio-economic advancement and the country's development process. There should be economic resources and opportunities for the lower social strata to improve their socio-economic status. When resources and opportunities for the masses are lacking, they will be dependent more on the state. The role and the responsibility of the state as a provider is critical. A lack of resources and opportunities for the masses also means that the economy has not gained growth momentum. In the absence of growth momentum the means by which the welfare state is sustained becomes a critical issue.

In underdeveloped economies, the welfare system becomes *irreversible* as well as *unsustainable,* reflecting a contradiction in delivering social services to the poor. The sustained provision of social services is problematic because the economic capacity of the welfare states is limited. The allocation of resources obviously depends not only on economic growth, but also on the commitment of the state. For this reason, at least in the short run, a developing country can maintain a certain level of welfare expenditure. However, a continuation and expansion of the provision of basic needs in the long-run, without adequate economic growth, is unrealistic. By nature, welfare measures are irreversible. It is easy to start providing social services when economic conditions are favourable, but difficult to stop when conditions become unfavourable. When the living conditions of the masses depend on welfare interventions, the irreversibility of welfare systems is acute.

The challenge facing welfare states has been to expand the welfare system in societies with growing populations. The problem is not limited to providing, continuing and expanding welfare systems. Rising social expectations are characteristic of such growing populations. The state cannot restrict itself to providing only basic needs. It should anticipate the rising social expectations of its people who are brought up in a welfare state yet are relatively deprived.

In many developing countries during the past few decades, systems of social services for a large part of the population were maintained (World Bank *WDR* 1990, UNDP *HDR* 1990). Yet the development problem has not been resolved. From the development point of view, as I have already mentioned, the expansion of welfare interventions increases the capacity of the masses to participate in economic development. The World Bank suggests that a welfare strategy for the rapid and politically sustainable reduction of poverty should be accompanied by the expansion of opportunities (*WDR* 1990). According to the World Bank, these opportunities are access to land, credit, infrastructure and technology. It cannot be denied that, from an economic point of view, these opportunities are crucial for the enhancement of the growth momentum with the productive participation of the poor in the development process. Nevertheless, the expectation of relatively deprived are not limited to a set of narrowly defined opportunities. People perceive themselves as entitled to and qualified for an advancement in their quality of life. The lack of opportunities is thus not the only factor which can prevent mass participation in the development process. The lack of opportunities of the kinds which are expected by society can be a critical issue faced by the state, and hindering development.

Contradictions in welfare democracy

Political systems can exacerbate the problems faced by a welfare state. Democratic and pluralist political structures are typically considered to be better than authoritarian political systems, because democratic and pluralist political systems are said to represent the will of the majority. Thanks to popular political participation, people can decide what is best for them. Modernization theory rationalizes the development of democratic and pluralist political structures in developing countries. According to Eisenstadt (1966), industrialization requires a parallel development of a democratic and pluralist political structure. As economic development is interpreted in terms of growth and improving mass welfare, 'to achieve the latter masses must have the right to participate in policy debate concerning the provision of basic needs' (Hunt 1989: 272). However, the idea that industrialization, economic growth and liberal democratic systems are interdependent does not hold even for Western European societies (Salmi 1993, Webster 1984).

Even under a political system characterized by popular participation, *popular will* will not necessarily make the sacrifices requires for long-term economic growth. The opposite is true. In an underdeveloped society where people are relatively deprived and where social aspirations are governed by local and global forces, people perceive their personal socio-economic advancement as what is best. If society is strong enough to influence the decision-making, people will be unlikely to agree with policy measures that reduce or rationalize the existing welfare systems. Moreover, within such a democratic and pluralist political system, politicians are able to manipulate the will of the underdeveloped society in order to fulfil personal political objectives, regardless of the country's long-term growth objectives. Furthermore, society is heterogeneous in terms of attitudes and ideological positions of individuals and social groups, who are influenced by various institutions. Therefore, in practice 'what is best' is unclear, and social and political consensus is often absent.

In authoritarian systems, where decision-making power is concentrated in the hands of one or a few political leaders, political commitment and capability depend largely on the personal qualities of the leaders. Unlike in pluralist systems, the state's commitment to long-term development objectives cannot be assumed. Some states in East Asia achieved economic growth under authoritarian political systems, while some states in Africa and Latin America did not. However, the political system and political stability are only part of underlying forces influencing a country's growth. A comparison between pluralist and authoritarian political systems does not lead to the conclusion that one is better than the other in terms of economic development. The major issue is not whether one is better than the other. In any system, the question pertains to the commitment and capability of the regime in power to achieve long-term development objectives.

Despite the liberal modernization and development view that pluralist and democratic political systems are either complementary to or prerequisites for economic growth, there are contradictions within any such political system. Therefore, liberal political systems encourage society to pursue socio-economic advancement without considering the means for generating economic resources and opportunities required.

The paradox of development: economic dimensions of political conflicts

The development paradox is that economic transformation in developing countries can produce various contradictory processes affecting the socio-economic advancement of different social segments. Although development widens the range of choices available, it can also diminish the range of socially expected choices. On the one hand, among the relatively deprived social groups, expectations of socio-economic advancement rise, in the context of the current local and global socio-economic environment. On the other hand, relatively deprived social groups experience a growing scarcity of economic resources and opportunities in relation to their expectations. Therefore, the strategic development problem faced by developing countries is the generation of economic resources and opportunities to meet rising social expectations, rather than a set of pre-defined basic needs.

Social exclusion and frustration

An inevitable outcome of the growing *relative* scarcity of economic resources and opportunities has been the exclusion of large social groups from socio-economic advancement. This relative deprivation can be analysed as 'social exclusion', a concept which has been used to discuss a wide range of problems relating to the social, political and economic disadvantages of individuals or groups.

> Social exclusion ... is seen as a way of analysing how and why individuals and groups fail to have access to or benefit from the possibilities offered by societies and economies. It is at heart a normative, heavily value-laden notion, evoking negative responses, in contrast to the positive image of inclusion or integration. (Rodgers et al. 1995: 44).

Evidently, social exclusion is a relative concept, because it is to be understood in relation to what other societies and what others in the same society have achieved. As relative deprivation exists at different levels of socio-economic advancement, the expectations of deprived social classes can differ at each level of deprivation. Even though basic needs are provided for, enabling escape from *absolute* poverty, people remain deprived in terms of their expectations for social status, income, consumption, education, career prospects and so on. They feel excluded when others and other societies have access to such opportunities.

In modernizing societies, the social status that people have at birth does not necessarily determine the status they can achieve. Increasing labour mobility coupled with high population growth resulted in a new social category which exhibits weakened ties to parental social class and high socio-economic aspirations. The socio-economic advancement of any individual or social group is virtually unimpeded by traditional social ties. Hence, social exclusion is no longer determined by status at birth in modern capitalist societies.

However, different economic, social, cultural, political and legal factors formally and informally determine social exclusion (Rodgers et al. 1995). The need for a wide range of *formal criteria* for social exclusion is legitimized by the internal contradictions in modernizing underdeveloped societies. Because social mobility is free from traditional social ties, new generations in developing societies typically form an expanding category of social classes striving for socio-economic advancement. In contrast, economic resources and opportunities required for their socio-economic advancement are already scarce in absolute terms, and are becoming scarce in relative terms due to globalization. The expanding new social classes constitute an acutely competitive society, unified under the modern economic, political and administrative system. From the state's point of view, increasing the quantitative and qualitative measures to curtail demand is a justifiable option. The deprived social classes feel socially excluded.

Even though the 'nation-states' are unified under a centralized administrative and political system, from an economic point of view, regional disparities in development result in the social exclusion of social categories in disadvantaged regions. Wealth, income and prices are economic criteria which deny consumption to low-income classes. Some important characteristics of commoditization, such as complementarity, indivisibility and the production of increasingly high exchange values (James 1993), confine material consumption to affluent minorities. 'The visible growth of mass consumption among affluent minorities clearly intensifies the sense of exclusion among other groups even if absolute poverty does not increase' (Rodgers et al. 1995: 45). The development of modern consumption patterns even in underdeveloped countries, as a result of global commoditization, inevitably results in social exclusion.

The problem of social exclusion should be viewed as a 'process' (Rodgers et al. 1995), as expectations rise according to levels of achievement. Therefore, socio-economic advancement cannot be considered to solve the problem of social exclusion. The idea of preventing social exclusion rationalizes the provision of basic needs as well, because social categories affected by the lack of basic needs are denied social mobility. Rather than solving the problem of social exclusion, the provision of basic needs itself becomes a source of social exclusion at a higher level. The provision of basic needs enables people to develop socially defined expectations for higher incomes, consumption and career prospects. When economic resources and opportunities fail to meet these high expectations, the provision of basic needs itself results in intensified feelings of social exclusion.

If the scarcity of resources and opportunities is acute in relation to rising competition due to the rapid expansion of social expectations, formal criteria of exclusion become inadequate. This, in turn, opens the possibilities to exercise *informal criteria*: characteristics such as race, ethnicity, religion, social background, kinship, friendship and political affiliation become important qualifications for access to economic resources and opportunities. Therefore, the distribution of scarce resources and opportunities is not only unequal but also unfair.

Social grouping: localization within globalization

Social exclusion in a unified and competitive economy with an increasing scarcity of resources and opportunities can become an important source of social frustration. One person's socio-economic advancement in a competitive society necessarily prevents that of others. Evidently, this problem is acute in the post-war developing societies, where new generations have been expanding quantitatively and qualitatively. Youths in underdeveloped societies increasingly experience social exclusion in the context of the post-war development process. This is because these generations face absolute and relative scarcity of resources and opportunities, competition amongst individuals and social categories, and consequently, unequal or unfair distribution.

Social exclusion resulting from the development paradox can explain the economic dimensions of political conflicts in developing countries, because social exclusion contributes to the formation of social categories. This is, in fact, a process of *localization* within developing societies increasingly exposed to a *globalization*.

> ... when relatively small groups or categories are incorporated in larger ones, they become more conscious of themselves, and they begin to emphasize an identity of their own they never felt before (Kloos 1993: 11).

Globalization increases the awareness of relatively small groups and societies of the socio-economic advancement of other groups and societies. Being exposed increasingly to the outside world, and facing increased competition in their own societies, small social groups perceive their social exclusion as well as their 'right' to social inclusion and integration. Analysing discontinuities in change, modernization theories postulated that people in traditional societies oppose change and consequently protest against modernization. Yet, the phenomenon of localization within globalization suggests that people tend to protest more due to their exclusion from change than due to their resistance to change.

According to Terhal (1992), there several social groups form in a rapidly growing economies. These groups are classified as disadvantaged, stagnating, mobile satisfied, and mobile unsatisfied. In addition, rapid economic growth has been seen as a source of political destabilization (Olson 1963). By taking economic growth in developing economies as autonomous processes of these societies, these conceptualizations present too narrow a picture of the relationship between the formation of social groups and economic growth. As I have discussed, *economic change* in a global environment, whether it is rapid growth or not, can result in social exclusion and the formation of smaller social groups. Societies experiencing rapid economic growth can lessen social exclusion resulting from the development paradox better than economies facing slower economic growth.

The formation of political conflicts should be understood as a process. The development paradox is also a process, which intensifies the sense of social exclusion. Socio-economic advancement increasingly comes to lie beyond the reach of deprived social groups. Thus, the emergence of intrastate political conflict is significantly associated with the development paradox.

There is no universal, unilinear correlation between the development paradox and the emergence of political conflict. Political conflicts involve not only economic, but also social, cultural and political factors. Even in multidimensional political conflicts, it is noteworthy that individuals and social groups stress their identity in terms of social, cultural and political factors when economic conditions frustrate their socio-economic advancement. No single factor taken in isolation provides a comprehensive explanation for political conflict, even in developing countries. Abstract specific conflict theories, which tend to see 'volcanic' relations of political conflict, are one-sided (Aya 1990, Rule 1988). Moreover, as Tilly (1978) pointed out, the escalation of political tensions into collective violence demands organization and mobilization forces, common interests and opportunity. Political conflicts are organized when people feel that they have no access to institutionalized non-violent means of representing their grievances, and when state authorities are believed to be directly responsible for their exclusion. Perhaps they may have access to such institutions, which is the case in many democratic states, but the non-violent means of expressing grievances may not be effective.

There is no single pattern of emerging intrastate political conflict in every developing economy, even in countries with similar patterns of economic change. This is because economic change coupled with cultural, political and social factors can be destabilizing. Likewise, any of these factors can be stabilizing, countering the negative consequences of others. Even though other factors are crucial in the emergence of potential political conflicts, the pattern of economic change can be a stabilizing force, depending on the ways in which it influences society.

Summary

In the preceding analysis, I have conceptualized the 'development paradox' as a contributing factor in political conflicts in developing countries. The development paradox pinpoints the irreversible escalation of social aspirations in competitive societies, resulting from the development paradigm itself. Development can widen the range of choices, but it is also possible that developing societies experience a contraction of choices in the process known as development. The increasing relative scarcity of economic resources and opportunities results in a decline of the possibilities to satisfy rising social aspirations.

Economic transformation in developing countries takes place in a global economic environment, where Western development plays an influential role. Western economic transformation introduces development problems and goals. Globalization through transaction, transportation and communication, plays an increasingly influential role, in combination with domestic forces, in conditioning the development problem. The development problem in developing countries has been how to generate economic resources and opportunities, rather than to provide a constant set of basic needs.

The normative term development stands for an idealized kind of society that is considered to follow on the increased creation of wealth and its distribution throughout society. Development is thus viewed as 'growth plus distribution' or a provision of basic needs, enabling people to overcome the problems of underdevelopment. The development paradox arises from the contradictions in economic change.

Commoditization, which is *the production of more and new things in less time*, is considered to be the means to the creation of wealth. But it is also the source of scarcity, by definition. Commoditization and its globalization created the problem of underdevelopment for developing countries by increasing the *relative* scarcity of resources in underdeveloped societies to cope with global commoditization. Consequently, income and consumer inequalities have worsened. Even though distribution in a developing country can be influenced by effective distributive policies, domestic equality makes little sense if the country is increasingly disadvantaged internationally. In the face of global commoditization and its social consequences, a constant set of strictly defined basic needs becomes meaningless. Development theories have failed to recognize the importance of people's perceptions of own development.

The provision of basic needs, as the development paradigm explains, expands the range of choices at an aggregate level. But it contracts the range of 'expected' choices in societies faced with a scarcity of economic resources and opportunities to meet the rising social expectations. Social aspirations escalate in relation to global and social economic change and in relation to development itself. As relative deprivation exists at different levels, the basic needs approach solves the problem of underdevelopment at a low level but contributes to problems at higher levels of deprivation. The provision of social services such as health care, nutrition and education are justified on the basis of their development interdependence and people's 'right' to them. People consider themselves entitled to more social mobility. Therefore, development creates problems of development that in turn must be resolved by development itself.

The provision of social services is a responsibility of modern welfare states. But the modern states in developing countries face limited economic capacity. Further, the population with advanced aspirations increases, both quantitatively, as the population grows, and qualitatively, as social preferences for socio-economic advancement change. New generations are more exposed to the global socio-economic environment than earlier generations, and their expectations are conditioned by state policies of human capital formation. The commitment and the capacity of both state and society determine the generation of economic resources and opportunities to satisfy rising expectations of socio-economic advancement.

Due to increased exposure to globalization and increasing development, younger generations in developing countries more are aware of the degree of their social exclusion than their former generations are. Social status at birth no longer determines socio-economic advancement, and the younger generations exhibit weakened ties to their traditional social class. One individual's achievements inevitably restrict those of others. This results in increasing social exclusion, both formally and informally, leading to the formation of frustrated social groups. This is a localization within globalization: social groups begin to realize and to emphasize their *social exclusion* as well as their 'right' to *social inclusion*.

Social exclusion resulting from the development paradox can result in political conflicts in developing countries. However, social exclusion and political conflicts should be viewed as connected processes, rather than incidents in a sense that the former triggers off the latter. There is no unilinear relationship between the two processes, for political conflicts and their escalation into collective violence involves many factors other than economic ones.

I have tried in this chapter to demonstrate the importance of an economic perspective on political conflicts, by focusing on some important contradictions in economic change in developing countries. In the light of this conceptual analysis, in the forthcoming chapters I investigate the experience of Sri Lanka.

Sri Lanka: Political Conflict in a Welfare democracy

V

In this chapter, my purpose is to discuss the political conflict in the post-colonial period in Sri Lanka in the context of the country's growing economic crisis. A unified competitive society has emerged, thanks to the liberal welfare state, which has continuously failed to achieve the economic growth required to sustain the competitive society. Mismanagement and the lack of political discipline have contributed the country's economic crisis.

In the first section of this chapter, I introduce the major characteristics of political conflict in Sri Lanka in order to highlight the feasibility and the significance of a single economic framework for analysis. In the second section, the increased demands of a consumer-oriented competitive society for economic resources and its underlying economic and political forces are discussed. In the third section, the state's failure on the supply side, and the economic and political factors of the failure, are analysed. I confine my analysis in this chapter to the simultaneous processes of the formation of political conflict and the growth of economic crisis. In the face of growing economic crisis, the exclusion of the country's increasing youth population from socio-economic advancement became acute due to the growing scarcity of resources and opportunities. The problem of distribution during economic crisis in a global context and the social categories that experienced exclusion are addressed in the next chapter.

The escalation of political conflict

For more than two decades after Independence in 1948, Sri Lanka was a relatively peaceful country. The defence expenditure was only 0.5 per cent of total government expenditure at Independence (Snodgrass 1966: 388). In 1970, defence expenditures accounted for 2 per cent of total government expenditure, and by 1995 this figure has risen to 18 per cent (CBSL: *ROE*). From Independence to the early 1970s, there were no major political conflicts, while the recorded incidents were neither armed conflicts nor large-scale violence against the state. Many early incidents were protests against particular constitutional changes or policy measures, and were limited in terms of their escalation and persistence. They did not challenge the state or the country's economy. Society as a whole did not suffer, as the incidents were rather localized. However, these events were of increasing tension, conflict, and violence. Much of the social science literature on the present political conflict in Sri Lanka suggests that today's political conflict is rooted in history, even in colonial times.[1]

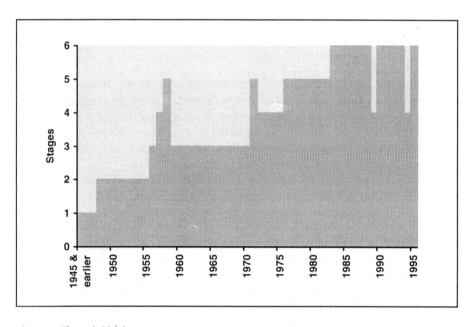

Source: Kloos (1996a)

Stage 1:   differences in culture;
Stage 2:   differences in interests;
Stage 3:   tension;
Stage 4:   conflict;
Stage 5:   irregular eruptions of violence;
Stage 6:   civil war.

The 1980s was marked by an escalation of political conflict in two armed struggles that, although unconnected logically, were connected historically. One is the separatist struggle of the Tamil youth, based on considerations of ethnicity. The other was the Sinhala youth insurgency of the *Janatha Vimukthi Peramuna* (JVP, People's Liberation Front) which had already launched its first insurrection for state power in 1971. The Tamil militant movements became dominated by a single group known as the Liberation Tigers of Tamil Eelam (LTTE). They fought for a separate Tamil state in the Northern and Eastern provinces of

1 For example Chandraprema (1991), Hennayake (1992), Hettige (1992b), Ivan (1989), Jayawardena (1990), Kloos (1993, 1996a), Manor (1984), Ponnambalam (1983), Silva (1995), Silva (1986), Spencer (1990), SSA (1985), Tambiah (1986), (1992), Wickremasingha (1995), Wilson (1988).

Sri Lanka. The two struggles are logically separate in terms of their objectives, geographical locations and cultural factors. They emerged independently, one among the Tamil community in the North and the other among the Sinhala community in the South. The two movements were not interrelated. Yet they appear to have been historically connected in the sense that they are facets of the same political conflict that had existed since Independence.

Chart 5.1 presents graphically the phases in the escalation of the country's political conflict from colonial times to the present. According to Kloos (1996a), differences in terms of cultural factors entail friction between and within societies and become the vehicle of differential interests. Then the stage for conflict is set, and conflict may lead to tension, sporadic eruptions of violence and finally civil war. The development of political conflict in the post-Independence history of Sri Lanka has proceeded according to these stages of escalation, as shown in the chart.

Chart 5.2   *Major events in the post-colonial political conflict in Sri Lanka*

Time	Event
1957/58	Sinhala - Tamil ethnic riots caused by the 'Sinhala-Buddhist' definition of the country
1960	Tamil protests in Jaffna against the attempted change of language of administration from English to Sinhala
1960s	Formation of the Sinhala youth group (JVP) in the South
1971	First JVP insurrection in the South
1972	Tamil protests in Jaffna against the new Constitution
1970s	Formation of the separatist Tamil youth groups, the LTTE and others, in the North
1975	Launching of a programme of political assassinations by the LTTE
1978	Proscription of the LTTE
1981	Anti-Tamil riots in Jaffna
1983	Anti-Tamil pogrom in Colombo; Proscription[JdV3] of the JVP; Beginning of the Eelam War, phase I
1987	Beginning of the second JVP insurrection in the South; Arrival of the IPKF in the North
1989	Death of the JVP leader
1990	Departure of the IPKF; Beginning of the Eelam War, phase II
1995	Beginning of the Eelam War, phase III

The major events in the post-colonial political conflict in Sri Lanka are summarized in Chart 5.2. Two points should be noted. First, some early historical incidents can be considered to some extent sporadic and isolated. Yet these events are historically connected to the political developments that took place since the 1970s. Second, the two facets of the country's political conflict, i.e. the Sinhala youth movement in the South and the Tamil youth movement in the North, are independent of each other. Yet they are historically connected. The two facets of the conflict are similar to a degree.

Growing conflict between and within communities

The differences in Sri Lankan society involve two basic issues. One is the ethnic division of society *between* Sinhala and Tamil communities, and the other is the division *within* these communities. Historically, the Tamil community was concentrated primarily in the Northern and Eastern provinces, and the Sinhala community in the rest of the island. By 'Tamil' I refer to the community that is classified in population censuses as 'Sri Lanka Tamil'; other Tamils, living mainly in the centre of the island, were classified as 'Indian Tamil'. According to the 1981 population census (DCS 1981), the Sinhala community accounted for 74 per cent, and the Sri Lanka Tamil community for 12.7 per cent of the total population of 14.8 million. Of the Sri Lanka Tamil community, about 72 per cent was in the Northern and Eastern provinces].[2] When colonization, which began with the arrival of Portuguese in 1505, Sinhalese and Tamils lived separately to some extent. At the time, the two communities were different in terms of their origin, ethnicity, language and religion, and in terms of political administration and geographical concentration. Yet there was no strict dividing line between the two communities, as historically the Sinhalese and the Tamil were not mutually exclusive ethnic groups, the present linguistic difference notwithstanding (Dewaraja 1988, Pieris 1956, Roberts 1982).Throughout Sri Lanka's history, even in ancient times, the two ethnic groups shared certain cultural, social and political characteristics.

The second difference exists *within* the communities: neither the Sinhala nor the Tamil population is homogeneous. Vast social differences exist within both communities. Historically, both communities have been divided along caste lines (Pieris 1956, Roberts 1982). The Tamil community resembles the South Indian caste system. The *vellala* is the highest caste—the caste of farmers—and was concentrated largely in Jaffna of the Northern province. There are differences between the Tamils of the Northern and the Eastern provinces, as well as between Sri Lankan and Indian Tamils. The Indian Tamil group, which belonged to a caste far lower than the caste of the Tamils in the North, migrated to Sri Lanka from the mid-nineteenth to the early twentieth centuries for plantation work (see Chapter VII). The Sinhala community is also divided along caste lines. One should also note the distinction within the Sinhala community between Up-country (Kandyan) and Low-country. The majority of the Sinhala community belongs to the highest caste, known as *govigama*, which is the caste of farmers. The colonial policy of education and employment has also resulted

2 The distribution of the population by community and district/province, and its changing patterns in the censuses of 1946-81 are presented in Appendix I.

in the rise of an English educated, Westernized, Christian and affluent minority within both Sinhala and Tamil communities (see Chapter VII). This minority group comprised the group of colonial servants and the middle class of the country, and emerged from the higher Sinhala and Tamil castes. As I will discuss later, the country's national political elite also emerged from this minority of both communities. There were few differences in culture and interests between the two communities in this minority group. The differences between the two communities were significant at the lower strata of the social hierarchy.

A major outcome of British colonial administration in Sri Lanka was the political and economic unification of the population, which opened up avenues for conflicts of interests. This effected divisions between the ethnic groups and within each of the ethnic groups. In the former case, because all communities were brought under a centralized administrative system, the Sinhala and the Tamil had to share political power. In the latter case, because the social mobility of any community became virtually independent of the traditional caste system, the Sri Lankan population became a unified competitive society. I focus on the formation of a competitive society in the post-Independence history of Sri Lanka in the next section. In the colonial period, however, the initiation of the modern education system, and the abolition or the disintegration of traditional tenure played a major role in formulating the competitive society. Thus, even in colonial times, the parameters for conflicting interests *between* and *within* communities were already visible.

An additional element of the conflict was the nature of political groupings in Sri Lanka since colonial times. The nature of political groupings before Independence shows two issues connected to differences *between* and *within* communities. As the political arena was a monopoly of the Anglicized elite of the Sinhala and Tamil communities (Jupp 1978 Wilson 1979), Sinhala and Tamil political elites had more in common with each other than with the rest of their own communities. Even Marxist-oriented parties were led by the country's elite (Obeyesekere 1974). Therefore, the structure of political groupings reflected the social hierarchy existing *within* the communities. The second characteristic was the ethnocentric nature of political groupings, which represented ethnic interests. In principle, neither the centre-right United National Party (UNP), founded in 1946, nor the centre-left Sri Lanka Freedom Party (SLFP), founded in 1951, had ethnic labels, but they represented the majority of the Sinhalese and their ideology. The Tamil Congress (TC) and the Tamil Federal Party (FP) were founded in 1944 and in 1949 respectively. Ethnocentric political groupings of the Tamil political elite, with clear ethnic labels, defended the 'minority rights' and illustrated a distinct Tamil consciousness. Although Sinhala and Tamil political elites had much in common, they established the basis for ethnic conflict between themselves. The ethnocentric nature of political groupings provided the people of Sri Lanka with a justification to identify themselves as 'Sinhalese' and 'Tamil' rather than 'Ceylonese'.

Soon after Independence, the ethnocentric nature of governance resulted in the alienation of Indian Tamils, and caused a split in the TC. In the first years after Independence, the House of Representatives passed numerous acts, including the Ceylon Citizenship Act of 1948, the Indian and Pakistani Residents (Citizenship) Act of 1949, and the Parliamentary Elections Amendment Act of 1949. The first two acts denied citizenship to the majority of Indian Tamils, and the third restricted the right to vote to citizens, disenfranchising non-citizen Indian Tamils. Citizenship was granted by 'descent' or on stringent conditions of 'registration'. Indian Tamils, who had been brought to Sri Lanka from Southern India by the British as plantation labourers, could hardly meet the criteria to obtain Sri Lankan citizenship by registration. The political motive of the government, dominated by the Sinhala centre-right United National Party was to prevent that '... the Kandyan electors would be politically swamped by the Indian vote' (Jayawardena 1990: 69).[3] In addition, the Trotskyist opposition, *Lanka Sama Samaja Party* (LSSP: Lanka Equal Society Party) had already been involved in politicizing the plantation community (Jayawardena 1987). Therefore, from the *centre-right* perspective of the UNP, the potential political strength of the Indian Tamil community implied increased Trotskyist opposition. From the UNP's ethnic point of view, which perceived the Sinhalese as an 'unfortunate' community (Jayawardena 1990), the potential political strength of the Indian Tamil community would further marginalize the Sinhalese. These early acts of the first UNP government did not pertain to the Sri Lankan Tamil community. Some Tamil politicians of the TC accepted the acts, but some did not. As a result, the TC split, and the Tamil FP was formed in 1949.

The political changes at the general elections of 1956 caused an upsurge of in political conflict. The change in government from the UNP to the *Mahajana Eksath Peramuna* (MEP: People's United Front), of which the SLFP was the major partner, was a reaction against a still Anglicized government and civil service. The leader of the SLFP, Bandaranaike, won the 1956 elections on the waves of a massive anti-Western, anti-Christian and Sinhala-Buddhist political resurgence, particularly among the rural intelligentsia. In the colonial period, the majority of Sinhala Buddhists had lost the social status that, they had enjoyed prior to colonization, due, it was argued, to the emergence and dominance of Westernized minority groups. The resurgence of Sinhala Buddhist nationalism was backed by contemporary national movements such as the Buddhist revival, and anti-Christian and temperance movements, which had come into being in the nineteenth century (Jayawardena 1985, 1990). The revival of Sinhala Buddhist nationalism coincided with *Buddha Jayanti Year* in 1956, which marked 2500 years of Buddhism. This event, which was celebrated by Buddhists throughout the world, strengthened the local appeal for the restoration of the position of the Sinhala Buddhists. As soon as the Sinhala Buddhists found the proper place to address their grievances, under the leadership of the MEP, they ousted the UNP from power.

---

3 According to 1946 census, the Indian Tamil community accounted for 11.7 per cent of Sri Lanka's population. They were concentrated largely in the tea estate areas of the Central, Uva and Sabaragamuwa provinces. In Nuwara Eliya district of the Central province, the Indian Tamil community accounted for 57.3 per cent of the population, outnumbering the Sinhala community (Appendix I).

Having come to power on the Sinhala Buddhist nationalist platform, the MEP government attempted to change the Westernized appearance and the dominance of the Westernized elites of Sri Lankan society inherited from colonialism. In this attempt, the 'mistake' was committed of ignoring the pluralist nature of indigenous society. Thus, Sri Lanka was defined as a 'Sinhala-Buddhist' country. In this regard, a major step was the introduction of the Official Language Act of 1956, which has become known as the 'Sinhala only' act. The attempts of the government to guarantee the supremacy of the Sinhala language and of Buddhism caused an escalation of ethnic tensions and violence in 1957-58 (Jupp 1978, Wilson 1979). A 1957 government agreement with the Tamil FP was to rectify the 'mistake' and devolve power regionally, under what was known as the Bandaranaike-Chelvenayakam Pact. This failed, due to Sinhala-Buddhist protests backed by the *Sanga* (Buddhist monastic order) and the opposition, the UNP. The Tamil Language Act of 1958 was proposed by the government, but never presented for approval. In 1959, Prime Minister Bandaranaike was assassinated by a Buddhist monk, and the MEP government was dissolved. Tamil *hartal* (general protests) erupted again in 1960, in response to the attempted change of the language of administration from English to Sinhala. In addition to the 'ethnic' events, there were a few other tense incidents in the 1950s and 1960s. The most important events were two abortive coups staged by Army and Police officers in 1962 against the SLFP government (1960-65), and in 1966 against the UNP government (1965-70).

New forces of the conflict: the emergence of radical youth

In the early 1970s, political conflict escalated. The JVP launched its first insurrection in April 1971. The militant Sinhala youth had been preparing for a revolt in the semi-clandestine JVP movement since 1965 (Dissanayake et al. 1995). The JVP movement was an extreme leftist movement based on Guevarist and Maoist ideas on violent revolution and the revolutionary role of the peasantry (Kearney 1973). When the first revolt erupted, the movement was known to people as the 'Che Guevara movement', reflecting Guevara's influence. The JVP insurgents expected to overturn the established political order by following a strategy of 'one-night revolution' (Kearney 1973: 202). Thus, the JVP was opposed to all established political parties, including those of Marxist orientation. The oldest political parties in Sri Lanka were Marxist: the LSSP had been founded in 1935, and the Communist Party (CP) in 1943. But these parties participated in parliamentary politics, and in many cases entered into the coalitions to form the governments. The first JVP insurrection aimed overthrow such a coalition government, which included the SLFP, the LSSP and the CP, elected in 1970.[4]

4 In the general elections of 1970, the SLFP won a landslide victory, winning 91 of the total of 151 parliamentary seats. The LSSP and the CP won 19 and 6 seats respectively. The opposition UNP, which had been in power in 1965-70, with 66 parliamentary seats, secured only 17 seats (Kearney 1973: 93).

The JVP insurrection was suppressed by government forces, and the leader of the movement was imprisoned. To some extent, one could argue, the ethnic riots in 1957-58 and the JVP insurrection in 1971 were isolated events. However, *political conflict* is a process, involving differences, tensions, and sometimes violence. Thus, the early ethnic riots and the first JVP insurrection are events of the same process of escalating political conflict, though the two issues were isolated and logically unconnected.

Soon after the first JVP insurrection, Tamil riots in the North erupted, in 1972, in response to the adoption of the new Constitution, which tried to guarantee Sinhala Buddhist supremacy. The Constitution also replaced the name Ceylon—the name by which the island was known to the rest of the world—by its traditional name 'Sri Lanka'. In the wake of the Tamil riots, political groups of militant Tamil youths were formed in the North and the East (O'Ballance 1989, Ram 1989, Wilson 1988). The Tamil New Tigers was the first of these groups; later it was divided into the Liberation Tigers of Tamil Eelam (LTTE) and the Tamil Eelam Liberation Organization (TELO). These militant Tamil groups agitated not only against the government but also against Tamil parliamentarians who shared the power in the House of Representatives.[5] Since the mid 1970s, a programme of assassinating the Tamil politicians and police officers was launched by the LTTE considering them as betrayers of the rights of the Tamil.

Chart 5.3   *Major partners of political conflict in Sri Lanka*

Sinhala establishment	Tamil establishment
United National Party Sri Lanka Freedom Party and other traditional parties	Tamil Congress Federal Party Tamil United Liberation Front
Ambitious Sinhala youth	**Ambitious Tamil youth**
Janatha Vimukthi Permuna (People's Libertation Front)	Liberation Tigers of Tamil Eelam and other militant groups

Source: Kloos (1995).

5 The TC and the FP, with 3 and 14 seats respectively after the general elections of 1965, entered into a coalition government with the UNP. In the 1970 elections, these Tamil parties were in the opposition with the UNP (Kearney 1973: 42).

The goal of the Tamil militant groups, but also of some of the Tamil parliamentarians, was a separate Tamil state in the North and the East of the island, known as 'Eelam'. The concept of a separate Tamil state in Sri Lanka was declared *officially* to the public by Tamil political leaders in 1976. It was argued that the idea of a separate Tamil state had existed among Tamil political leaders even in the early twentieth century, but it had not been declared officially as a goal of traditional Tamil politics (Silva 1995). The Tamil United Liberation Front (TULF), formed by traditional Tamil parliamentarians established in 1976, pledged to establish a separate Tamil state, but continued to work along democratic lines. The militant Tamil youths were determined to achieve the goal by military means. The LTTE later assassinated the leader of the TULF.

In the early 1970s, there were two major facets of the country's political conflict, which in turn could be divided into a conflict between *established* and *non-established* conflicting parties. The formation of the JVP by the Sinhala youth meant a split in the Sinhala community, between the traditional parliamentary politicians and the militant Sinhala youth. In the same way, the formation of the militant separatist groups among the Tamil youth also meant a split in the Tamil community, between the traditional elite politicians and the radical ambitious youth. Chart 5.3 presents these major political groups.

After 1977, political violence led by Tamil militant groups gained momentum. The new UNP government, elected in 1977, proscribed the LTTE and other Tamil militant groups, and started to fight them, strengthening the army presence in the North. In response, Tamil separatist groups continued to organize and to target the armed forces in their guerrilla activities. After a number of political assassinations of UNP and TULF politicians by Tamil separatist groups, a military and police operation took place in Jaffna. This also followed anti-Tamil riots in Jaffna. A major breakthrough in the Tamil separatist movement occurred in 1983. Following an LTTE ambush that killed thirteen soldiers in Jaffna, urban Sinhala mobs went on an anti-Tamil pogrom in Colombo. Unlike in earlier riot situations, the government did not attempt to stop the mobs, which were allegedly backed by some of the politicians in power. The LTTE and other Tamil separatist groups benefited greatly from the Colombo pogrom in 1983, because the recruitment of the Tamil youth for the separatist movement gained momentum.

The episode of a twin civil war

After the early 1980s, violence and war spread to every corner of the island. The Tamil separatist war started in 1983 in the North and the East of the island. The JVP, which was proscribed in 1983, launched its second insurrection in the rest of the country, carrying out political assassinations after the mid-1980s. The government responded with violence. As a result, the terror of violence quickly eroded the country's democracy, and even its human right record (Kloos 1995, Moore 1992). After the Indo-Lanka Peace Accord was signed in 1987, the Indian Peace Keeping Force (IPKF) arrived in the North and the East of the island. Following this peace agreement, Tamil separatist militant groups other than the LTTE agreed to some regional power devolution, and ceased their military activities, joining the country's democratic process. Due to the arrival of the IPKF in the North and the East, the government was able to station its armed forces in the rest of the country to fight the JVP.

The period of 1987-89 was marked by a complete breakdown of civil society in the Southern areas of the country, due to the violence of the JVP and of the official and unofficial armed forces (Chandraprema 1991). The JVP insurrection was apparently (but temporarily) resolved through repressive measures in 1990 that brought the country back to some state of normalcy. This was followed by the extra-judicial killing of the leader of the JVP in November 1989, who had been released from the prison in 1978 (Chandraprema 1991). The ruthless repression of the JVP insurrection somehow led to a lessening of the political crisis in the Sinhala community.

The new president of the UNP government, R. Premadasa, who was elected in 1989, was willing to negotiate with the LTTE, and forced the IPKF to leave Sri Lanka. At this time, the LTTE was the only Tamil military group involved in the separatist war, as others had joined the democratic process, if they had not been destroyed by the LTTE. The IPKF left in 1989. The negotiations between the government and the LTTE lasted more than a year, until, in June 1990, the LTTE unilaterally terminated negotiations and started Phase II of the Eelam war, as it is usually called. President Premadasa was assassinated in 1993, allegedly by the LTTE. In 1994, a coalition named People's Alliance (PA), of which the SLFP was the major partner, came to power, defeating the UNP which had ruled the country since 1977. Chandrika Bandaranaike Kumaratunge, the new president, also invited the LTTE to unconditional peace negotiations, according to a promise she made in her electoral campaigns. After a truce of four months, the LTTE unilaterally withdrew from negotiations in April 1995, and started Phase III of the Eelam war. It is difficult to judge whether the probability of a resurgence of political conflict in the rest of the island declined following the military repression of the JVP. Thus, the threat of political conflict persists.

The historical pattern of the country's political conflict points to some important issues. First, the sporadic events in the history are not isolated. They clearly show the escalation of political conflict since Independence. The conflict went through different stages, from differences *between* and *within* communities to tension, conflict, irregular eruptions of violence, and, finally, civil war. Second, a major breakthrough in the escalation was due to the emergence of a struggle for power between the traditional established and the radical, unestablished political groups. This occurred in both the Sinhala and the Tamil communities. Thus there are two facets of the political conflict, i.e. the one in the North involving the Tamil community and the other in the South involving the Sinhala community. This also demonstrate the weakness of any study that attempts to isolate the events and facets of the conflict.

Factors beyond ethnicity

Many studies on the political conflict in Sri Lanka have attempted to isolate or to emphasize the so-called 'Sinhala-Tamil' issue, which is only part of the conflict. This has inevitably led them to reduce their analysis to an examination of ethnic factors. An analysis of isolated events or facets of the conflict is less meaningful than an analysis of the whole process of the political conflict. The importance of the escalation of youth agitation in both the Sinhala and the Tamil communities, and its simultaneous evolution into a twin political war cannot be ignored. Important factors other than ethnicity should receive due consideration.

Even though part of the conflict has been characterized as an 'ethnic conflict', this does not mean that there is conflict between all individual Sinhalese and Tamils (Kloos 1993). For the Tamil separatist movement, ethnicity is an effective instrument for the mobilization of the community. Politicizing cultural cleavages is a typical mobilization strategy in political conflicts (Schlichte 1994, Singer 1994). Studies of the Tamil conflict usually emphasize the Sinhala dominance in decision-making processes and Sinhala-Buddhist nationalism (e.g. Silva 1986, Spencer 1990, Tambiah 1986, 1992, Wilson 1988). The analyses of Tamil political conflict are coloured by a focus on a homogeneous ethno-nationalism: as a result, it is designated as 'ethnic conflict'. This claim is not unsupported, because in the first place Tamil militants belong to the Tamil community and fight the Sinhala-dominated government. Tamil militants believe that they are discriminated against by the Sinhalese-dominated governments. This belief provided a reasonable justification for the mobilization of the Tamil youth on an ethnic basis. Sinhala Buddhist nationalism as well as Tamil nationalism constituted the cultural factors of the Tamil conflict. There is a wide range of literature on this issue, particularly on Sinhala Buddhist nationalism (e.g. Jayawardena 1985, Silva 1986, Spencer 1990, SSA 1985, Tambiah 1986, 1992, Wilson 1988), which is not part of the focus of this study. However, as many of these studies have claimed, Sinhala Buddhist nationalism was sponsored by the Sinhala-dominated states, and consequently changes in state policies affecting the allocation of resources in favour of the Sinhala occurred (Ponnambalam 1983; Wilson 1979).

According to Oberst, 'in the case of the Tamils, the majoritarian system of government has allowed Sinhalese dominance of the political system and thus, it was easier to blame the Sinhalese dominated government for the failure of the system' (1991: 15). Not only Tamils blame the post-colonial governments for the failure. Regardless of the Sinhala dominance of the political system, the Sinhala youths have been organized as the JVP since the mid-1960s, that is, even before the separatist Tamil youth movement emerged. A long history of the organization of the JVP movement in the Sinhala community would suggest that the growing tension in the Sri Lankan economy cannot be reduced to factors of ethnicity. Moreover, both the Sinhala militant movement and the Tamil militant movement are nationalist. According to Kloos, both the JVP and the LTTE are '... far more nationalist than the majorities' (1993: 13). This aspect has not yet researched adequately, while the Sinhala struggle has attracted less academic interest than the Tamil struggle.

Some other characteristics are shared by the Sinhala and Tamil militant movements. Both movements draw their membership mainly from the educated and unemployed segments of the youth population, which belong largely to socially and economically depressed lower castes (Chandraprema 1991, Kloos 1993, Moore 1993). The JVP was a product of the unrest of educated and unemployed or underemployed youth from the rural peasantry, normally in the lower strata in the Sinhala caste hierarchy. Opinions continue to differ, however (Hettige 1992a, Moore 1993, Obeysekere 1974, Wriggins & Jayewardene 1973). Nevertheless, it is commonly agreed that the JVP was a youth movement, as much as it was the Tamil struggle. In the North and the East, groups of Tamil youth organized themselves into an armed guerrilla movement with the goal of forming a separate state because they perceived themselves to be the active political representatives of their community (Uyangoda 1992). Similarly, the Sinhala youth of the JVP also aimed to overthrow the existing political order and establish a new one according to their own specifications and standards.

The *Report of the Presidential Commission on Youth* (PCY 1990) has highlighted the heterogeneity of different social classes in every community, and its relation to the development of both Sinhala and Tamil youth unrest. These heterogeneous features were identified by the Commission as economic, social and cultural differences, and caste and regional disparities. Moreover, in the post-colonial period, these differences were exacerbated by political and economic changes introduced by various governments. This resulted in the alienation of a substantial youth population in both communities from the socio-economic advancement that they expected.

If the heterogeneous and plural character of Sri Lankan society transcends mere ethnic division, the claim that 'the Sinhalese gained and the Tamils lost' is rather narrow. It is true that Tamils had an additional disadvantage due to the 'Sinhala Buddhist' definition of the country, a definition that denied its plural character. Yet the issue is whether this is a sufficient argument to postulate that 'the Sinhalese gained, excluding the Tamils'. A basic point against this argument is the emergence of the political conflict in the Sinhala community as well as in the Tamil community. Therefore, a distinction should be made not only *between* but also *within* the communities in the case of the political conflict in Sri Lanka. To explain how Sri Lankan society as a whole has experienced the losses and gains historically, I shall now focus on economic change.

Increasing demand: growth of a competitive society

At of Independence, diverse social segments and isolated regions were unified into a single competitive society, competing for economic resources and opportunities for socio-economic advancement. The process started in the colonial period, with the gradual erosion of traditional Sri Lankan society and the unification of regions in a centralized administrative system. Moreover, the development of a welfare economy and a pluralist political system have become the cornerstones of the competitive society. The emergence of a competitive society can be seen in two respects. Different communities were unified, creating scope for competition *between* them. The Tamils in the North and the Sinhalese in the South hardly had anything to compete with each for other prior to colonization. They became significant contenders of the unified competitive society, however. On the other hand, various social segments of each of the communities were unified, creating scope for competition *within* the communities. Traditionally, different social strata hardly had anything to compete with each other for. However, various social segments within the same community gradually became competitors, competing for the same resources required for socio-economic advancement.

The growing competition for economic resources and opportunities has constituted a significant part of the country's economic crisis. The issue in question involves complex combinations of various economic, political, social and demographic forces. In many respects, Sri Lanka was an exceptional country at Independence (Bhalla 1988 Isenman 1980 Jupp 1978 Kearney 1973 Sen 1983). Manor mentioned that Sri Lanka was '..the scene of a number of important political, social and economic experiments and problems' (1984: 2). One consequence of these specificities was the rapidly growing *demand* for economic resources and opportunities, in quantitative and qualitative terms. I do not use the term 'demand' here in an economic sense, which describes the 'willingness to pay' at different prices. I use the term 'demand' to indicate *political and social demand*, which is a 'compulsion' of individuals or society to obtain access to economic resources and opportunities for socio-economic advancement.

The economy at independence

The Sri Lankan colonial economy has often been described as a 'dual export economy' which comprised the export-oriented plantation sector and the subsistence peasant sector (e.g. Oliver 1957, Snodgrass 1966). With the expansion of the plantation economy under colonial rule, the island's self-sufficient agricultural economy deteriorated. Tea, rubber and coconut plantations became the backbone of the economy.[6] There was no significant manufacturing sector in the country other than that which involved the processing of export crops.[7]

6 Tea plantations were founded in the latter half of the 19th century, while those for rubber were founded in the early 20th century. Coconut was a traditional crop in Sri Lanka, known from ancient times, though the plantation system of cultivation emerged in the British colonial period. At Independence, the plantation sector contributed 36.7 per cent of GDP at current factor cost. The export of tea alone accounted for 61.1 per cent, and the exports of tea, rubber and coconut together for 88.4 per cent of total export earnings. Employment in the plantation sector was 45 per cent of total employment in agriculture, and 26.8 per cent of total employment in the country. Tea, rubber and coconut occupied 63.6 per cent of the total cultivated area (Snodgrass 1966).
7 In fact, there were a few state-owned industrial ventures producing manufactured goods such as plywood, acetic acid, drugs, ceramics, glass, steel, paper, leather and textiles. These industries emer-

According to estimates by Snodgrass (1966), in 1950 only 4 per cent of GDP at current factor cost was contributed by the manufacturing sector. Economic activity seemed to be based largely on merchant capital. As a result of colonial influence on economic ideology, the natural preference of the indigenous capitalist class was also for 'safe investment' in plantation agriculture and related trade and service sectors (Athukorala 1987). In fact, the Minister of Finance of the first national government pointed out that '... investment by the private sector of the economy has, in the recent past, always been small if not negligible' (Jayewardene 1951: 38). Service sectors such as trade, banking, insurance and transport were a by-product of the colonial plantation economy. Hence the service sector, which contributed 46 per cent of GDP in 1950 (Snodgrass 1966), served the interests of the plantation sector more than those of the rest of the economy.

Table 5.1   *Trade balance and trade indexes in Sri Lanka 1940-1960*

Year	Price indexes[a] (1953 = 100)		Trade balance	
	Imports	Exports	Rs. mn.	as % of GDP[b]
1940	26	32	–	–
1945	71	52	–	–
1950	86	104	239	5.7
1951	102	126	238	4.8
1952	110	98	-297	-6.4
1953	100	100	-138	-2.8
1954	88	112	340	6.7
1955	89	117	415	7.2
1956	99	109	196	3.8
1957	96	104	-95	-1.7
1958	83	102	-89	-1.5
1959	91	106	-183	-3.0
1960	91	106	-203	-3.1

a. Census and Statistics Price Indexes
b. GDP at current market price
Source: Data from Snodgrass (1966).

ged during the Second World War, in response to the disruption of the flow of import of commodities. As the supply of imports returned to normal after the war, this 'war-generated' manufacturing activity began to suffer from numerous operational problems and was closed down in the 1950s (Oliver 1957).

A prominent feature of the Sri Lankan economy at Independence was its relatively favourable economic status (Bhalla 1988, IBRD 1953, Jayewardene 1951,
NPC 1959). From the perspective of external and government finance, the Sri
Lankan economy enjoyed economic prosperity until the end of the 1950s. In the
case of external finance, as Table 5.1 shows, the country's terms of trade were
favourable for its primary exports, recording a positive trade balance in the
early and mid-1950s. Further, as I discuss below, there was a large stock of
external assets. In real terms the country was not able to accumulate external
assets in relation to its growing import price index after the early 1950s.
Moreover, the Sri Lankan government maintained a sound budgetary position in
this period, due perhaps to the influence of colonial principles of budgetary
management. In the mid-1940s and mid-1950s, there were even budgetary sur-
pluses (Snodgrass 1966: 388-89). The World Bank mission that visited Sri Lanka
in 1951, made the following assessment of the country's economic condition:

> In the past 75 years the population of Ceylon has trebled. Yet typical living
> standards, while low in comparison with the West, have been maintained
> and almost certainly improved; at present they are among the highest in
> Southern Asia. (IBRD 1953: 1)

This advancement was attributed by the World Bank mission to a virtual 'revolution' in Ceylon's agricultural export sector in the preceding century. At the
expense of the indigenous agricultural economy and the ancient irrigation network in the country's Dry Zone, the production of plantation crops has been
expanded dramatically (Snodgrass 1966). The economic prosperity of Sri Lanka
in the 1940s and the 1950s can be attributed largely to favourable world market
conditions for these exports. The country enjoyed favourable terms of trade, a
sound trade balance and an accumulated large stock of external assets.

A distinguishing feature of the country's international trade was that the favourable movements of the terms of trade, trade balance and external reserves
always corresponded with random events in the world economy, which affected international trade rather, than with improvements in the production capacity of the domestic economy. The decline of the import volume due to the
Second World War resulted in an accumulation of foreign exchange reserves in
the second half of the 1940s (Jayewardene 1951: 10).[8] According to estimates by
Snodgrass (1966: 377), in the five year period of 1940-45, Sri Lanka's total external assets increased by 289 per cent (from Rs. million 324 to 1260). Similarly,
corresponding to the Korean war in 1950-51 and tea price hike in 1954-55, Sri
Lanka's terms of trade improved largely due to an increase in export price
index. Therefore, the trade balance was boosted and external reserves accumu-

8 The impact of the Second World War on the accumulation of Sri Lanka's external reserves could
have been more than the actual accumulation, through a 'war-generated tea price boom', but this
was prevented by Britain, compelling Sri Lanka to sell all its tea to Britain at fixed prices. A free market price for tea would likely have been higher than the fixed price, because when the contract system was abolished, tea prices markedly increased (Wickremeratne 1977: 132).

Table 5.2   *Sri Lanka among Asian countries:
human development record 1960*

Country	Crude death rate (per 1000)	Infant mortality rate (per 1000)	Life expectancy at birth (years)	Primary school enrolment (%)	Adult literacy rate (%)
Sri Lanka	9.2	70.6	62.0	95	75.0
India	21.8	165.0	43.2	61	27.8
Pakistan	24.3	161.5	43.3	30	15.4
Indonesia	22.5	149.9	41.2	71	39.0
Thailand	14.9	103.0	52.3	83	67.7
The Philippines	14.6	105.8	52.8	95	71.9
Malaysia	15.7	72.4	53.0	96	52.8
South Korea	13.4	78.3	54.4	94	70.6
Hong Kong	7.9	36.7	66.7	87	70.4
Singapore	7.9	35.7	64.5	111	–
Japan	7.6	30.4	68.0	103	97.8

a.   The primary school enrolment ratio is given as a percentage of the population aged between 6 and 11. In some countries, this ratio exceeds 100 because children in primary education can be below or above the given age limit due to different school systems.
Source: World Bank (WDR 1983).

lated. Yet when these random events in the world economy disappeared, the country's external trade prospects regressed to 'normal' in external trade in primary commodities, recording deteriorations in the external reserve position and the trade balance. In most of the 1950s, for example, the trade balance was negative. The favourable economic conditions at Independence were a result of haphazard events in the international economy, rather than the achievement of an export-agricultural revolution.

The welfare state

The 'easy phase' of the economy enabled successive governments to maintain an exceptional type of a 'welfare state'—an exception when compared to most other Third World countries. The country's per capita income in terms of GDP, over US $150 in 1960, was the highest in South Asia and was higher than even some of the East Asian countries which experienced rapid economic growth in the subsequent period (Table 5.2). Some of the newly industrialized countries

9 For instance, in both South Korea and Sri Lanka, GNP per capita was about US $150, and manufacturing GDP was about 12 per cent in 1960. Three decades later, in 1990, the per capita GNP of South Korea was US $5400, while that of Sri Lanka was US $ 470; the manufacturing share of GDP was over 30 per cent in South Korea while that of Sri Lanka was 15 per cent (Abeyratne 1993: 8).

(NICs), had almost the same per capita income and the same production structure in 1960 as Sri Lanka did (Abeyratne 1993).[9] Although Sri Lanka had a high income level, compared to many Asian countries, and, for that matter, compared to many developing countries in general, it was relatively low compared to that of industrialized countries. Nevertheless, the economy could achieve health, education and other welfare standards almost at the level maintained in some industrialized countries (Isenman 1980, Sen 1983). A comparison of Sri Lankan human development indicators with those of some other Asian countries (Table 5.2) shows that the record of human development in Sri Lanka in terms of nutrition, health and education has been exceptionally high.

The welfare programmes were initiated in Sri Lanka in the early twentieth century in the context of the British social policy (Alailima 1997). From the mid-1940s onwards, Sri Lanka expanded the welfare programmes. They included, among others, free health care (both curative and preventive) and free education (including free meals and milk at schools) throughout the island, state subsidies on food and other essential goods and services (such as transport) for the whole population, plus some other social services (Jayewardene 1951, Karunatilake 1987). Sri Lanka's record on welfare expenditure, '...highly impressed most financial observers from abroad. It stands out in distinct contrast to other countries in South East Asia' (Jayewardene 1951: 14). Under the national governments after Independence, particularly in the 1960s and the early 1970s, the welfare expenditure of the government further increased.

Table 5.3 *Expenditure on selected welfare programmes 1949/50 - 1995 as a percentage of total government expenditure*

| | Social services | | | Food |
Year[a]	Education	Health	Total[b]	Subsidies
1949/50	–	–	26.2	4.5
1954/55	14.4	10.1	29.1	3.4
1959/60	15.9	8.1	26.1	10.4
1964/65	18.7	8.8	29.8	23.6
1969/70	18.1	9.7	30.2	20.3
1975	13.4	7.8	23.2	23.4
1980	13.7	10.0	25.7	2.3
1985	8.1	3.8	22.0	2.7
1990	9.6	5.0	27.5	5.1
1995	9.4	5.5	33.7	0.9

a. After 1973, the calendar year was adopted as the financial year.
b. In addition to education and health, the total figure includes, social expenditure on housing, welfare and community services.
Source: CBSL (*ROE* annual issues).

Table 5.3 shows the share of government expenditure on selected welfare programmes since Independence. The share of total expenditure on social services
accounted for 26.2 per cent in the financial year 1949/50 and increased to 30.2
per cent in 1969/70. A significant proportion of the social service expenditure
was on education and health. Even though expenditure on education and
health decreased after 1980, the total expenditure on social services has not
shown a substantial decline. Expenditure on food subsidies was 4.5 per cent of
total government expenditure in 1949/50. A substantial proportion of food subsidy consisted of expenditure on the programme of rice ration for the whole
population. According to the UNDP (1990:49), the proportion of rationed rice
to total rice consumed in Sri Lanka exceeded 70 per cent at one time, and even
after the decline after 1966, remained about 50 per cent. Nevertheless, the share
of expenditure on food subsidies increased, and remained over 20 per cent in
1964/65, 1969/70 and in 1975. A substantial decline in the share of expenditure
on food subsidies was evident only after 1980. This was largely a result of
replacing the system of rice ration, which was an overall food subsidy programme, with a targeted 'food stamp' system under the post-1977 market-oriented economic policy. Even though the welfare programmes were subject to
various changes after Independence, and were scaled down in some cases in
the recent past, the relatively high welfare expenditures continue to exist.

Pluralistic and competitive democratic model

The relatively favourable economic status of the economy and the welfare system were coupled with a Westminster type of democracy. The Sri Lankan political system was highly pluralist and competitive (Kearney 1973). For the purpose of analysis, I focus on two aspects of this political system.These two aspects are the multi-party system, and the high degree of popular political participation.

In independent Sri Lanka, a multi-party democratic political system evolved,
although there are controversies over the erosion of democracy since the late
1970s (e.g. Manor 1984, Moore 1992, 1990, Piyadasa 1984, Tambiah 1986, Wilson 1988). The two dominant political parties, that is, the centre-right UNP
(1946) and the centre-left SLFP (1951), have been in power alternately due to
regular general elections.[10] No Marxist party could achieve the required majority of votes to form its own government. But as partners in coalition governments of the SLFP or of even the UNP,[11] the Marxists and the Marxist parties

10 Between 1948 and 1994 there were 11 general elections. Five of these general elections witnessed major changes in political power between the two major political parties, which participated in
these elections either on their own or in coalition with other parties. The longest period that one
single party (the UNP) wielded power in the country was 1977-94.
11 Under the leadership of Philip Gunawardana, a Marxist, the MEP, was a partner in the UNP-led
coalition government of 1965-70. The Sri Lanka Freedom Socialist Party (SLFSP), based on a socialist political ideology, was also a partner in this UNP-led coalition government.

played an influential role in determining the country's economic and political process.

Tamil political parties were minorities in parliament, as the major UNP and the SLFP became Sinhala-dominated. The Tamil political parties and the Muslim parties have, however, shared power with either the UNP-led or the SLFP-led coalition governments.[12] According to Oberst, 'as a British-styled democracy, Sri Lanka tried to set up political arrangements that would provide representation to all ethnic communities in the society' (1986: 140). Their incorporation in the government has increased the support for the government in parliament. For the same reason, Tamil parties could play an influential role in Sri Lankan politics, because eventually their support was important in determining who held the government decision-making power. Thus, it is difficult to maintain that Tamil political parties were excluded from decision-making in Sri Lankan political history. But as the Tamil representation in parliament was always smaller than the Sinhala representation, usually the Tamil or any other minor parties had less influence than the 'Sinhalese' parties.

Political power in Sri Lanka has often been considered a monopoly of the Anglicized elite (Jupp 1978, Wilson 1979). Political parties, including the Marxist ones, were factions of the country's elite (Obeyesekere 1974). But the situation did not remain as it was at Independence. The political elite did not remain Anglicized, nor were politicians always from the elite. The important point is that, even though politics was a monopoly of the country's Anglicized elite, governing the state did not become a monopoly of the elite. Decision-making since Independence was a result of the complex and conflicting interests of a variety of political and semi-political power groups and institutions.

The relatively high degree of political consciousness in Sri Lankan society was an important source of influence on the decision-making in the country. Through the constitutional changes in 1931—about two decades before any other Asian country—Sri Lanka legislated universal adult suffrage.[13] The Sri Lankan population was highly literate, politically conscious and widely exposed to mass media, compared to other developing countries (Jupp 1978, Kearney 1973, Obeyesekere 1974). Sri Lanka's long practice of universal franchise in combination with its multi-party democratic political system and high standards of education made the society extremely politically conscious.[14] As a result, popular participation in decision-making was at a remarkably high level.

12 In the governments from 1948 to date, except for the period 1956-65, the Cabinets included Tamil representatives, too. In addition, there were other Tamil and Muslim Ministers representing either the UNP or the SLFP parties.

13 Since the early 1900s, Sri Lankans had begun to acquire decision-making powers in the State Council. Even in 1910, some Sri Lankans had the right to elect a limited number of members to the State Council. But the majority were British members. In 1921, members elected by the Sri Lankans plus appointees outnumbered British members, while in 1924 elected members alone were the majority (Oliver 1957).

14 For example, at the first general election held to choose the national government in 1947, the turnout of votes was 61.3 per cent of eligible votes, while it increased to 74 per cent in 1952, and exceeded 85 per cent at the general elections in 1970 (Jupp 1978: 370-71).

Political power groups in Sri Lanka comprised centre-right, centre-left including Marxist, and ethnic-based political parties, trade unions, student unions and other institutionalized pressure groups, which have had direct links with political parties (Jupp 1978, Kearney 1971). All these enjoyed relatively high degrees of political freedom. Striking features of the resistance created by most of the power groups and institutions were that they were politically oriented by action and consumer-oriented by objective. The role of political parties based on Marxist ideology was highly influential in the expansion and continuation of welfare services, and the politicization of the urban working class in both public and private sectors. Consequently, one could argue that the Marxist parties also retarded the country's capitalist development. Although the urban working class was well-organized and influenced decision-making through trade unions, the peasantry, which was the largest occupational group, exerted little organized influence. There were also semi-political power groups and institutions which enjoyed political support as well. Ethnocentric or religious movements, the press and some other power groups and institutions at both national and local levels operated in the political field (Jayawardena 1985, Wilson 1979). Therefore, governance in Sri Lanka since Independence was influenced by various political and semi-political forces, although the UNP and the SLFP alternated in dominating the successive governments.

Politicizing the competitive society

The democratic political system was instrumental in politicizing not only the welfare state and consumerism but also nationalism. A major characteristic of the parliamentary multi-party democracy in Sri Lanka was the holding of regular general elections. Thus,obtaining popular support was a priority for the ruling party as well as for the opposition. Post-Independence governments could hardly ignore the pressure of political and semi-political power groups or of public opinion. Governments were often under pressure to maintain a balance between the long-term growth objectives of the country and their short-term political objectives. As a result, successive governments were compelled to satisfy the growing demand at any social or economic cost.

The British rulers have introduced the welfare state, while the favourable economic conditions at Independence enabled its maintenance and expansion. The rapid expansion of welfare services for all social segments of population was also a bid for popular support (Alailima 1997). Political and semi-political pressure groups often defended the welfare state and consumerism, but rarely promoted production and productivity. According to Alailima (1997: 143), the demand for welfare services was '...abused unscrupulous politicians who made extravagant promises to a gullible electorate'. Whenever, the government decided to curtail welfare expenses, political parties in the opposition, with support of pressure groups outside the House of Representatives, opposed it to gain political mileage. However, on returning to power, the parties formerly in the opposition had to face the same problems leading to cuts in welfare, while the parties which had become the opposition from earlier government practiced the same strategy of opposing welfare cuts. The standards of living of the masses increasingly depended on welfare measures, yet the UNP and the SLFP played the 'political game' of promising to grant *more* than what was granted by the other in order to win elections. It is difficult to know whether voters took these election promises into account in deciding which party should be elected for power. The election promises were obviously beyond the country's economic capacity.

Sinhala and Tamil politicians engaged nationalism to win popular support. The parameters for the politicization of nationalism had been set before Independence. A major breakthrough came in 1956, with a splendid victory of the MEP on the platform of Sinhala Buddhist nationalism. Independence did not mark a major breakthrough in response to the deeply rooted Sinhala Buddhist demand for the restoration of their lost position. Until 1956, the Sri Lankan economy, society and culture were little different from those under colonial rule. After 1956 the political participation of the majority Sinhala Buddhist people increased, and governments were no longer in a position to ignore Sinhala Buddhist grievances which had evolved during colonial rule.

As a result of intra-communal political competition, both the UNP and the SLFP attempted to be more Sinhala-Buddhist than the other, to win popular support. As the Sinhala-Buddhists constituted the majority of the population, their support at the elections determined whether the UNP or the SLFP would rule. Just as Sinhala politicians used Sinhala-Buddhist nationalism for their political power, Tamil politicians used Tamil nationalism to lobby for political power. The Tamil political elite had been organized on ethnocentric nationalistic grounds since the early twentieth century. The goal of a separate Tamil state, and the official declaration of that goal in 1976 were essential factor in the politicization of Tamil nationalism.

Welfare and nationalism are closely related to the formation of a consumer-oriented competitive society. The widespread social and political demand for economic resources and opportunities for socio-economic advancement has escalated. Traditional politicians began to compete amongst themselves to be more welfare-oriented than rival politicians. Both factors are, of course, rationalized in terms of 'development', as I have discussed in the previous chapter. At one level of socio-economic advancement extensive welfare services relieved the masses from the problems of poverty and deprivation. But the problem which was hardly anticipated was that welfare, while promoting 'development' on the one hand, escalated demand and hence competition for economic resources and opportunities on the other hand. Socio-economic advancement is no longer restricted to the higher social classes, as the lower social classes which were helped by welfare services emerged to compete with them.

The formation of the competitive society was fuelled by the resurgence of Sinhala Buddhist nationalism. The link between the promotion of nationalism and the formation of a competitive society emerged through the development of popular political participation. As I discussed in the previous chapter, an increase in popular political participation is justified by the development paradigm. In the Sri Lankan context, to a great extent nationalism was the platform for popular political participation. Nationalism increased popular political participation by increasing the demand for economic resources and opportunities based on nationalist sentiments., Nationalism also became a factor in creating competition between communities.

The increase in the demand for economic resources and opportunities was quantitative as well as qualitative. It was *quantitative* in a sense that the demand increased in volume due to the rise of the masses and increased political participation. The increase in demand was *qualitative* in terms of changing preferences. The rising masses no longer demanded socio-economic progress in the context of their traditional society. Their aspirations were for socio-economic advancement in a modern society. The quantitative as well as qualitative expansion of the competitive society was coupled with demographic trends, intensifying competition.

The expansion of the youth population

An outstanding feature of the demographic trends in Sri Lanka is the rapid growth of population for a period of about two decades before the early 1970s. The country's population almost doubled in 25 years time, and was nearly trebled in 50 years. In 1971, the Sri Lankan population was 12.7 million, while at present it is estimated to be over 18 million. The country's rapid population growth in the 1950s and 1960s and its continuous decline from the 1970s onwards have been a great concern (Abeykoon 1993, Hettige 1992a, Kiribanda 1997).[15] There According to Table 5.4, the population increased by an average annual rate of 2.8 per cent in the period 1946-53, while it continued to be over 2 per cent until the census year 1971. As population censuses show, from the late-nineteenth to the mid-twentieth century, even with a high immigration rate,[16] population growth was under 2 per cent. It has been argued that the high population growth in the 1950s and 1960s was largely due to the health care and nutrition guaranteed by the Sri Lankan welfare state, and the resulting declines in the crude death rate and infant and maternal mortality rates. Although the crude birth rate started to decline from its five-year average of 38.9 per 1000 in 1946-50, it was above 30 per 1000 until 1961-65 (DCS 1981: 27). The fertility rate was 5.3 in 1953, 4.2 in 1971 and 3.3 in 1981 (DCS 1981: 27). High fertility accompanied by a decline in mortality contributed to a high population growth and to a substantial change in the age composition of the population.

As a result of the continuation of what Joan Robinson labelled a 'primitive birth rate with the modern death rate' (Kiribanda 1997: 226), there was a

---

15 Also see Economic Review, 20(8), 1994, Peopleís Bank, Colombo for an analysis of this problem.
16 Population increase due to immigration, as a percentage of intercensal total population increase, which was 66.7 per cent in the period 1871-1881, dropped to 18.7 per cent in the period 1921-31. It remained around 5 per cent in the period 1931-53. After 1953, population increase due to immigration was negative as migration was higher than immigration (DCS 1981; Siddhisena 1994).

Table 5.4 *Intercensal population increase 1946-1981*

Census year	Population (million)	Intercensal increase (%)	Inter-censal average annual growth rate (%)
1946[a]	6.7	25.4	1.5
1953	8.1	21.6	2.8
1963	10.6	30.7	2.6
1971	12.7	19.9	2.2
1981	14.8	17.0	1.7
1991[b]	17.3	16.2	1.5

a   Figures for 1946 in the last two columns refer to the intercensal period 1931-46.
b   Estimate for mid-1991 from Siddhisena (1994)
Source: DCS (1981).

remarkable and continuous increase in the population of the youth after the mid-1960s. According to Table 5.5, the population of the age groups 10-19 and 20-29 together increased from 37.7 per cent of total population in 1963 to 40.9 per cent in 1971, and to 41.0 per cent in 1981. It is important to note that the population of the age group 0-9 increased by 5.3 per cent per annum, the highest rate of growth among all age groups, in the period 1946-53. In the subsequent period of 1953-63, the population of the age group 10-19 increased by 4.5 per cent per annum. The increase of the age group 20-29 in 1963-71 (4.5 per cent per annum), and that of the age group 30-39 in the subsequent period of 1971-81 (3.5 per cent per annum) were the highest rates of increase in age groups in the respective periods. Thus, the growth of the younger generation has been higher than the growth of the total population. This created the pres-

Table 5.5 *Composition and growth of age groups of population, census years 1946-1981*

Age group	Age group as % of population					Average annual growth rate (%)			
	1946	1953	1963	1971	1981	'46-53	'53-63	'63-71	'71-81
0 - 9	25.1	28.3	28.9	26.3	23.8	5.3	3.3	1.1	0.6
10 - 19	22.3	20.1	22.3	23.4	22.2	1.4	4.5	3.2	1.1
20 - 29	18.3	18.3	15.4	17.5	18.8	3.1	1.0	4.5	2.6
30 - 39	13.8	13.0	12.5	11.5	13.3	2.1	2.6	1.3	3.5
40 - 49	9.6	9.2	8.9	8.9	8.8	2.4	2.6	2.5	1.6
50 - 59	5.5	5.7	6.0	6.1	6.4	3.7	3.8	2.7	2.3
60 & over	5.5	5.4	6.0	6.3	6.6	2.8	4.5	3.2	2.3

Source: DCS (1981: 82).

sure on the economy and on the welfare state and exacerbated the expansion of demand for economic resources and opportunities.

The expansion of social services had to cover not only the existing population, but also the rapidly increasing number of young people. Chart 5.4 shows the increase in school enrolment in relation to population growth for selected years of 1953-92 over the 1946 level. In twenty-five years since 1946, the population less than doubled (1.9), but school enrolment trebled (3.0). In thirty-five years, that is, 1946-81, the population increased by 2.2 times, but school enrolment by 3.7 times. The increase in school enrolment at a rate much higher than the increase in population was a result new generations entering the formal education system, which is free and accessible throughout the island. As a result of high population growth of the 1950s and the 1960s, the population of the young generation increased at the same time and the formal education system had expanded enough to absorb the new generation.

Chart 5.4   *School enrolment and population, selected years 1953-1992:*
                ratio of increase over 1946 level

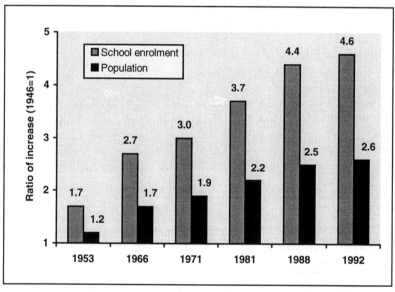

Source: DCS: *Statistical Abstract*, annual issues; CBSL: *ROE*, annual issues.

The youths no longer remained in their traditional family-based economic activities in terms of occupation, and they ceased to rely on their birth status as a source of identity (Hettige 1992a). Education has become the major avenue for upward social mobility (Jayaweera 1986). With an increasing demand for economic resources in the post-Independence period, effective means of supplying economic resources and opportunities were required. That required both rationalizing the demand side and increasing the economic potential of the country. The evidence conclusively suggests that the Sri Lankan state continues to fail to meet the needs of the expanding competitive society.

Chart 5.5   *Main features of the post-colonial political economy of Sri Lanka*

Period	Legitimized political economy	Social implications
'48-56	• Political liberalism • Economic liberalism • State welfare	• Increasing political consciousness • Increasing expectations • Depletion of economic resources
'56-77	• Political liberalism • Economic control • State welfare strengthened	• Increasing political consciousness • Increasing expectations • Deepening economic crisis • Laborious maintenance of welfare • Decreasing economic capacity • Emergence of youth agitation
'77-94	• Political control • Economic liberalism • Growth orientation • State welfare weakened	• Repression of rival politics • Repression of pressure groups • Moderate economic increase • Aggravating distributive equity • Escalation of civil wars

Decreasing supply: the crisis in a competitive society

The decreasing supply of economic resources and opportunities constituted a fundamental contradiction in Sri Lanka's economic change. I use the term 'supply' in a broader sense than its economic meaning. For the purpose of my analysis, supply means not the 'willingness to sell at a given price', but the economic capacity of the state to meet the political and social demand of society. Since Independence, the state's economic and political philosophy has changed. The changes in the economic and political philosophy occurred in a framework which was corresponded with the political-economic ideology of the ruling party. Chart 5.5 summarizes these changes and their social implications. The post-colonial period is divided into three phases according to distinguishing features of government ideology in the respective periods. There are variations in each period, which I will discuss. Also, the changes in social implications of the state political and economic philosophy should be viewed as an historical process connecting all variations in each of the periods classified.

Decline in economic prosperity

There was a degree of state mismanagement throughout the economic and political arena since Independence. First, Sri Lanka's potential to become a developed industrial economy was overlooked at policy and political levels until the late 1950s. Even after this period, although the need to restructure the colonial economic system was accepted, the economy appeared to be mismanaged in the face of changing global economy. The country's political liberalism enabled a consumer-orientation of society, at the expense of production-orientation. According to the ILO (1971: 4), '... Ceylon has been living far beyond her means'. The country's social achievements, which can be attributed wholly to temporary economic prosperity, were exceptional. In contrast, however, there was no emphasis on the question of how to sustain these social achievements of the welfare state. Sri Lanka gradually moved into a crisis in economic, political and social terms. The formation of the country's political conflict occurred in the 1960s and the 1970s, when the economic crisis deepened, and its escalation into a civil war occurred in the 1980s, deepening the political crisis.

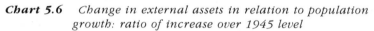

Chart 5.6   *Change in external assets in relation to population growth: ratio of increase over 1945 level*

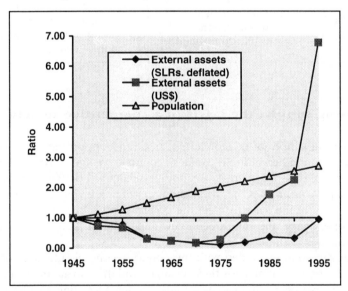

Notes   a.   Population for the first three years refers to 1946, 1949 & 1954.
        b.   External assets in SL rupees were deflated by import price index (1945 = 100).
Source: CBSL (*ROE* annual issues); Snodgrass (1966: 313) for population in the first three years.

Soon after Independence, the imminent end to Sri Lanka's economic prosperity was already evident. The economic and political philosophies of the governments, accompanied by an anti-growth consumer orientation, were soon reflected in economic distress. The subsequent deterioration of the external assets position indicates this tendency. Chart 5.6 shows the change in the country's external assets in relation to population growth over 1945-95. The ratio of increase in population and in external assets, shown in the chart, indicates the increase in the value of these variables over their 1945 level. Against the steady growth of the population, the amount of external assets remained below its 1945 level, while its lowest critical level was recorded in 1970. In terms of US dollars, until 1980, the amount of external assets did not increase to its 1945 level. Given that the increase in import prices is considered, it has taken 50 years to build up the country's external assets to the level of 1945. Nevertheless, the increase in external assets by 1995 to the 1945 level still lags behind the population increase in the same period.

Table 5.6   *Change in external assets, selected years 1945-1995*

Year	in SL Rupees, deflated byimport price index (1945=100)		in US dollars	
	Total (SLRs.mn)	Per capita (SLRs.)	Total (US$ mn)	Per capita (US$)
1945a	1260	189.3	379	57.0
1950a	1100	147.6	279	37.5
1955a	980	115.1	258	30.3
1960	422	42.7	114	11.5
1965	312	28.0	92	8.3
1970	197	15.7	68	5.4
1975	133	9.8	108	8.0
1980	244	16.6	376	25.6
1985	463	29.3	672	42.4
1990	415	24.4	857	50.4
1995	1195	66.0	2570	141.9

a. Population for the first three years refers to 1946, 1949 & 1954.
Source: CBSL (*ROE:* annual issues); Snodgrass (1966: 313), for population in the first three years.

Table 5.6 shows the change in the *per capita* and *total* external assets, in terms of US dollars and constant Rupee values. The per capita value of external assets has continuously declined from US $57 in 1945 to 5.40 in 1970. The per capita value of external assets deflated by import price index (1945=100), has declined from Sri Lanka Rupees 189.30 in 1945 to 9.80 in 1975. Even though it has increased in the period since, the per capita value of external assets in 1995 (SL Rs. 66) shows that it failed even in 1995 to reach the 1945 level. Along with the depletion of the country's foreign assets, trade surpluses turned into growing deficits with deteriorating terms of trade. The successive governments after the 1950s also faced the aggravating problem of financing the growing budget deficits. After the 1960s, a new dimension was added to Sri Lanka's economic crisis, that is, the growing foreign debt burden.[17]

The trade balance never recorded a surplus after 1956, except in 1977.[18] As Table 5.7 shows, the trade deficit as a percentage of GDP remained at double digit level after 1982, the year that recorded the highest trade deficit of 21.5 per cent. The country's stock of external assets was sufficient to finance 10 months of imports in 1955, but gradually deteriorated to less than 2 months of imports by the 1970s (Abeyratne 1997). Without a corresponding export expansion, imports grew rapidly. Even though non-traditional exports grew modestly, the increase in total exports fell far short of the sharp rise in the import bill. Despite sporadic minor recoveries, on average the terms of trade deteriorated until the mid-1980s, as the increase in import prices was higher than the increase in export prices.

Table 5.7   *Trade balance and budget deficit, selected years 1960-1995*

Year	Budget deficit (−)		Trade balance	
	SLRs. million	% of GDP (factor cost)	SLRs million	% of GDP (factor cost)
1950	-172	–	239	–
1955	91	–	415	–
1960	-417	-6.6	-210	-3.3
1965	-430	-5.7	-13	-0.2
1970	-936	-7.1	-316	-2.4
1975	-2103	-8.2	-1421	-5.5
1977	-2127	-6.1	350	1.0
1982	-17479	-18.5	-20322	-21.5
1987	-21749	-12.2	-20005	-11.3
1992	-33908	-8.8	-45699	-11.8
1995	-58335	-9.7	-71203	-11.9

Source: For 1950 and 1955, Snodgrass (1966); For the years after 1960, CBSL (*ROE*: annual issues).

A comparative survey of GDP per capita data for Asian countries, given in Table 5.8, shows clearly that the economic performance of Sri Lanka for the period of

17 The foreign debt burden became a major political issue and was highlighted by the opposition in its political manifesto against the UNP government in the general elections of 1970. A vivid description of this problem was also provided in the first *Budget Speech* (Minister of Finance 1970) of the new SLFP government.

18 The trade surplus in 1977, which was 1 per cent of GDP, was considered to be a result not of natural market conditions or successful export promotion policies, but stringent import controls and the temporary improvement in tea prices on the world market in 1975-77.

1960-90 lagged far behind that of many other Asian countries, as compared with conditions in 1960. Sri Lanka's GDP per capita of US $152 in 1960 was the same as that of South Korea and almost half of that of Hong Kong. Three decades later, in 1990, South Korea's GDP per capita was about 13 times that of Sri Lanka, and the per capita GDP of Hong Kong was about 25 times higher than that of Sri Lanka. In principle, nutrition, health and education are closely linked with economic development through their positive impact on productivity and output. Hence, it is economically desirable to invest in human capital formation. However, the experience of Sri Lanka, which has maintained high standards of human development for more than five decades since the mid-1940s, hardly supports such a positive relationship between human capital formation and economic growth.

Table 5.8   *Sri Lanka among Asian countries: GDP per capita (US$) for selected years 1960-1990*

Country	1960	1970	1980	1990
Sri Lanka	152	177	255	427
India	68	97	207	299
Pakistan	76	151	259	317
Indonesia	91	82	472	603
Thailand	95	198	716	1424
The Philippines	255	182	734	713
Malaysia	280	785	1715	2387
South Korea	152	288	1528	5514
Hong Kong	310	878	4015	10459
Singapore	428	914	4592	12791

Source: World Bank (WDR: annual issues), (*World Tables*: 1983)

It was observed that the country's economic policy has been closely linked to the changes in the political arena. As there were regular general elections in independent Sri Lanka, changes in power caused substantial changes of economic policy from time to time, at least until 1977.[19] Furthermore, as the Sri Lankan governments operated in a context of a Westminster-type democratic model, decision-making has been influenced to a great extent by political and semi-political interest groups and institutions. In addition, the ruling parties

---

19 For the first time after Independence, the change in political power from UNP to an SLFP- dominated coalition, i.e. People's Alliance (PA), in 1994 did not mark a drastic change in the country's economic policy. The UNP regime of 1977-94 has become known as an 'open economy', while the PA government used to describe its regime as an 'open economy with a human face'. The newly added term 'human face' has never been interpreted, but generally it was used to distinguish the new 'open economy' phase from its old one, which was accompanied by a deteriorating human rights record and a corrupt political culture.

were due to face regular elections, so maintaining a balance between short-term political popularity and long-term growth objectives was of great importance.

Continuation of the colonial economy: 1948-1956

After the first general elections in 1947,[20] the UNP remained in power until 1956, having been re-elected in 1952. The leadership of the first government expected to continue with the economic and political structure inherited from the British colonial administration (Jayasekara & Amerasinghe 1987, Lakshman 1997, Oliver 1957, Ponnambalam 1980, Wickremeratne 1977). Thus, economic and political liberalism and the welfare state continued to dominate the socio-economic and political structure. The UNP government adopted a *laissez-faire* ideology regarding economic activity. Given its dependency on social democracy for political survival in a society used to basic welfare provision, the UNP retained the welfare state structures established in colonial times (Lakshman 1997: 6). In 1935 an attempt was made in 1953 to eliminate the consumer subsidy on rice, but the government had to abandon this due to widespread political protests, known as *hartal in 1953*. The mix of economic and political liberalism, accompanied by an extensive welfare system was due, as we have already seen, to an increased political consciousness and social expectations. At the same time, the UNP government not only ignored the means of generating economic resources and opportunities to sustain the consumerism but also encouraged the exhaustion of accumulated resources.

The continuation of the colonial economic structure was not a haphazard incident, but the result of political and economic forces. Basically, the new rulers accepted the continuation of colonial economic structure based on the fortunes of plantation crops, even accepting the British control of the plantation sector. Consequently, they neglected the need for industrialization. Rather, the development strategy of the UNP was limited to agricultural development to attain self-sufficiency in food production, as the country was spending its foreign exchange largely on the import of foodstuffs. Also, the local cost of consumer items was less than market prices due to mass subsidy schemes. This policy was in conflict with the basic development strategy of the UNP government, which focused on self-sufficiency in the country's food requirements.

In fact, there was much concern about the need for industrialization (Jayewardene 1951, Oliver 1957: 66). Yet, the political leadership was led by its class interests in maintaining the existing economic structure, and feared that industrialization would strengthen the working class movement backed by Marxist parties (Jayasekara & Amarasinghe 1987, Ponnambalam 1980, Wickremaratne 1977). The UNP government was confronted with widespread working class and peasant unrest (Jayawardena 1985, 1990), which the government hoped to

---

20 Although the country gained political Independence on February 4, 1948, the first national government of the post-Independence period was elected in 1947.

end by striving for self-sufficiency in agriculture (with no industrialization) and the expansion of welfare measures. It was assumed that the economic prosperity based on plantation agriculture was permanent.

A World Bank mission that visited Sri Lanka at the request of the government, was in complete agreement with the development ideology of the government. The mission felt that the economic development of the country in 1953-59 should be based primarily on agriculture, because Sri Lanka did not possess the required technological facilities and capital for a programme of industrialization. Consequently, investment in industry, proposed at 6.3 per cent of total *public* investment in the *Six Year Development Plan 1951-1957*, was reduced to 4.7 per cent by the World Bank for the period 1953-59 (IBRD 1953). Thus, industrialization did not appear on the agenda of the UNP government as a priority.

The industrialization history of many Western and Asian industrialized countries shows that the surplus generated in the agricultural sector formed a significant part of industrial investment in the initial stages of industrialization. The economy of Sri Lanka prior to 1955, unlike that of other countries in South Asia, had accumulated a large volume of agricultural surplus in the form of foreign exhange reserves. A socio-economic survey of the Ministry of Finance of the first national government of Sri Lanka pointed out that most other South East Asian countries had been faced with a third difficulty of shortage of foreign exchange, 'fortunately, in Ceylon we do not face this difficulty' (Jayewardene 1951: 34). However, Sri Lankans knowingly or unknowingly exhausted the foreign exchange reserves for domestic consumption. The survival of the welfare state was to become a critical issue, as resources generated were inadequate to sustain the consumer society.

Political liberalism and economic control: 1956-1977

For about two decades after the general elections in 1956, the country was ruled by four governments of party coalitions headed either by the SLFP (1956-59, 1960-65 and 1970-77) or the UNP (1965-70).[21] A shift in government economic strategy from *laissez-faire* towards a state-controlled economy was a significant change. The new development strategy for industrialization, one of *import substitution*, was concerned with delinking trade ties of developing countries with the industrialized world, and achieving a high degree of self-sufficiency, particularly in manufacturing production.[22] This policy reflected not only government

21 The government of 1956-59 was formed by a coalition of parties, the MEP, of which the major partner was the SLFP. Following the political confusion in 1959, resulting from the assassination of the Prime Minister, Bandaranaike, the UNP was elected in 1960. But this government did not have the majority in parliament, and therefore lasted only a few weeks. At the next elections in 1960, the SLFP was elected.
22 The theoretical framework for import substitution was based on the structuralist economic perspective of development thinking that emerged in the early period after the Second World War in the pioneering works of Nurkse (1958), Prebish (1959), Singer (1950) and ECLA (1950).

commitment to change the classic colonial economic structure, but also indicated the government's intention to resolve the growing balance of payments
crisis (Abeyratne 1997). Although the UNP has always favoured a market-oriented, liberal, private enterprise system, the UNP government of 1965-70 was
not willing to make a drastic change in the major development framework of
import substitution. In the period of 1965-70, the UNP government carried out
a partial liberalization programme, abandoned nationalization and relaxed restrictions on private business, but all within the framework of import substitution (Abeyratne 1997, Cuthbertson & Athukorala 1991). Thus, the basic economic policy framework continued for about two decades, until 1977.

Table 5.9   *Real growth of GDP and production sectors 1960-1994*
             percentage average annual rates of growth

Category	1960-65	1966-70	1971-77	1978-87	1988-94
Agriculture, forestry & fishing	3.2	4.2	2.1	3.0	3.0
Mining & quarrying	1.6	15.1	56.8	7.4	5.3
Manufacturing	5.4	7.3	1.1	5.7	8.3
Services	4.7	5.4	3.2	6.0	4.9
GDP	4.2	5.3	2.9	5.2	5.2

Source: CBSL (*ROE* annual issues).

The initiation of a new development ideology in the late 1950s was not acci-
dental. External and internal forces pointed to the worsening economic conditions of the country. The economic policies of import substitution were found
to be entirely consistent with these forces and conditions, as was the case in
many other developing countries gaining political Independence at the time.
Import substitution was the policy prescription of contemporary development
thinking (ECLA 1950). The policies of import substitution were attractive to new
states in the developing region which were eager to change their colonial image
in general, and colonial economic and trade patterns in particular.

Economic ideology since Independence was based largely on nationalist
sentiment. 'All ranks of Ceylonese politicians and writers, from conservative to
communist, have shared this nationalist emphasis in economic opinion ...' (Oliver 1957: 13). Import substitution was consistent with nationalist appeals and
ambitions. Nationalist sentiment in economic ideology, which started to appear
even in the conservative UNP government's economic vision, intensified after
1956. Even under the UNP government (1948-56), which was reluctant to make
radical changes in the colonial economic structure, the nationalist sentiment
behind economic policy was evident. Sri Lanka's export trade was dominated
by the British, and import trade by Tamils, Muslims and others of South Indian
origin (Wilson 1979). The UNP did not touch export trade, dominated by the
British, but attempted to change import trade dominated by South Indians. The

Table 5.10   *Export composition, selected years 1965-1994
as percentage of total exports*

Year	Traditional exports[a]	Non-traditional exports[b]		
		Manufacturing	Other	Total
1965	91.8	–	–	8.2
1970	88.5	–	–	11.5
1975	78.6	12.4	9.1	21.4
1977	74.3	14.2	21.5	25.7
1982	47.4	38.6	14.1	52.6
1987	38.2	48.6	13.2	61.8
1994	17.9	73.6	8.5	82.1

a. Traditional exports include tea, rubber and coconuts.
b. Non-traditional exports includes minor agricultural products, manufacturing, gems and others.
Source: CBSL (*ROE* annual issues).

UNP government's attempt to create a self-sufficient agricultural economy also indicates the influence of nationalist sentiment in policy-making.

As I have discussed earlier, the MEP coalition government came to power on the Sinhala Buddhist nationalist platform. At Independence, Sinhala Buddhists, who were left in subsistence traditional agriculture, were largely absent in the modern plantation and commercial sectors. Restrictions on import trade and on the use of foreign exchange decreased the non-Sinhala control over the economy. Sri Lankans, as others in South Asia, were also conscious of the Americans '… whom they suspect of wishing to move in as the British moved out, or of seeking political influence and economic control in the area' (Oliver 1957: 12). The new development strategy, with additional socialist elements, was believed to minimize the political and economic influence of the indigenous non-Sinhala communities, but also Western influence. Marxist parties agreed with the ruling party regarding import substitution, not because of any 'nationalism' on their part, but because they opposed the capitalist influence of the Western bloc.

As the country started to experience growing balance of payments difficulties and depleting foreign exchange reserves, the governments after 1960 considered import substitution the best strategy. Import substitution would enable the government to expand its economic activities and control the private sector. Following the period of state disengagement in industry under the UNP governments of 1948-56, there was a gradual intensification of 'state entrepreneurship' not only in industry but also in other forms of economic activity in the two decades after 1956 (Lakshman 1979). The United Front (UF) coalition of SLFP, LSSP and CP (1970-77) declared a commitment to achieve a socialist economy (Minister of Finance 1970, MPE 1972).[23] Policies included the nationalization of

23 The important cabinet posts, such as the Ministry of Finance, were assigned to Marxist parties in this government.

private business, restrictions on high income classes, the expansion of welfare programmes, intervention distribution, and central economic planning. The influence of the Marxist political policies was strong.

While the import substitution regime was responsible for initiating a significant change in the classic colonial economic structure, it appeared a failure, in Sri Lanka as elsewhere in the developing world. The import substitution strategy was accompanied by restrictions on international trade with little attention to export promotion. In Sri Lanka, as elsewhere, exports were virtually discouraged and the terms of trade deteriorated, and balance of payments became a critical problem hindering economic growth and employment creation (Abeyratne 1997, Cuthbertson & Athukorala 1991, Rajapathirana 1988). Consequently, Sri Lanka not only missed the opportunities that it could have otherwise gained from international markets (Abeyratne 1989), but also aggravated its economic crisis. An outstanding feature of the economic philosophy, which was also influenced by the Marxist political parties, was the government's commitment to achieve a socialist economy by restricting the expansion of the private sector and continuing the country's extensive welfare system. The distributive orientation of the economic policy in the context of a growing economic crisis compelled Sri Lankan society to share not growth, but poverty. The gap between social expectations and resources and opportunities widened.

The deepening of the economic crisis and the formation of militant youth groups were simultaneous processes in the 1960s and the 1970s. The youth population had to face growing resource scarcity against rising social expectations As I have noted earlier, the youth population was unusually large, due to the population boom in the 1950s and the 1960s. In addition, it was relatively healthy and educated. Moreover, owing to the pluralist and competitive democratic political system tradition and to the education system, the youths were highly politically conscious. Thus they were ambitious to move away from their parent's traditional economy towards a modern economy. Yet, the stagnant economy of the 1960s impeded their socio-economic advancement and the participation of the youths in the country's development process. An increasing proportion of the country's youth began to experience social exclusion in terms of socially valued income and consumer aspirations and education and career prospects (see Chapter VI). It is difficult to know whether the policy commitment of the 1970s to achieve *equal distribution*, and the growing scarcity of economic resources and opportunities, could have lessened the growing youth agitation.

Political control and economic liberalism: 1977-1994

There was a radical shift in economic and political philosophy when the UNP government came into power after a landslide victory in the general elections of 1977. The UNP remained in power until 1994. This change was a reaction to the traditional political economic system of Sri Lanka in the pre-1977 period. The new government intended move from *liberalism to control* politically, and from *control to liberalism* economically. The new leader of the party, J.R. Jaye-wardene, understood the problems of the country's *anti-growth* economic and political philosophy and was determined to deal with them. There was also an attempt to understand these problems by comparing Sri Lanka's difficulties with the impressive successes of East Asian NICs. The new UNP government, which had not had any coherent economic vision since its establishment in 1945, thus started to introduce radical policy reforms aimed at a substantially liberalized and international market-oriented trade regime. This was to be done in the context of a supportive political structure, ensuring long-term political stability of the UNP government and firm decision-making power.

The important elements of the economic policy reforms were the substantial liberalization of import trade and exchange payments, incentives provided for export promotion, measures to encourage the private sector including foreign private capital, and reduction of government intervention in the economy (Lakshman 1997). The poor growth performance in Sri Lanka as in many other developing countries under import substitution policies, and the successes of the export-oriented economies such as the NICs,[24] provided a clear economic justification for a radical shift in development strategy. The new strategy was also in line with development thinking and was advocated through loan conditionality of capitalist donors and international financial institutions such the World Bank and the IMF.

The policy commitment of the UNP regime was to reshape the country's economic and political atmosphere for *growth rather than distribution*. This meant that the country could no longer have state-sponsored welfare as a priority. According to the UNDP (HDR 1990: 49), '... Sri Lanka shifted from a regime of moderate growth with a good distribution of income to one of better growth with a poorer income distribution'. However, the country's experience showed that the sustainability of an extensive welfare system is unrealistic if there is inadequate economic growth. All achievements in the name of 'development' are dependent on growth. Furthermore, a resource-scarce underdeveloped and small economy cannot be growth-oriented under a strategy of isolating the domestic economy from the global economy.

The 1977-94 regime, however, led to the escalation of a number of controversial economic, social and political issues. These issues were debated widely by social scientists.[25] Following the policy reforms, achievements in economic growth and export expansion were better than those of the pre-1977 periods, as

24 In the post-war debate among economists on the choice of trade strategy, there is disagreement regarding the conclusion that ISI strategies failed everywhere. Whatever the market it serves, the expansion of industrial activity is necessary for economic growth. Even from a theoretical point of view, much of the controversy about the relative worth of strategies of import substitution and export promotion can be attributed to 'interpretations' or 'misinterpretations' of trade strategy on the part of the protagonists of the two perspectives in this debate (Abeyratne 1993; Chapter 3).

25 The studies on economic, social and political issues of the 1977-94 policy regime in Sri Lanka are numerous. A few are noted here. Studies on economic aspects include, Abeyratne (1993) Athukorala (1986) Cuthbertson & Athukorala (1991) Dunham & Abeysekera (1987), Lakshman (1997), Lal & Rajapathirana (1989), and Rajapathirana (1988). On social and political aspects: Gunasinghe (1984), Lakshman (1986, 1992), Manor (1984). Moore (1990, 1992) and Tambiah (1986).

shown in Tables 6.9 and 6.10. According to different arguments, the kind of economic growth that was generated was not sustainable (Athukorala 1986, 1987); it led to the collapse of domestic infant industries (Osmani 1987); and the distribution of the benefits of growth was highly unequal (Lakshman 1986). Aggregate growth indicators do not, however, show these structural problems.

The issues relating to the post-1977 UNP regime involved, in addition to economic matters, political and social problems. Accustomed to state-sponsored welfare and political liberalism, the population was not ready to accept the growth-oriented and authoritarian political economy. The post-1977 regime was marked by political reforms, actions, corruption and even violence of the ruling UNP, aimed at ensuring the political power of the party (Manor 1984, Tambiah 1986, Vittachi 1995). To achieve political stability and authority, the UNP government attempted to control the country's pluralist and competitive political system. One of the first steps was to change the Constitution in 1978, creating an executive presidency. The leader of the UNP became the first president of Sri Lanka. Since then, there were numerous attempts to repress rival political parties, including the SLFP, semi-political groups, including trade unions, and other pressure groups, including the press (Vittachi 1995). Actions were taken by President Jayewardene to silence dissent even among the members of parliament. The movement away from the country's popular democratic model was believed to enhance the growth momentum. The objective of economic growth was achieved to a certain extent, but growing political turmoil was the consequence.

Growing economic inequality and changes in the country's traditional political culture gave rise to widespread social agitation (Manor 1984, Moore 1993, Tambiah 1986, Vittachi 1995). Thus, the government had to face protests and violence since the late 1970s. In response, the government also showed an increasing tendency to use violence. It was in this context of widespread social agitation, that the civil war of the Sinhala JVP in the South and that of the separatist Tamil militant groups in the North gained momentum. Although not all of the events of the widespread social agitation were necessarily related to the twin civil war, in general the social agitation was conducive to the escalation of the country's political conflict into civil war. Thus, the political violence and war, in which the state, the JVP and the LTTE were involved, went hand in hand in the UNP regime.

Summary

My purpose in this chapter was to provide an overview of the relationship between the escalation of the political conflict and the growth of the economic crisis in Sri Lanka, which have plagued the country since Independence.The period since the 1960s was marked by an intensification of the economic crisis which continued in the 1970s. At the same time, youths in both the Sinhala and the Tamil communities have agitated against the democratic state. After 1977, there were government attempts to move from 'political liberalism with economic control' towards 'political control with economic liberalism'. This episode created a social and political crisis and fuelled youth agitation. In the new economic and political regime, the organized youth agitation in both Sinhala and Tamil communities escalated into civil war in the early 1980s. Thus, the country's double-sided political conflict shares a single economic background.

Political conflict escalated over the last five decades, moving from differences in culture and interests, through tension, conflict, and irregular eruptions of violence, finally to civil war. Generally, I used the term 'political conflict' to denote this whole process. The country's political conflict has disclosed two important interrelated, characteristics: a development of the political conflict *between* the communities in showing features of an 'ethnic conflict', and *within* the communities in showing features of a conflict between 'social classes', and a breakdown of the conflicting parties into *established* political groups of traditional parliamentary politicians, which represented the state, and *non-established* political groups of radical and ambitious youth.

The growth of economic crisis, was discussed in the context of an *inner-contradiction*. With a growing social and political demand for economic resources and opportunities for socio-economic advancement, a unified and consumer-oriented competitive society emerged—a process which had started in colonial times. The development of Sri Lanka as an exceptional case of a welfare state, in which popular political participation was remarkably high, provided a substructure for the competitive society. On the one hand, the exceptional welfare levels and the high degree of popular political participation are justified in development thinking. On the other hand, the decision-making power of the post-Independence governments was continuously under the pressure of the political, semi-political and other groups and institutions, which strove achieve a 'consumer-oriented' competitive society. Different communities, that is, mainly Sinhala and Tamil, and different social classes in each of the communities competed for economic resources and opportunities in the unified competitive society. Under the pluralist and highly competitive democratic political system of the country, each traditional political party strove to be more *welfare-oriented* than the others, and to be more nationalist than the others, to win popular support.

An unsustainable paradox of the Sri Lankan democratic welfare state was created by the growing scarcity of economic resources and opportunities relative to the escalating social and political demand. Economic mismanagement failed to produce the growth required to sustain the competitive society. The social segments confronted by the crisis of the country's growing competitive society consisted of the youth. This youth population was proportionately large due to high population growth in the 1950s and the 1960s, and was educated and politically conscious. The youth population, with high aspirations for socio-economic advancement, was confronted with an increasing scarcity of economic resources and opportunities. This phenomenon revealed the economic forces underlying the emergence of political conflict. In the next chapter, I will focus on the question of social exclusion as a result of distributive implications of the resource-scarce competitive society, placing 'scarcity' in global context.

Economic Crisis in Sri Lanka: Social Aspirations and Exclusion

VI

In this chapter, I focus on implications of the distribution of economic resources available for socio-economic advancement. In the decades following Independence, political conflict and economic crisis escalated. This was facilitated by the long tradition of Sri Lanka's state welfare and political liberalism, coupled with economic mismanagement, as I discussed in the previous chapter. The term 'socio-economic advancement' is used for the dynamic achievement of valued social and economic status. This is governed by both local and global factors most of which are is beyond the control of the people or even the state. For analytical purposes, I use a set of interrelated macroeconomic variables, namely consumption, income, employment and education, to indicate how economic resources and opportunities for socio-economic advancement have behaved. The analysis deals with increasing social expectations for the achievement of socio-economic advancement, and the distributive implications of economic resources and opportunities in the post-colonial development history of Sri Lanka.

The quest for education, income, consumption, and higher career prospects in an economy characterized by a growing scarcity of economic resources and opportunities results in some critical phenomena. First, society experiences a growing international inequality as the economy loses its economic ability to meet global technological challenges. Secondly, competition among individuals or social segments, inspired by their exposure to socio-economic changes in the global context, increases. Third, certain affluent social groups will succeed in excluding large segments of their own society. Thus, the sense of social exclusion escalated not only due to the increasing competition for economic resources and opportunities but also due to their unfair distribution. I argue that social exclusion and frustration in the quest for socio-economic advancement constitutes a fertile basis for the escalation of intrastate conflict. However, I confine the analysis of this chapter to social exclusion resulting from the growing scarcity of economic resources and opportunities and the competition for socio-economic advancement. I do not mean that frustration due to social exclusion is the reason people become 'rebellious', but it forms a fertile economic basis for the recruitment of people on a large-scale for anti-state political conflict. This I will discuss in the final chapter.

The first section of the analysis is concerned with the development of consumption aspirations and inequalities due to changing consumption patterns of the country over the past few decades, against the background of local and global economic changes. Second, I explore income inequality, which is necessarily associated with consumption inequality. In the final section, I explore the problem of unemployment and its structural characteristics with special reference to education. The chapter concludes that in the face of local and global economic changes, expectations for socio-economic advancement were escalating. However, due to the inadequate generation of means to satisfy these expectations, large segments of society increasingly experienced a sense of social exclusion and frustration. The new generations constituted a significant part of these social segments, excluded and frustrated.

Change in consumption aspirations

The conventional approach to the issue of inequality was based on analyses of the pattern of income distribution. With respect to the theoretical groundwork established in Chapter IV, I approach the issue from the point of view of the patterns of consumption as well. Income has a direct link with consumption, because consumption is the final achievement expected through income. Besides, methodologically, the level and the distribution of consumption are more relevant to my purpose than income distribution exclusively. An income approach generally deals with *only* those who earn incomes, and it says little about levels of or changes in consumption.

It is apt to open with a remark made by Meyer (1984: 150) on the escalation of political conflict in Sri Lanka:

> The display of luxury goods such as audio-visual appliances in shop windows contrasted sharply with the austerity of ten years before and created insupportable frustration amongst a youthful population which was still largely under-employed.

In fact, the remark refers to the period of trade liberalization following economic policy reforms in 1977. Technically and contextually, 'under-employed' may not be an appropriate term. Similar ideas were often heard in Sri Lanka following trade liberalization.[1] For my purpose, this remark serves as an important point of departure. Technically, the term 'under-employed' covers those who are 'employed' but below the level of *optimality* in terms of labour time, skills, training, experience and educational or other qualifications. Contextually, the problem addressed by Meyer is much more critical than stated. Even the majority of the employed in Sri Lanka cannot afford audio-visual appliances, which cost several months or perhaps even years of earnings. If this is the case of even the employed, one van easily understand the lack of purchasing power of the 'underemployed or the unemployed. In contrast, an employed person who earns even the lowest income in a 'developed' country can afford not just one,

---

1 The literal translation of a local expression widely used goes like this: *find money, no matter even if it is by killing dogs.*

but several audio-visual appliances, and perhaps even more, just from one month's income.

Both commodity types and prices are increasingly globalized. They encompass almost all nations in the world via a single global market. The income patterns of the nations are, however, localized (Chapter IV). According to the conventional classification of nations in terms of national incomes, Sri Lanka is one of the poorest in the world. Its per capita income, which was US $400 in 1986, was only 3 per cent of the average per capita income of industrially developed economies (World Bank *WDR* 1988). Nevertheless, the consumption pattern, as in other developing countries, is not significantly different from that of high-income countries. The differences exist only in terms of the degree of consumption, not in the pattern. Almost all commodities sold in the market of a high-income country can be bought in Sri Lanka as well. Why does a low-income country make the consumption pattern of a high-income country available to its ciizens, and how is it made possible?

Meyer's (1984) remark above can be expanded to a global level. People born in a so-called developing region, and earning incomes determined by localized income patterns, are exposed increasingly to global 'shop windows' that exhibit the outcome of the complex process of commoditization. The development of aspiration is fundamentally free from economic means. When the issue is approached from a wider perspective, covering the historical commoditization and the formation of a global market, changes in trade policy in a small economy such as that of Sri Lanka are of little importance. No doubt, the shift in economic policy towards a 'liberalized' trade regime in 1977 speeded up the integration of the economy with the global economy. The pre-1977 inward-oriented trade policy, with an emphasis on equal distribution, was a futile attempt to delink the country's trade from the global market. What the policy eventually proved was that the intrinsic ability of the economy to cope with global technological challenges actually decreased due to poor growth performance. Even in a regulated economy, the human 'needs' or consumption aspirations, and hence consumption and production patterns are governed and determined by forces beyond the control of people and states in developing countries.

A few decades ago the consumption pattern of people in Sri Lanka, as anywhere else, was relatively 'simple' in terms of both the range of choices available and the amount of resources needed to afford these choices. A few centuries ago, it was extremely 'simple'. People have change their consumption patterns as they are confronted by the continuous enlargement of the range of choices. The change in consumption pattern is, on the one hand, *quantitative*, in terms of the increase in the amount of resources required to satisfy consumption, namely the opportunity cost of consumption. On the other hand, the change in consumption is also *qualitative*, in terms of changing consumer preferences. An important feature of the change is the increasing tendency to produce and to consume 'secondary' commodities, namely non-food and durable consumer items.

The increase in the consumption of selected consumer durables in urban and rural sectors (excluding the estate sector) in Sri Lanka for selected Consumer Finance Survey (CFS) years is given in Table 6.1. These indicators are quite a simple approximation of the increase in the consumption of manufactured consumer durables. They can be used as a proxy to show the increase in the volume and the variety of consumer durables consumed over the past few decades. The percentage of households having the consumer durables has increased, but there the number of items increased as well, particularly after the late 1970s, reflecting mainly the impact of trade liberalization. Also, there was a significant disparity between urban and rural households having consumer durables. The most important is that the majority of households had no access to most of the items listed; in many cases this well over 90 per cent of total households reported. There is no reason to assume that the majority of people did not posses them because they did not want to have consumer durables. T he majority had to go without them for other reasons. The survey data show the *actual* increase in consumption. This is determined by a number of factors such as the availability of complementary commodities, the speed of diffusion, the government's trade and distributive policies, the rate of income growth, and the awareness of the people.

The consumption of many consumer durables requires the supply of other complementary goods. For example, the supply of electricity is required for the use of many electrical goods, and roads for motor vehicles. This is an important complexity associated with technological transformation (Chapter IV). This need for other complementary goods for the use of consumer durables, in turn, increases the cost of their consumption to a level well above the actual cost of the commodity. The increase in the consumption of a significant number of consumer durables which require electricity was slow in Sri Lanka due to the lack of electricity in many households. Televisions were not available for mass consumption, as the broadcasting stations were not established until the early 1980s, or they were unable to broadcast throughout the island. As shown in the table, 36 per cent of urban households and 2 per cent of rural households obtained access to electricity in 1963. By the survey year 1986/87, electricity was available to 63.9 per cent of urban households and 18.3 per cent of rural households. In fact, according to the UNDP (*HDR* 1992), Sri Lanka still ranks poorly in terms of the availability of electricity (and telephone facilities). The insufficient expansion of electricity could have restricted the potential increase in the consumption of consumer durables.

Technological change is such that certain commodities that we find today, did not exist a few decades ago. A number of consumer durables, such as televisions and washing machines, as shown in the table, were not available for mass consumption in Sri Lanka. Moreover, the commodities that existed changed due to technological change. The speed of the diffusion of products of technological change can also determine the increase in consumer durables. Many consumer durables in developing countries are imported. The pre-1977 governments, with their inward-oriented trade policies, generally considered consumer durables 'luxury' imports, and restrictions were imposed on their impor-

Table 6.1   *Increase in consumption of selected consumer durables, CFS years 1963-1986/87; number of households as a percentage of total*

Consumer durables	1963 Urban	Rural	1973 Urban	Rural	1978/79 Urban	Rural	1986/87 Urban	Rural
Sewing machine	40.0	19.0	38.6	24.8	43.8	31.0	56.7	34.8
Radio	37.0	17.0	39.5	23.4	56.5	51.5	76.4	66.5
Cooker (electric/gas)	19.0	2.0	7.0	2.2	6.6	0.7	16.1	0.6
Refrigerator	6.0	0.3	4.9	0.5	8.3	0.6	28.4	3.8
Telephone	4.0	0.3	1.0	0.1	3.0	0.1	6.4	0.4
Motorcar	–	–	–	–	4.7	1.2	9.0	1.8
Motorcycle	–	–	–	–	1.8	0.7	7.9	5.1
Television	–	–	–	–	–	–	48.1	14.5
Washing machine	–	–	–	–	–	–	4.0	0.2
Electricity	36.0	2.0	32.0	2.5	38.1	6.7	63.9	18.3

Source: CBSL: CFSs.

tation in order to save scarce foreign exchange. Trade liberalization resulted in an increase in the flow of 'more' and 'new' consumer durables from industrialized countries, thus promoting Western consumerism. Finally, income generation in the domestic economy is an important determinant of the increase in the consumption of consumer durables. As I have highlighted in the previous chapter, the Sri Lankan economy experienced sluggish growth and export expansion with inadequate structural change for about three decades after Independence. A number of factors determined the level of consumption, so the *potential* increase in consumption could be different from the *actual* consumption pattern.

The expansion of the range of choice available inevitably had repercussions on income distribution at the national level. An expansion of the range of consumer durables requires a corresponding expansion of national income. If the economy generates insufficient income, the important question is how the range of consumer durables sold within the economy has expanded. The only way to sustain such an expansion was through increasing income inequality, which in turn lead to an increase in consumption inequality. The question is important, as it is one of the characteristics of commoditization—the increasing cost of not only consumer durables but also their consumption. A fundamental characteristic of commoditization is the tendency to produce commodities with increasing exchange values, and an enhanced character of complementarity and indivisibility. Both features of technological transformation directly raise the opportunity cost of non-food and durable commodities. The issue is more critical than stated, when consumption of these commodities is largely import dependent.

Chart 6.1   *Ratios of import price and volume indices for other consumer goods over food and drink, selected years 1950-1995 (1950=100)*

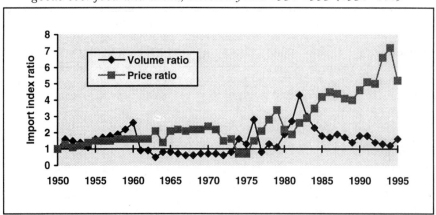

Note: Other consumer goods include consumer durables and other non-food manufactured consumer goods, excluding textiles.
Source: Appendix II.

Technological transformation is a fundamental feature of advanced countries or their multinational corporations. According to James (1990: 1), 'for one thing, with modernization usually goes an exposure ... to the technical change in products that are so fundamental a feature of developed economies, but which are for the most part absent from traditional societiesí. The latecomers to the globalizing market, which first producing first primary goods, and later ëlightí manufactured products, began to exchange them for consumer durables which were changing fast in character. Chart 6.1 shows the ratios of volume and price indices in respect of imports of 'other consumer goods' to those of food and drinks. According to the usual practice in the compilation of import trade data by the CBSL, the category *other consumer goods* includes consumer durables and other non-food manufactured consumer goods except textiles.[2] The year 1950 is considered the base (1950 = 100) for the trade indices. An increase (or decrease) of the ratio of the import price index above (or below) unity should be interpreted as an increase (or decrease) in the *relative* price of other consumer goods in terms of food and drink. In the same way, an increase (or decrease) in the ratio of the import volume index above (or below) unity shows an increase (or decrease) in the *relative* volume of other consumer goods in terms of food and drink.

The movement of the import price and volume ratios in Sri Lanka in 1950-95 shows the twin problem which is fundamental to developing countries facing

2 The sub-groups included in the category of *other consumer goods*, are (a) motorcars and motorcycles, (b) radio receivers and televisions, (c) rubber tyres and tubes, (d) medical and pharmaceutical products, and (e) other consumer goods (CBSL *ROE* 1992: 97). According to the present system, the imports of textiles are included in the 'intermediate' category, and not in the 'consumer' category. The same classification method is used in the analysis.

global technological change. One of the problems is the increase in the volume of non-food manufactured consumer goods imports as compared with those of food and drink. This change in the pattern of consumer goods imports general-ly points to the fact that for Sri Lankans over the past four and a half decades since 1950, the range of imported non-food manufactured consumer goods has generally widened relative to the range of imported food and drink. Also, the increase in domestic production should be taken into account. In response largely to contemporary import substitution industrialization policies, domestic production of commodities of the same types, which were imported previously expanded.[3] Thus, decline in import volume has, at least partially, been offset by increasing domestic production.

Despite annual variations of the ratio, generally the import of non-food man-ufactured consumer goods has increased over the period after 1950, with the exception of the period from the early 1960s to the late 1970s. In this period, the decrease in the ratio of import volume index below unity reflects largely the impact of trade restrictions of the contemporary development strategy on the importation of such non-food manufactured consumer items. A relative decline in the volume of food and drink can also result in a corresponding increase in the ratio of import volume index, but this has not been the case in Sri Lanka until the late 1970s. According to trade indices of Sri Lanka, import volume index of food and drink remained above 100 for most of the period of 1950-77, but decreased below 100 for the period of 1978-92 (Appendix II), possibly due to an increase in domestic production.

As shown by the ratio of import price indices, the second problem is the increase in import prices of non-food manufactured consumer goods relative to those of food and drink. The ratio of import price indices was below unity only in the mid 1970s in response to the increase of import price of food and drink (perhaps, due to contemporary world food shortage) as compared with those of non-food manufactured consumer goods. The expansion of the range of im-ported non-food manufactured consumer goods due to trade liberalization in 1977 has resulted in an upward movement of the ratio of import price indices at a higher rate than its increase in the period before that. Trade liberalization can result in an increase in the import price index as 'new' commodities enter into imports and the improvement of quality and change in characteristics of the imported commodities. As I have shown earlier, both factors associated with a continuos increase in 'exchange values' of the imported commodities. Evident-ly, the shift of trade policy towards a market-oriented economy has brought about many 'new' commodities from industrialized countries into the domestic market. Yet, there is a technical problem as well. It should be pointed out that

3 It has often been argued that the import substitution regime in Sri Lanka, and in many other coun-tries, has given rise to production of capital-intensive non-essential manufactured commodities, be-cause they were the items which came under strict import controls and hence, naturally, received higher incentive to produce domestically than essential commodities. According to Athukorala (1986:70), during the import substitution regime in Sri Lanka '... much of the industrial capacity es-tablished was intended to cater to requirements of upper-income domestic consumers'.

the extent of these 'new' commodities is taken into account in the index can have implications on aggregate indicators of data.

Table 6.2   *Expenditure on imports of consumer goods, selected years 1960-1990*

Imports	1960	1970	1975	1980	1990
As a % of imports of consumer goods					
Food and drink	75.3	91.4	95.8	76.0	55.0
Other (excluding textiles)[a]	24.7	8.6	4.2	24.0	45.0
As a % of total imports					
Food and drink	38.4	46.2	48.0	18.9	14.5
Other (excluding textiles)[a]	12.6	4.4	2.1	6.0	11.9
As a % of GNP at current factor cost					
Food and drink	12.0	8.2	9.9	10.4	5.5
Other (excluding textiles)[a]	3.9	0.8	0.4	3.3	4.5

a. Other consumer goods include consumer durables and other non-food manufactured consumer goods excluding textiles.
Source: CBSL (*ROE* annual issues).

Generally, the patterns of change in price and volume of imports of non-food manufactured consumer goods and of food and drink in the period after 1950 involved important repercussions on the domestic economy. The range of the imports of non-food commodities has widened relative to the range of the imports of food and drink. The expenditure on the imports on non-food commodities has also increased, on the other hand, in response to different patterns of price changes between the two types of commodities.

Even though there were positive achievements of the then popular post-war development strategy of an import substitution industrialization in developing countries, there is little doubt that this strategy did not bring about a sustainable reduction in the amount of consumer durables imported into these countries. Table 6.2 provides information on Sri Lanka's import of consumer goods for selected years in 1960-90. Imports of *other consumer goods* which basically include consumer durables and other manufactured goods, measured as a percentage of imports of consumer goods, total imports and that of GNP, shows a substantial reduction in 1970 and 1975. This was largely a result of gradually tightened import restrictions on consumer durables in reaction to the deteriorating balance of payments position rather than positive achievements of import substitution policies. Once foreign trade was liberalized in 1977, imports of consumer durables and other manufactured goods recorded a rapid escalation. The imports of consumer durables and other manufactured goods in 1990 amounted to 4.5 per cent of GNP, an increase from 0.4 per cent in 1975. It is important to note that the recorded level of imports of consumer durables and other manufactured goods in 1990, measured as a percentage of GNP exceeded the level of 1960.

Table 6.3   *Change in consumption expenditure per spending unit[a],*
CFS years 1953-1986/87; as a percentage of total expenditure

Commodities	1953	1963	1973	1978/79	1981/82	1986/87
Food	66.8	64.9	60.2	57.5	57.7	52.7
Non-food	30.0	34.7	33.8	37.9	35.8	42.1
Housing	3.6	7.4	6.8	5.6	5.8	7.9
Clothing	8.0	9.6	7.6	10.4	7.1	7.6
Transport & communication	2.6	2.2	3.4	4.5	3.9	5.0
Education	2.0	1.8	2.2	1.7	1.6	2.1
Recreation	1.3	0.7	0.8	1.4	1.2	2.0
Social functions	1.9	1.6	2.2	3.1	3.1	3.9
Gifts & donations	1.8	1.1	1.3	1.9	1.7	1.9
Personal expenditure[b]	2.0	0.2	1.4	1.9	2.3	2.3
Medical	1.3	2.9	1.6	1.7	1.6	2.2
Consumer durables	3.2	0.4	6.1	4.6	6.5	5.2
Jewellery	1.2	0.1	0.6	0.6	1.6	1.1
Other[c]	2.0	0.3	5.5	4.0	4.9	4.1

a. According to the definition of the CFSs (CBSL 1993: 7), a spending unit is formed by one or more persons who take independent decisions with respect to spending their income with their dependants.
b. Personal expenditure includes those expenses on tailoring, toiletries, cosmetics, hairdressing, shaving equipment and other.
c. Other consumer durables include all electrical appliances and other durable manufactured goods.
Source: Appendix III.

The changes in consumption patterns are reflected by the changes in the shares of consumption expenditure between food and other commodities, namely non-food and consumer durables. Table 6.3 shows changes in the pattern of consumption expenditure of an average 'spending unit' of the country. According to the definition of the CFSs (CBSL 1993,7), a spending unit is formed by one or more persons who take independent decisions with respect to spending their income with their dependants. The share of expenditure on food per average spending unit has consistently declined from 66.8 per cent in the CFS year 1953 to 52.7 in 1986/87, despite a slight increase in 1981/82. In contrast, the share of expenditure on non-food and consumer durables, though not constant, has increased remarkably in this period. Expenditure on non-food consumption has increased from 30.0 per cent of total expenditure per spending unit in 1953 to 42.1 per cent in 1986/87. Among consumption items classified in the non-food category, the shares of expenditure on housing, transport and communication, recreation, and social functions shows significant upward trends. Moreover, expenditure on consumer durables other than jewellery which includes all electrical appliances and other manufactured goods has increased from 2.0 per cent of total expenditure in 1953 to 5.5 per cent in 1973, and then, has slightly declined to 4.1 per cent in 1986/87. These data on the changing consumption pattern in Sri Lanka does not, however, show the changes in consumption pattern among different market segments, as they indicate only the changes in the shares of consumption expenditure per *average* spending unit. Yet, they show that generally people have reduced the share of expenditure on food and increased that on non-food and consumer durables.

There are some controversial issues regarding the changing patterns of consumption expenditure. The expansion of consumption towards 'secondary' types of commodities—non-food and consumer durables, is a typical characteristic of changing consumption patterns. As the consumption capacity is dependent primarily on income, according to Engel's law, at higher levels of income people spend a larger share of it on non-food and consumer durables. For this reason, one could argue that the changing patterns of consumption expenditure in Sri Lanka are an indication of rising income. Evidently, consumption is positively correlated with income. Yet, it is an important question whether people only attempt to change their consumption patterns if income rises. It is difficult to deny that, for m reasons, people may take the irrational decision to purchase consumer durables even at the expense of basic necessities. For example, Wells (1977) found that, in Brazil, increased spending by the poor on consumer durables was accompanied by a decline in nutrition levels. The traditional consumption theory, which formulates consumption in principle as a dependent variable of income, has however come under strong criticisms in terms of its empirical validity (James 1990, Miller 1995). Most importantly, this theory assumes 'a constant range of consumer choices' on the one hand, and 'a rational behaviour of consumers' on the other hand. The former assumption leads to the ignoring of the impact of commoditization and globalization on the range of consumer choices, while the latter to the exclusion of the influence of cultural, social, political and other economic factors on consumers' decision-making, reflecting an irrational behaviour (Chapter VI). Moreover, statistically the changes in the shares of consumption expenditure can also be a result of the changes in the *relative prices*, even without an income growth. Most important commoditization was accompanied by a tendency to produce high exchange values. If the production of high exchange values is more intensive in the non-food and consumer durable sectors than in the food sectors, the share of consumption expenditure on the former category of commodities can rise at the expense of expenditures on the latter. Therefore, it should be noted that the changes in the patterns of consumption expenditure constitute an issue more complex than is assumed by a simple income-consumption relationship. Given the specific theme and the scope of this study, however, I will not address these issues of consumer behaviour in the Sri Lankan context.

It is now time to return to our basic problem. The range of consumer choices, also partly import-dependent, increased in the domestic market and was accompanied by a tendency to increase cost of consumption and a change in consumption expenditure. Therefore, an increasing share of expenditure on non-food consumer goods should be drawn from an already low level of national income, thus increasing consumption inequality in society. Even though national income is growing, an increasing share of it should be taken by the high income classes to sustain the increasing *range* of consumer goods and the increasing *cost* of such consumer goods. This is how a low-income country affords the consumption patterns similar to those in a high-income country. The growing consumer inequality, and hence, an increase in *social exclusion* is the result (see Chapter VI). The rest of society, other than people who improved their level of consumption, was confronted by to the consumer advancement of some parts of society. The social segments which were excluded from consumer advancement became frustrated. Evidently, it is difficult to anticipate that policy restrictions on consumer advancement in society in terms of import controls, income ceilings and taxation coupled with distributive policies, can solve the problem of social exclusion from consumer advancement. Most importantly, as I discussed in Chapter VI, such a regulated economic system contributes to, rather than solves, the problem of growing *international* consumer inequality in the context of the current global economy.

Income and consumption inequality

Affordability is important in changing consumption patterns, since the change is not simply a matter of choice between 'old' and 'new' things. Changing consumption patterns, in an increasingly complex consumer society, demand an increase in income. The changing of consumption patterns, which is a global phenomenon, must be sustained through income generation, which is a local phenomenon (Chapter IV). If consumption capacity depends basically on income, then income generation should be in line not only with the quantitative and qualitative changes in human 'wants', but also with the increase in exchange values. From the point of view of a developing country, the need for income generation in the economy and the distribution of income among different social segments are thus justified by changes in consumption patterns. Even though the required level of income generation is difficult to establish, developing countries are provided with a model of Western development principles and standards. This model shows the level of income growth that developing countries must achieve and maintain to meet the challenges of global economic change. For reasons that I discussed in Chapter V, the Sri Lankan economy experienced a growing economic crisis in a competitive society. The crisis was characterized by a growing social and political demand for economic resources and opportunities on the one hand, and a deterioration of the country's economic capacity to generate these resources and opportunities on the other hand. In the context of the economic crisis, the Sri Lankan economy can hardly be considered to have achieved the required levels of economic growth in the post-Independence period.

Income generation and distribution

Evidently, one of the key issues of income growth and distribution in the post-Independence development history of Sri Lanka was the shift in the trend of income growth and distribution in the late 1970s. Prior to this period, income growth was relatively low, but the redistribution of income was relatively fair, compared with the change in their trends in the period after that. It was argued widely that the policy shifts following political changes in 1977 constituted the major factor of these changes in trends of income growth and distribution (e.g., Lakshman 1997, UNDP *HDR* 1990). Table 6.4 provides information on real income generation for the period of CFS years 1963-86/87. Real income data were derived using the GNP deflator (1960 = 100) to adjust nominal income data from the CFSs for each of the consumer units given, that is, a household, a spending unit, an income receiver and a person. In this period, the striking feature was that the real income did not even double for any unit of consumers. Furthermore, the real income per consumer unit in 1973 was actually lower than in 1963. Annual national accounts data also confirmed a significant decrease in the rate of economic growth in the early 1970s.[4] The decline in economic growth could be attributed largely to the weaknesses of the contemporary ëinward-orientedí policy and stringent state intervention. In addition, other explanations can also put forward, namely the youth insurrection of 1971, the world oil shock of 1973-74, the world food shortage of 1973-74, and the frequent droughts and consequent crop failures. A relatively considerable increase

Table 6.4   *Change in real income per various consumer units, CFS years 1963-1986/87; at 1960 constant prices*

CFS year	GNP deflator[a] (1960=100)	One month income (SLRs.) per			
		Household	Spending unit	Income receiver	Person
1963	98	213.0	196.6	136.4	37.0
1973	169	193.8	183.9	134.6	34.5
1978/79	336	302.3	274.7	183.9	55.4
1981/82	549	315.4	298.0	202.5	60.3
1986/87	866	339.8	315.2	210.0	66.7

a.   GNP deflator for 1978/79, 1981/82 and 1986/87 is the average of annual deflators for the respective two years.
Source: Appendix IV.

4 In the early 1970s, the economy recorded little progress, along with rising population. The rate of income growth adjusted for population growth was negative (-0.6 per cent) in 1971 and 0.5 per cent in 1972 (CBSL ROE 1974: 3). Even during the rest of the period until 1977, the rate of economic growth was low and, consequently, the average annual rate of economic growth, which is not adjusted for population growth, was only 2.9 per cent during the SLFP regime of 1970-77 (see Chapter V).

in real income was recorded after 1978/79. This change was due to the growth-oriented policy changes. However, income distribution was more unequal after 1977 than it was before then.

Table 6.5   *Change in income distribution among income classes,*
CFS years 1953-1986/87; percentage of total income of the groups
of spending units, ranked according to income

Ranked spending units	1953	1963	1973	1978/79	1981/82	1986/87
Lowest 10 per cent	1.9	1.5	2.8	2.1	2.2	1.9
Second 20 per cent	7.4	8.0	10.0	8.3	8.0	7.2
Third 20 per cent	11.6	11.5	14.0	12.3	11.6	11.0
Forth 20 per cent	15.2	16.5	18.7	16.3	15.7	16.1
Fifth 20 per cent	23.3	26.7	26.6	25.2	25.2	26.3
Highest 10 per cent	40.6	36.8	28.0	35.8	37.3	37.4
Gini coefficient	0.46	0.45	0.35	0.44	0.45	0.47

Source: CBSL: *CFSs*

Table 6.5 presents changes in income distribution among income groups of spending units for the CFS years 1953-86/87. A striking feature of change in income distribution is that the pattern of changing income distribution from 1953 to 1973 was in favour of lower income classes, at the expense of the highest income class. As was shown by the figures for the years after 1973, there was a reversal in this pattern of income distribution. For the period of 1973-86/87, the income shares of the highest two classes of spending units increased, while those of all other lower income groups declined. The Gini coefficient for income groups of spending units decreased consistently, from 0.46 in 1953 to 0.35 in 1973, indicating a change in income distribution towards equality. In the period of 1973-86/87, it increased to 0.47, reflecting an unequal distribution. Generally, the change in state policy from one of redistribution to one of growth-orientation in 1977 can largely explain the change in the income distribution pattern. Nevertheless, an analysis of income distribution without reference to the income generated does not make sense. In a situation of unequal income distribution, the living standards of the poor in a growth-oriented economy can be higher than those in a redistributive economy, because of the differences in the level of income generated and distributed. The increased equality of income distribution does not necessarily improve the average living standards. As the Sri Lankan economy did not grow adequately, the policy commitment to achieve distributive equality resulted in an episode of sharing poverty. In contrast, the relatively high income growth in the post-1977 period was not shared by the lower income classes. In particular, the income share of not only the lowest, but also the middle income groups declined after 1973. This indicates that the development of an unequal distribution pattern affected the majority of the lower and middle income classes relative to the increase in the income share of the highest income group of spending units.

Regional inequality

The CFS data sources provide some useful information on regional income inequality. The classification of regions is somewhat aggregate, but shows the income disparities according to 'urban-rural-estate' differences and according to 'zone' differences. The CFSs divide the into 5 zones as follows:

Zone 1:
Districts of Colombo excluding the Colombo Municipality, Gampaha, Kalutara, Galle and Matara.

Zone 2:
Districts of Hambantota, Monaragala, Ampara, Polonnaruwa, Anuradhapura and Puttalam.

Zone 3:
Districts of Jaffna, Mannar, Vavuniya, Mullative, Trincomalee and Batticaloa.

Zone 4:
Districts of Kandy, Matale, Nuwara Eliya, Badulla, Ratnapura, Kegalle and Kurunegala.

Zone 5:
Colombo Municipality.

Two important points should be noted. First, the Colombo Municipality area was considered a separate zone in the CFSs after 1973 only. Prior to that, it was included in zone 1. Secondly, the data for zone 3 are not reported for the CFS year 1986/87, because the CFS was not conducted that year in zone 3 due to the ongoing Tamil separatist war. The changes in regional income disparities prior to the war are more important to my analysis than those in the war period.

Regional disparities are important in an analysis of the country's political conflict. First, both the JVP and the Tamil separatist movements were basically organizations of educated rural youth (Chapter V). Therefore, it is important to investigate whether the rural sector was neglected or more disadvantaged than the urban sector. Secondly, this question can be extended to deal with zone differences. The Tamil separatist movement emerged in the North and the East. As those districts (excluding Ampara in the East) are in zone 3, it is important to note zone disparities affecting zone 3. Such a consideration does not mean that other zones were free of conflict. With regard to the JVP insurrection, in particular, an identification of the zones in terms of income disparities is complex, for the JVP activities were rather diffuse, particularly in the 1980s. Violent incidents relating to both the JVP and the LTTE took place in Colombo, because the most effective political, economic and even civilian targets for attack were found in Colombo. However, according to Hettige, the highest 'intensity of JVP attacks against police stations' in the first JVP insurrection in 1971 was found in Moneragala, Anuradhapura, Polonnaruwa and Galle. The first three of these districts are in zone 2 and Galle, is in zone 1 (1992a: 71). The second-highest rates of incidents were reported in Vavunia, Trincomalee, Kurunegala, Kegalle, Nuwara Eliya, Matara, Hambantota and Ampara. Hambantota and Ampara also belong to zone 2, while Kurunegala, Kegalle and Nuwara Eliya are in zone 4. Thus, it appears that relatively high rates of JVP incidents were reported from zones 2 and 4. Nevertheless, it is also true that in these zones there were some districts with relatively low rates of JVP incidents, such as Puttalam in zone 2 and Matale, Badulla and Ratnapura in zone 4. The zone-wise classification does not, however, permit exploration of intra-zone disparities of economic change.

Table 6.6a   *Change in average monthly income per income receiver at constant prices, CFS years 1963-1986/87 (GNP deflator: 1960 = 100)*[a]

Zones/Sectors	1963[b]	1973	1978	1981/82	1986/87[c]
Zone 1	171	155	187	205	232
Zone 2	142	155	212	215	229
Zone 3	161	162	221	206	–
Zone 4	105	106	151	179	162
Zone 5	–	163	338	361	444
Urban	260	187	246	296	337
Rural	130	138	184	196	193
Estate	66	70	89	82	93

a. GNP deflator, as of Table 6.4.
b. Colombo Municipality was included in zone 1 in the CFS year 1963. This was considered a separate zone since 1973.
c. The CFS of 1986/87 was not conducted in zone 3 due to the on-going war in this zone.
Source: Appendix IV.

Inter-regional income differences and their changes are presented in Tables 6.6a and 6.6b. The former shows regional changes in average monthly income per income receiver at constant prices, assuming 1960 as the base year. The latter shows regional deviations in average monthly income per income receiver from the all-island average, assuming the all-island average is 100. A comparison of zone-wise changes in income (Table 6.6a) shows a few important points. Although income increased in each zone, the increase was greater in zone 1 than in other zones. This clearly shows that advantages in terms of income generation were concentrated in the Colombo Municipality area. In addition, zone

3 shows an important change in income for the period 1963-81/82. In terms of average income, zone 3 appears to have enjoyed conditions comparable to those of Colombo Municipality in 1973. Until 1978, it recorded the second highest monthly income per income receiver. The income of other zones increased after 1973, but the income of zone 3 actually declined by 1981/82. The income of zone 2 was higher than that of zone 1 in 1978. But in terms of income growth by 1981/82 and by 1986/87, zone 1 had surpassed zone 2. The changes in urban-rural income disparity indicate that the average monthly income per income receiver in the urban sector has always been substantially higher than that of the rural sector. Although the urban rural income disparity declined between 1963 and 1973, since then the disparity has grown continuously.

The changes in regional income disparity in relation to the all-island average further indicate the advantage of zone 1 and of the urban sector (Table 6.6b). The incomes of zones 3 and 5 were the highest, and 120 and 121 respectively compared to the average of 100. In the course of economic change in the subsequent period, the economic conditions declined relative to those of the Colombo Municipality. The income deviation of zone 3 from the all-island average remained constant until 1978, and declined to 102 by 1981/86. But that of zone 5 increased to 184 relative to the all-island average in 1978. Although this recorded a decline in 1981/82, it was 211 in 1986/87. Another important income disparity was noted regarding the average income in zone 4. The average income in this zone has always been below the all-island average, perhaps due to the low average income in the estate sector which is included in zone 4. The urban-rural disparity also decreased until 1973, but increased continuously in the subsequent period. The average income of the rural sector, which was 103 in 1973, was equivalent to the all-island level of 100 in 1978. By 1986/87, it was

Table 6.6b   *Index of average monthly income per income receiver, CFS years 1963-1986/87 (All-island = 100)*

Zones/Sectors	1963[a]	1973	1978	1981/82	1986/87[b]
Zone 1	125	115	102	101	110
Zone 2	104	115	116	106	109
Zone 3	118	120	120	102	–
Zone 4	77	78	82	88	77
Zone 5	–	121	184	178	211
Urban	191	139	134	146	160
Rural	95	103	100	97	92
Estate	48	52	49	40	44

a.   Colombo Municipality was included in zone 1 in the CFS year 1963. This was considered a separate zone from 1973 on.
b.   The CFS of 1986/87 was not conducted in zone 3 due to the ongoing war in this zone.
Source: Appendix IV.

92, while that of the urban sector was 160, indicating an increase in urban-rural income disparity.

The decline in urban-rural income disparity in the period 1963-73 can be attributed to the distribution-oriented economic policies prior to 1977 and the attempts of the governments to achieve self-sufficiency in agricultural production. The urban-centred development in general, and the Colombo-centred development in particular, were led by the substantial growth of infrastructure, industry and service sectors following the policy changes in 1977. For example, 87 per cent of the industrial firms, registered under the Ministry of Industries in 1996, were located in the districts of Colombo and Gampaha of the Western province (CBSL *ROE* 1996: 64). However, the impact of the 1977 'open economy' model on the rural agricultural sector '… is necessarily a complex, uneven and contradictory development' (Gunasinghe 1986: 66). In relation to some aspects of trade liberalization, domestic food production faced competition that curtailed the *absolute* income and profit margins of rural farmers. The farmers in the North, whose income was dependent on certain agricultural products such as chillies and onions, were affected to a great extent (Gunasinghe 1986). Even in the industrial sector, urban-centred, large-scale economic activities increased, while small-scale production activities and cottage industries deteriorated (Athukorala 1986, Osmani 1987). But there was no significant expansion of other economic activities to absorb the rural population. A large section of the rural areas was left untouched by growth. In some cases, large-scale development projects such as the Mahaweli scheme were implemented to assist the rural sector, with mixed results (Lakshman 1997). Large-scale development projects such as the Mahaweli scheme had an economic impact, but also created numerous social problems, including violence (Schrijvers 1993).

Evidently, there were significant variations within the rural sector in terms of conditions affecting income growth. But aggregate data do not show these variations. However, the faster growth of urban-centred and Colombo-centred economic activities is confirmed by these data, as shown in the tables. Such an urban-biased and Colombo-biased development can have widened the regional income disparity, even though absolute income in the rural sector was on the rise. In general, it is difficult to maintain that the Sri Lankan economy has ever developed preconditions ensuring a reasonable profit margin and accumulation in the rural sector, as compared with industrial and other urban-based service sectors.

Social exclusion from consumption

The empirical data analysed so far reveal that consumption pattern in Sri Lanka, as in other developing countries, was changing towards a pattern that can be afforded only in high-income countries. The speed of change can be controlled by the state, but the expectations for change cannot be controlled. The speed of changing consumer patterns, however, was enhanced by trade liberalization in 1977, and the impediments to the integration of the domestic economy with the global economy declined. Trade liberalization eliminated restrictions imposed on international imports. Relatively high economic growth and the expansion of export earnings increased the affordability of changing consumption patterns. But in reality, the Sri Lankan economy, as a developing country, does not have the income to afford the mass consumption of a modern consumer society. Instead of developing a mass consumption pattern, what a developing economy can achieve at best is a highly fragmented consumer society with highly unequal income distribution. According to Hettige 'perhaps the most significant changes occurred after 1977 in the sphere of private consumption when import liberalization coupled with growing income inequalities gave rise to marked disparities between the rich and the poor in terms of ownership of assets and consumer durables ...' (1995: 100). If this was the case, then the question is whether the imposition of restrictions on trade and the implementation of policies for distribution could be the solution.

The choice of trade strategy can affect the speed of changing consumption patterns, while policies for equality can minimize income and consumption inequality (see Chapter IV). But it does not solve the problem of the escalation of expectations. The restrictions imposed on import trade naturally create an impetus for the domestic production of the same types of commodities as those that could otherwise be imported from industrialized countries. By definition, 'import substitution' industrialization implies producing domestically, what was previously bought from outside. The problem is acute when the economy is experiencing slow economic growth. The pre-1977 period, which was characterized by state intervention to control trade and distribution coupled with slow economic growth (Chapter V), provides an example in this regard. An examination of changing consumption patterns in Sri Lanka in this period shows that, generally, society continued to share poverty, as state intervention retarded the growth of modern consumer patterns. Nevertheless, the pre-1977 development experience indicated that the possibilities to achieve a 'closed' economy in a globalizing world were declining, not only in economic but also in social and political terms. Thus, as I have shown in Chapter V, a regime of sharing poverty has resulted in an increasing international consumption inequality.

In the post-1977 period, these restrictions were removed, and consequently, minority sections of population developed modern consumer patterns, aggravating income and consumption inequality. Advancing consumption is an important method of upward social mobility, because consumption is no longer a means of survival. It raises social status and shows 'what the person is' to the rest of society. In response to commoditization, thus, an endless increase in consumption can be seen among the affluent minority, which absorbs an increasing share of national income at the expense of the rest of society. The rise of income and consumption inequality was not necessarily a result of economic growth. A striking example was the development of above average consumption of politicians in power and their associates, not due to the generation of resources from investments, but by simply using political power. This development should be considered in contrast to the increasing difficulties struggle of the majority of employed and rural peasants, faced with relatively stagnant incomes, and with growing unemployment. Having no means to afford consumer advancement, a majority of society increasingly experienced a sense of social exclusion and frustration. The most frustrated belonged to the new generations. The new generations were more sensitive than their former generations to the possibilities of consumer society. This was because their awareness of the changes was relatively high, and their ties to traditional society were loose. Both were a result of the increasing exposure to the changing environment locally and globally, and of widespread education.

Employment and education

The growing unemployment problem became a critical policy issue faced by every post-colonial government in Sri Lanka. With special reference to the contemporary high population growth of the country, the problem of unemployment along with the foreign exchange crisis has received a considerable attention from analysts, policy-makers and governments (ILO 1971, MPE 1971, NPC 1959). Just as other development issues, the unemployment problem is largely a modern one in developing countries because it became critical only with the beginning of the labour flight from, and the depletion of economic activities of, traditional societies (Chapter IV). In the traditional occupation system a person inherited categories of work at birth. New generations in traditional societies were gradually moved into the world of adults, doing work the same as or similar to that of their fathers. For the same reason, in traditional society, unemployment, was not an issue.

Growth of modern unemployment

Statistics on employment and unemployment in Sri Lanka should be interpreted cautiously due to inconsistencies in definition, measurement and methodology in data sources and in different survey years. The data sources used in this study are the population censuses of the Department of Census and Statistics (DCS) and the CFSs of the Central Bank of Sri Lanka (CBSL). Changes in the labour force and unemployment in the post-Independence history of Sri Lanka are shown in Table 6.7a according to the census data of the DCS, and in Table 6.7b according to CFS data of the CBSL. The statistics presented in the two tables are not comparable, owing to differences in the data sources. For example, the lower age limit of the labour force is 10 years in the population census, and 14 years in the CFSs. In addition, the concepts of employment and unemployment vary even within one data source. Therefore, changes in employment or unemployment statistics are due not only to real changes in the size of the employed or unemployed populations, but also to changes in concepts and definitions. These limitations should receive due consideration.

Evidently, underemployment is acute in Sri Lanka. A situation of underemployment, or in other words that of employment below the level of optimality, can result from many causes other than the period of time that a person is employed. As I have shown earlier, these factors include skills, training, experience and educational or other qualifications. But owing to the problem of measurement of employment, the definition of underemployed in the data sources is confined to the period of time employed. The CFSs considers as unemployed people working less than 20 hours per week. This is not a satisfactory indicator of underemployment, so in this section I focus on unemployment only.

According to the DCS census data, in the three and a half decades of 1946-81, the labour force in Sri Lanka approximately doubled, but the number of unemployed people trebled (Table 6.7a). However, the unemployment statistics in the population census cannot be compared over time, for the reasons mentioned above. In particular, those who seek employment at the time of enumeration were treated differently in different census years. Moreover, in the first census years after 1946, the unemployed population was defined as those who had had employment previously, but not at the time of enumeration. In the CFSs since 1953, however, the population seeking employment was treated as unemployed. The CFS data were, however, based on sample surveys. According to the CFS data (Table 6.7b), the rate of unemployment declined from 16.6 per cent in 1953 to 13.8 in 1963. In the next CFS year (1973), 24.0 per cent unemployment was reported, the highest rate of in the post-Independence period. It is noteworthy that according to both data sources, the highest rate of unemployment was in the early 1970s. As the CFS data revealed (Table 6.7b), unemployment recorded a substantial decline, to 11.7 per cent in the 1981/82, but increased again in 1986/87 to 15.5 per cent.

Table 6.7a   *Labour force and unemployment: DCS data for 1946-1992*

Year	Census data (number in 1000s)			Rate of unemployment (%)
	Population	Labour force	Unemployed	
1946	6657	2612	287	11.0
1953	8908	2993	335	11.2
1963	10582	3452	265	7.7
1971	12690	4488	839	18.7
1981	14847	5014	895	17.9
1992	17405	5756	832	14.5

Source: DCS (Census years), *Population Census* for 1946-1981; DCS (1992), *Labour Force Survey* for 1992.

Table 6.7b   *Labour force and unemployment:*
CFS data for 1953-1986/87

Year	Sample data		Rate of unemployment (%)
	Labour force	Unemployed	
1953	3254	540	16.6
1963	9097	1255	13.8
1973	9695	2326	24.0
1978/79	15678	2205	14.1
1981/82	14205	1658	11.7
1986/87	13734	2130	15.5

Source: CBSL: *CFSs*

The changes in the rates of unemployment do not, however, indicate the size of the unemployed population. The changes in unemployment should, therefore, be studied relative to the increase in the size of the population and of the labour force as well. According to the population census (Table 6.7a), both the population and the labour force have increased by 1.7 times in the period of 1953-81. This is an approximate population increase from 9 to 15 million, while the labour force increased from 3 to 5 million. In the early 1970s, when the highest unemployment rate were recorded, the unemployed population exceeded 1 million. As the population and the labour force were consistently increasing, even a decline in the rate of unemployment does not necessarily show a corresponding decline in the number of unemployed people.

The growth of the unemployment problem in post-Independence Sri Lanka was cumulative (Kiribanda 1997). Rapid population growth, the rapid expansion of formal education and the sluggish growth of the economy were the major causes. Every successive government had to confront the problem of trying to create employment for the backlog of the unemployed population, but also for the new members of the labour force.

Due to the rapid expansion of the formal education system after Independence, large numbers of people left the traditional economy to seek employment in the modern economy. During colonization, the occupation system in Sri Lanka began to modernize. A person's occupation is no longer determined at birth. In principle, avenues are open to anybody from any social background to choose an occupation that can change his or her income, consumption pattern, identity, social relations and status. The type of occupation is a major avenue for attaining the desired consumption pattern, and positions the individual in the social hierarchy. The hierarchical order of society does not value all occupations equally. White collar jobs become more highly valued and rewarded than blue collar jobs. The origin of the 'white collar syndrome' can be traced back to the early years of British colonial rule, when native chiefs and petty feudal functionaries were co-opted into an underclass of the emerging colonial bureaucracy (Hettige: forthcoming). The value attached to jobs is determined by factors such as the level of payment, the level of education required, the knowledge of English required, the place and the type of work, the ability to supervise over others, and so forth.

In modern Sri Lanka, a farmer or a fisherman or a person with such an occupation hardly expects his son to choose his own or a similar occupation. The son himself hardly ever considers becoming a farmer or a fisherman, unless he has no other option. Generally, even though traditional rural occupations are undervalued in the modern occupational system, if the work involves the use of modern technology, particularly new instruments and machines, it is not considered to be a traditional occupation. Owing to the low level of income generation in the traditional sectors, however, his type of change is still unlikely for the majority of people in Sri Lanka.

The role of the post-Independence state was full of contradictions. The failure of the state to satisfy the expanding demand for modern categories of employment was a result. The post-colonial governments were unable to create an economic environment that could absorb the expanding labour force. In the welfare state, the government was considered to be the 'provider' of almost all economic needs. The government increased its involvement in economic activity. Thus, the provision of welfare services, but also the provision of other economic needs, particularly employment, became the responsibility of the government. Traditionally, society looked to the government for jobs. Moreover, the Sri Lankan society used to prefer government sector jobs, as these ensure a regular income, job security, social status, and a relatively high degree of freedom and flexibility. Widespread education created an increasing demand for certain types of employment, in contrast to the opportunities that the government could offer. The government's ability to provide employment that matched the expectations of the unemployed were limited to the public sector, and these opportunities were numerous. Having no other employment opportunities to offer, every government used public sector institutions to provide jobs, particularly for political supporters (Gunasinghe 1984). Thus, in time, political affiliation became an important, perhaps the most important, qualification for obtaining a job. Political patronage was not limited to the labour market. The government's ability to continue to supply even the smaller necessities of life was limited. Therefore, these, too, were allocated through political patronage.

Social groups in unemployment

As was discussed in the previous chapter, the economic ideology of the UNP and the SLFP governments was a major cause of unemployment. Until 1977, the UNP did not appear to have a coherent plan for the country's economic development. The UNP governments of 1948-56 and of 1965-70 focused more on agricultural self-sufficiency than on industrialization, even though they preferred a more liberal economic policy. The basic ideology of the UNP governments to develop the rural agricultural sector was in conflict with both the decline of the traditional economy and the aspirations of the new generations in

the rural sector. In contrast, the SLFP governments did have a plan for industrialization, but the expansion and the viability of the domestic market-oriented
industrialization eventually became a critical policy issue. On the contrary, the
massive investment in education in the post-Independence period qualified the
younger generations for modern employment. They demanded white collar
jobs in particular.

Although unemployment is not an unusual phenomenon in developing economies, and even in developed economies, the changing pattern and structure
of unemployment in Sri Lankan development history, is striking. These features
can be attributed largely to the country's free education system. There is little
doubt that in Sri Lanka education became the only avenue for socio-economic
advancement for the majority of the people. In transferring the new generation
from the traditional economy to the modern economy, the free education system has no doubt been instrumental. In the post-colonial period, an increasing
proportion of the younger generation received formal education. As I showed
in Chapter V, since 1945 the population almost doubled, while school enrol-

Chart 6.2   *Growth of unemployed youth population,*
for selected CFS years, 1963-1981/82 (age group of unemployed
as a percentage of total unemployed labour force)

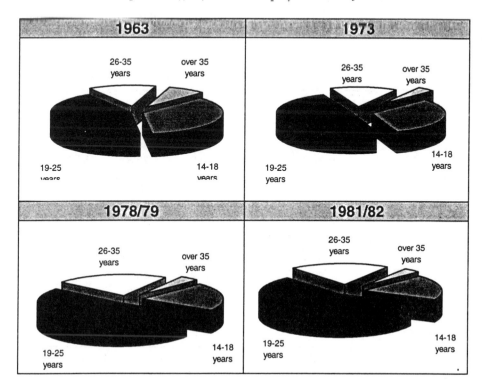

Source: Appendix V.

ment trebled. This new generation became unusually large. Thus, in terms of structural features, unemployment in Sri Lanka has become a problem of the increasing unemployment of the youth population on the one hand, and that of the educated population on the other hand. Chart 6.2 shows the increase of the unemployed youth labour force for selected CFS years between 1963 and 1981/82. Most unemployed people are in the 19 to 25 age group. The share of this group in the total population of unemployed youths increased between 1963 and 1981/82, with a corresponding decline in the size of the unemployed population between 14 and 18 years of age. In 1981/82, the share of youths in the unemployed population shows a slight decline, but it remained the largest share.

Table 6.8 shows detailed statistical indicators of the age distribution of unemployed population in two ways, as a percentage of the labour force in each age group, and as a percentage of the total unemployed labour force. The striking feature of the age distribution of the unemployed population is that, in both cases, the highest unemployment rates can always be observed for the two youngest groups (14-18 and 19-25). Unemployment rates of different age groups vary. In 1973, unemployment was highest both for the young labour force and for the labour force in general. Overall, the unemployment rate rose from 13.8 per cent in 1963 to 24.0 per cent in 1973, while the unemployment rate of the labour force of all age groups under 45 increased as well. Some 65.8 per cent of the labour force in the age group of 14-18, and 47.5 per cent of the labour force in the 19-25 age group was unemployed in 1973.

Table 6.8   *Age group of unemployed population; CFS years 1963-1986/87*

Age group (years)	1963	1973	1978/79	1981/82	1986/87
as a % of labour force in each age group[a]					
14 - 18	47.5	65.8	29.6	30.1	48.0
19 - 25	30.3	47.5	30.0	28.8	35.3
26 - 35	7.8	15.2	12.5	8.8	10.6
36 - 45	2.4	3.9	2.6	1.7	3.2
46 - 55	2.7	1.2	0.6	0.5	0.7
over 55	1.9	0.8	0.2	0.1	0.6
as a % of total unemployed labour force[a]					
14 - 18	35.5	32.0	21.3	19.5	26.4
19 - 25	43.2	49.4	52.2	56.8	50.9
26 - 35	13.4	14.7	22.6	20.4	17.4
36 - 45	3.5	3.1	3.2	2.7	4.2
46 - 55	3.0	0.6	0.5	0.5	0.7
over 55	1.4	0.3	0.1	0.1	0.4

a.   The employed population under 14 years of age, which is negligible, is excluded.
Source: Appendix V.

The largest share of the unemployed labour force belongs to the age group 19-25 years in all the years under consideration. This share increased, from 43.2 to 49.4 per cent of the unemployed labour force between 1963-73, and was over 50 per cent after 1978/79. By contrast, the total share of unemployed people over 35 years of age did not exceed the single digit level, either as a percentage of labour force of the same age group, or as a percentage of the total unemployed labour force.

As was mentioned above, an important characteristic of the unemployment problem was the increase in the size of the unemployed educated population. Evidence suggests that the number of unemployed reported in the surveys consisted to a certain extent of underemployed as well. This is because many underemployed persons prefer to respond to survey questionnaires as unemployed. This is of particular relevance to a discussion of the unemployment of educated youths. Chart 6.3 presents the changing pattern of the unemployed labour force according to levels of education in the CFS years from 1953 to 1981/82. In 1953, as the opportunities for the educated labour force were relatively high, the unemployed population was characterized by low levels of education. Yet in time, this situation reversed, and, the unemployed labour force with a sec-

Chart 6.3   *Growth of educated unemployed population, selected CFS years 1953-1981/82 (percentage of total unemployed labour force)*

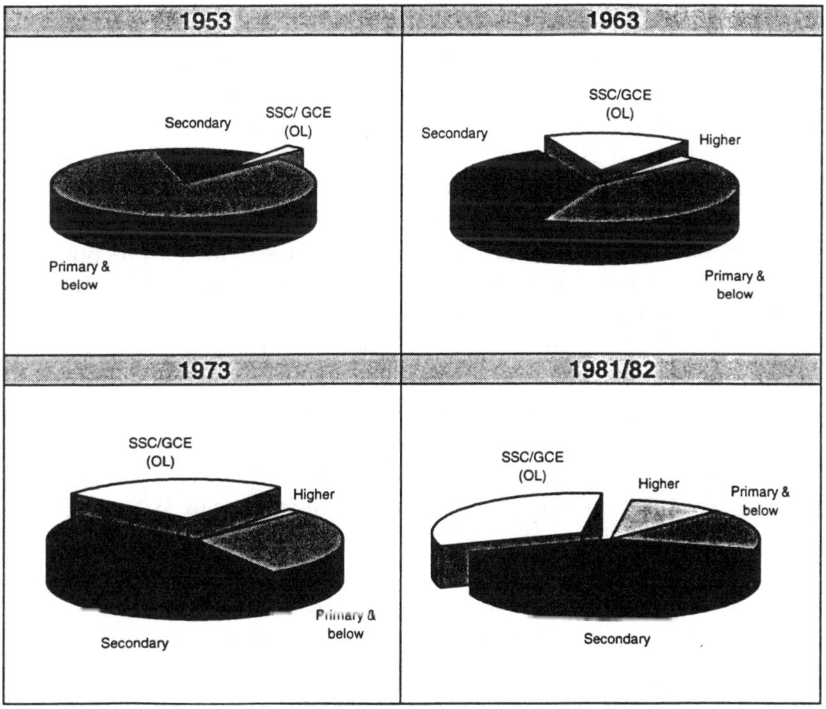

ondary level education or SSC or GCE (OL) increased. The unemployment of
those with levels of education higher than secondary also increased, but still
accounted for a relatively small share. Therefore, in the 1970s and the 1980s
unemployment was higher among the population with 'middle' levels of education than among the rest of the population (those with no school education,
'low' levels of education, or 'high' levels of education).

Table 6.9 shows changes in unemployment according to education level and
changes in unemployment classified by education levels as a percentage of total
unemployment. A striking feature of the unemployment pattern since 1953 was
the reduction of the unemployment rates among people with lower levels of
education, and the corresponding increase of unemployment among those with
higher levels of education. The year 1973 shows a critical escalation of unemployment at all education levels. In 1973 the unemployment rate of the labour
force with SSC or GCE (OL) was for 47.4 per cent, and that of the labour force
with HSC or GCE (AL) was 44.4 per cent.[5] In 1953, 25.0 per cent of unemployment was shouldered by the labour force with SSC. However, the variation in
unemployment rates of the labour force with low levels of education was small.
The unemployment rate of the labour force with secondary education was 17.9
per cent, while those of the labour force with primary education or no schooling were 16.4 per cent and 16.6 per cent respectively. In the three decades since
then, the unemployment situation changed dramatically. The general pattern is
that unemployment has primarily affected the labour force with middle levels of
education. In 1981/82, the unemployment rates of the labour force with primary
education or no schooling were 5.0 per cent and 2.9 per cent respectively. Also,
the unemployment rate of the labour force with a university degree was 9.7 per
cent in 1981/82, declining to 7.6 per cent in 1986/87. The labour force with middle levels of education suffered severely from unemployment. Among those
with a middle level of education, the highest rate of unemployment (35.0 per
cent) was recorded in the labour force with HSC or GCE (AL).

Since 1953, the share of the unemployed population with low levels of education decreased substantially, while the share of the unemployed population
with high levels of education increased. In 1953, 35.2 per cent of the unemployed had no formal education, while 48.9 per cent had only primary education. Until 1986/87, the shares of the unemployed population with no formal
education or with only primary education declined to 1.9 per cent and 10.1 per
cent respectively. A corresponding increase in unemployment can be observed
among the labour force with higher levels of education. The unemployed population with a secondary education increased from 13.1 per cent in 1953 to 44.1
per cent in 1986/87, while the unemployed population with SSC or GCE (OL)

5 The GCE (OL) examination, which was formerly known as the SSC, is an 'achievement test' of a
student at the end of secondary school. At present, the duration of secondary school education is
five years from grade 6. The GCE (OL) examination provides a qualification for students to study for
higher secondary education and some other vocational training as well as to apply for certain jobs.
The GCE (AL) examination, which was formerly known as the HSC, is an 'achievement test' at the
end of higher secondary education of which the duration is about two years. The university admissions are also based on the results obtained at the GCE (AL) examination.

Table 6.9   *Education of unemployed population, CFS years 1953-1986/87*

Education level[a]	1953	1963[b]	1973	1981/82	1986/87
as a % of labour force at each education level					
No schooling[c]	16.6	6.1	8.0	2.4	2.9
Primary	16.4	10.5	14.1	4.8	5.0
Secondary	17.9	23.0	37.1	14.6	19.8
Passed SSC or GCE (OL)	25.0	39.3	47.4	24.5	28.5
Passed HSC or GCE (AL)	3.0[d]	13.9d	44.4	35.0	36.8
Obtained degree	–	–	16.2	9.7	7.6
as a % of total unemployed					
No schooling[c]	35.2	12.8	6.2	2.7	1.9
Primary	48.9	30.9	22.5	14.3	10.1
Secondary	13.1	37.3	44.7	40.0	44.1
Passed SSC or GCE (OL)	2.6	16.9	24.8	32.8	32.2
Passed HSC or GCE (AL)	0.3d	2.1d	1.5	9.3	11.1
Obtained degree	–	–	0.3	1.0	0.7

a. Figures for the unemployed population with technical and other levels of education are not given.
b. In 1963, the category of 'unstated' education levels in the original source is excluded from estimations.
c   Includes both literate and illiterate categories.
d. For 1953 and 1963, 'Passed HSC' refers to any level of education higher than SSC.
Source: Appendix VI.

rose from 2.6 per cent to 32.2 per cent in the same period. Although there are problems of classification regarding the labour force with HSC or GCE (AL) for the early periods, its share in unemployment increased from 1.5 per cent in 1973 to 11.1 per cent in 1986/87.

The unemployment of the educated and the youth labour force came to dominate the unemployment problem. As an ILO study observed, 'about 250,000 are now [in the early 1970s] coming out of the schools each year, the great majority of them looking for work and one-third of them with at least ten years of education, including many who have passed one or more subjects at "O" level' (1971: 4). Those with no education or a relatively 'low' level of education had no means to obtain white-collar jobs. They were left to do the jobs that were considered to be lower than the white-collar categories or which they inherited from the traditional economy. Most importantly, this category of youths, with no education or with a low level of education, was shrinking, due to the expansion of free education since the mid 1940s. Thus, the competition for the categories of work for which they are eligible also decreased. 'There were jobs available at any rate in some areas and in certain sections;   young people with some years of secondary education feel that they are above this and entitled to a white-collar job' (ILO 1971: 4). As the size of the youth population with higher levels of education increased, so did the demand for a limited number of jobs. The state was confronted by the challenge to provide not just jobs, but also the right kind of jobs. Political patronage and the favouritism of other types of particular features intensified the problem. The final result was that the great majority of those who emerged from the formal education system found that their academic qualifications had no value, while a minority succeeded due to political connections.

Table 6.10a   *Median income index for the level of education, CFS years 1963-1986/87; one month median income for No schooling (illiterate) = 100*

Education level	1963	1973	1978/79	1981/82	1986/87
No schooling (illiterate)	100	100	100	100	100
No schooling (literate)	144	152	145	140	143
Primary	157	175	146	152	142
Secondary	242	229	187	190	189
Passed SSC/GCE (OL)	447	314	274	273	289
Passed HSC/GCE (AL)	–	385	273	262	258
Undergraduate	–	–	266	186	329
Graduate	–	741	402	401	362
All levels	–	182	167	152	173

Source: CBSL (1984: 202), (1993: 271)

It is generally believed that the higher the level of education the greater the financial reward. The positive correlation between the two variables was studied extensively in literature on human capital formation (e.g. Becker 1974, Polachek & Seibert 1993). Table 6.10a shows the median income indices for different levels of education in Sri Lanka for selected years of 1963-86/87. Assuming the median income for the education category of *no schooling (illiterate)* equals 100 for each of the years given, the indices show that the median income varies according to level of education. Generally, the median income rises with the level of education, but certain deviations from this pattern can also be observed, particularly in levels of education higher than SSC or GCE (OL) in 1978/79, 1981/82 and in 1986/87. Obviously, as the CFS data reveal (CBSL *CFS*), there are wide variations in the incomes of the people with the same level of education. Nevertheless, it cannot be denied that the general belief that education is the main avenue for socio-economic advancement has a strong economic basis.

Striking features can be observed in the income distribution according to education levels. In relation to a *unitary* increase of median income for the educational category *no schooling (illiterate)*, the ratios of income increase for the rest of the educational categories, are shown in Table 6.10b. In the period 1963-73, the ratio of increase was lower for higher levels of education than for lower levels of education. Furthermore, it is striking that in the period 1973-78/79, the ratio of income growth for all levels of education was lower than

Table 6.10b   *Ratio of median income growth for the level of education,
CFS years 1963-1986/87; Ratio of median income growth for
No schooling (illiterate) = 1.00*

Education level	1963-73	1973-1978/79	1978/79-1981/82	1981/82-1986/87
No schooling (illiterate)	1.00	1.00	1.00	1.00
No schooling (literate)	1.06	0.95	0.97	1.02
Primary	1.11	0.83	1.04	0.93
Secondary	0.95	0.82	1.02	0.99
Passed SSC/GCE (OL)	0.70	0.87	1.00	1.06
Passed HSC/GCE (AL)	–	0.71	0.96	0.98
Undergraduate	–	–	0.70	1.77
Graduate	–	0.54	1.00	0.90
All levels	–	0.92	0.91	1.14

Source: Table 6.10a.

unity, while those most disadvantaged in this regard had an education higher than SSC or GCE (OL). For the subsequent two periods of 1978/79-81/82 and 1981/82-86/87, the ratios of income growth were closer to unity for all levels of education, reflecting a more or less similar pattern of income growth, except for the undergraduate category. The distributive implications of the differences in the income levels according to education should, however, be considered in relation to the country's overall growth performance. Just as in the case of Sri Lanka's unemployment, the changing pattern of income distribution also presents a specific structural problem. In a situation of slow economic growth, at least until the late 1970s the problem of income generation was more severe for those with high levels of education than for those with low levels of education. If the pattern of income generation among the income earners with different levels of education is taken separately, after the late 1970s, income generation is quite similar among many of the categories.

Summary

In the preceding analysis, I explored some vital economic sources of widespread social exclusion and frustration in Sri Lankan society. The analysis was approached in both the local and global contexts, in the sense that rising socio-economic expectations are governed by global and local social, political and economic environments. Therefore, the development problem in developing countries is simply how to improve people's access to basic needs. Rather, the question is how to generate economic resources to match the increasing expectations. In Sri Lanka, a developing economy with a low per capita income, the case is critical. The generation of resources and opportunities and the rising expectations for socio-economic advancement were in conflict with each other. Increasing social exclusion and frustration resulted. The government, which traditionally was the 'provider' of the means for socio-economic advancement, failed to provide the resources and opportunities to meet the rising expectations. As a result, the resources and opportunities became scarce, and consequently, their distribution was unfair.

I discuss the aspects of social inequality associated with the distribution of economic resources with reference to consumption, income, employment and education. However, data on income were used as a variable, supporting the analysis on consumption distribution. In the same way, education was examined in relation to employment and unemployment. People in modernizing societies integrating with the world economy, increasingly expect to move away from the traditional economy, and they develop aspirations for socio-economic advancement similar that enjoyed in high-income countries..

The effects of commoditization were the dissemination of new and more commodities, with a tendency to equalize prices throughout the world. This process is rooted in technologically advanced countries. In contrast to this global phenomenon, the income patterns of various countries are a local phenomenon. The development of consumption aspirations is largely a response to global technological change, and a reflection of the degree of local exposure to global change, because consumption is no longer a means for survival. The material aspirations of Sri Lankan society do not reflect its economic ability. Therefore, matching rising consumer expectations is a critical issue. Nevertheless, the consumption pattern did change, as an important component of socio-economic advancement of individuals. The country was spending from its limited income to increase consumption levels. The range of new commodities was expanding. Also, the share of consumption expenditure on food declined. This trend has not been a socially 'neutral'. Inevitably, if income is low in comparison with consumption levels, the increase in consumption must be sustained by absorbing increasing amounts of income, and in turn alienating large segments of society.

Among those who witnessed the increased consumption of some social groups, there was a large population of unemployed and educated youths with sufficient qualifications for socio-economic advancement but no opportunities. Unemployment exhibited two structural features. Unemployment was increasing for younger generations on the one hand, and for educated generations on the other hand, while these groups overlapped each other. Many young, educated Sri Lankans experienced social exclusion and frustration.

It is also highly misleading to expect that those who were able to find employment were better off. The upward social mobility in the advancing consumer society was still a quite distant objective for the majority of income earners who were faced with the problem of managing the basic needs out of their low earnings. The discrepancy between the rising expectations and decreasing economic opportunities produced an acutely competitive society. The social exclusion experienced by the younger generation was fertile ground for political conflict.

Ethnicity and Scarcity in Sri Lanka: Regional and Communal Competition

VII

I examine in this chapter the discrepancy between rising expectations of socio-economic advancement and declining economic opportunities, with reference to the competition between regions and ethnic communities. Analyses, based on regional (provinces and districts) and ethnic (Sinhala and Tamil) factors overlap to a significant extent, as regions differ from each other in their ethnic composition. In the previous chapters, I discussed the deepening economic crisis and its implications for distribution, which resulted in an increasing alienation of the youth. In view of the so-called Sinhala-Tamil 'ethnic' conflict, it is also necessary to discuss the problem of distribution in a communal context. Many studies claim that 'the Sinhalese gained and Tamils lost'. If Sri Lanka has undergone a deepening economic crisis throughout its post-Independence development, obviously, the Tamils and Sinhalese should both have suffered a loss of means for socio-economic advancement. Therefore, it is difficult to analyse the distribution of economic resources and opportunities along ethnic lines.

Given the basic problem of increasing demand and decreasing supply, I concentrate on the historical patterns of change in the distribution of losses and gains among the communities. I also focus on the impact of the post-Independence state policies on this competition. However, I confine my analysis to an exploration of the economic realities behind the frustration among the younger generations of different communities, and not of their value judgements. In other words, I attempt to establish what happened and how it happened. It is true that the state, various social groups, those who lost or gained, and finally those individuals who sympathize with any of these parties can certainly have their own value judgements and rationalizations. However, dealing with these is not part of my objective.

I emphasize communal and regional disparities in education and employment for two reasons. First, education is believed to be the major avenue for socio-economic advancement. Secondly, the communal and regional competition for opportunities is more overt in education and employment than in other areas.

First I discuss the formation of an 'uncompetitive' privileged group in the colonial period in terms of socio-economic advancement. The ethnic characteristics of this group are discussed. Second, I depict the challenge to the old privileged group arising from the expansion of education to all social groups and all communities. Regional inequality in education is shown to support the dominance of the old privileged groups. Third, I show how, by restricting the number of students admitted to university, governments affected the ethnic communities. Fourth, I focus on the Indian Tamil community in the plantation sector which has not yet become a significant part of the competitive society, and briefly outline its chances of joining it. I conclude by emphasizing that new generations have experienced an increasing loss of means of socio-economic advancement at two levels: the old elite lost some of its, advantages, and, and 'newcomers' faced increasing scarcity. In both cases, ethnicity was an important factor.

The 'uncompetitive advantage' of the old elite

Prior to colonization, different communities in Sri Lanka, particularly Sinhala and Tamil communities, had no reason to compete for the same types of economic resources for socio-economic advancement. This was because regional populations including both communities were spatially separated and did not form part of one and the same competitive economic and political system (Chapter V). The concept of socio-economic advancement hardly existed, because what a person would become was determined at birth in traditional society. Nevertheless, the foundations of a competitive society, unifying all the regions and the communities within the same economic and political system, were already laid in the colonial periods. Various communities merged as competitive groups vying for resources, largely as a result of colonial education policy. Colonial education policy was implemented with a view to creating a qualified indigenous labour force for colonial administrative purposes. Thus, at Independence, a social group comprising Sinhala, Tamil and other communi-

Table 7.1   *The ethnic composition of provinces in 1946 (percentages)*

Province	Sinhala	Sri Lanka Tamil	Indian Tamil	Moor[a]	Other[b]
Western province	82.5	3.3	4.8	5.5	3.9
Central province	54.5	3.5	34.9	5.9	1.2
Southern province	94.8	0.6	1.5	2.6	0.4
Northern province	2.0	92.0	1.8	3.8	0.4
Eastern province	9.9	47.1	1.6	39.0	2.3
North western province	88.5	3.0	2.0	5.8	0.7
North central province	79.7	6.7	2.2	10.7	0.7
Uva province	57.4	4.2	34.2	3.2	1.1
Sabaragamuwa province	79.2	1.0	16.5	2.8	0.6
All island	69.4	11.0	11.7	6.1	1.7

a. Moor includes both Sri Lanka and Indian Moor communities.
b. Other includes Burgher and Eurasian, Malay, Veddah, European and other.
Source: Appendix I.

ties, free from their traditional socio-economic ties, had already emerged as competitive community groups. This development continued after Independence. New generations entered in the competitive society in growing numbers, while economic resources dwindled.

Competitive social groups did not emerge from various communities during the colonial period in a uniform pattern. There were geographical, and hence, communal disparities in terms of the distribution of colonial influence, as the duration and pervasiveness of colonial rule were different among the provinces. Since 1505, the Western and Southern maritime areas, and some areas of the Northern and Eastern provinces were under Portuguese, Dutch or English rule. Mostly the s low-country Sinhalese lived in the Western and Southern provinces. The Northern and Eastern provinces were inhabited mostly by Sri Lanka (Ceylon) Tamils. According to Table 7.1, in 1946 in the Western and the Southern provinces the Sinhalese community accounted for 82.5 per cent and 94.8 per cent respectively, while the Northern province, 92.0 per cent of population consisted of Sri Lanka Tamils. In terms of the duration and the degree of colonial penetration, the Kandyan Sinhalese who lived mostly in the central provinces were the least affected.

Table 7.2 *Indicators of the distribution of economic resources between Sinhala and Tamil in 1953*

	Kandyan Sinhala	Low-country Sinhala	Sri Lanka Tamil	Total population
Share of community in total population (%)[a,b]	26.6	42.8	11.2	100
Unemployment as a % of labour force	15.6	18.9	8.4	16.6
Underemployment[c] as a % of employed people	19.8	22.5	2.2	14.5
Average monthly income (Rs.)				
per income receiver	90.7	26.0	115.9	34.2
per person	124.7	43.2	107.4	35.4

a. Population data can differ slightly from those of DCS (1953) used elsewhere in this study.
b. The total includes the Indian Tamil, Moor, Malay, Burgher, European and other minorities.
c. working less than 20 hours per week.
Source: CBSL, *CFS 1953.*

Colonial influence and domination were distributed unequally over regions and communities, leading to different levels of socio-economic advancement. Socio-economic disparities at Independence, caused by social, economic, political and cultural factors, are widely cited in the Sri Lankan literature (Jupp 1978,

Manor 1984, Sivanandan 1984, SSA 1985). First, a tiny minority that had close links with British rulers emerged as a dominant group. This social group from the country's affluent and high-caste strata. Their distinctive features were close political affiliation to the colonial rulers and education, received mostly in Britain. Although this group came from both Sinhala and Tamil communities, they had much more in common with each other than with ordinary people in their own communities. Almost all features of this elite, such as Western-oriented socialization and education, wealth, caste and political affiliation, made them stand together (Chapter V). Below this social group, in the urban middle class people who often became Christians were able to advance in socio-economic terms, over the rural peasantry and over Buddhists, Hindus and Muslims (Silva 1974).The rise of the middle class was also facilitated by the Christian missionary and English-language education system under the colonial government and by employment in the modern sector, particularly in the colonial administration system. In fact, a variety of groups in all communities were able to benefit and advance, though at different levels, as a result of this colonial education system. These groups were mainly from the capital Colombo in the Western province and Jaffna in the Northern province, and belonged to Westernized and affluent social groups. Thus, a new social stratification was established in the colonial period, with education playing a leading role in upward social mobility.

Now let us turn to socio-economic disparities *between* the communities. In the new social hierarchy, there was an unequal distribution of resources and opportunities between communities. In other words, some had more and some had less than one would expect on the basis of their share in the total population. An inquiry into this issue reveals a disproportionately large part of economic resources and opportunities at Independence in the hands of the Tamil community. Table 7.2 shows certain aggregate data on unemployment, education and income among different communities in 1953. The lowest unemployment and underemployment rates, 8.4 per cent and 2.2 per cent respectively, are found in the Sri Lankan Tamil community.[1] Unemployment and underemployment in the Kandyan Sinhala community, 15.6 per cent and 19.8 per cent respectively, were lower than the 18.9 per cent unemployment and 22.5 per cent underemployment among the Low-country Sinhala community. Most likely this is a result of the fact that, unlike the Low-country Sinhalese, the Kandyan Sinhalese were still largely involved in the traditional agricultural economy, where unemployment was of little importance.

According to Table 7.2, monthly average income per *income receiver* and per *person* in the Tamil community was Rs. 124.7 and Rs. 43.2, respectively. The incomes for the Low-country Sinhalese averaged Rs. 115.9 per income receiver and Rs. 34.2 per person, while those for the Kandyan Sinhalese were Rs. 90.7 and Rs. 26.0, respectively. In terms of economic advantages enjoyed by communities, proportionately the position of the Kandyan Sinhalese was lower than

---

1 According to CBSL (*CFS 1953*: 11), unemployment amongst the Sri Lanka Tamil would have been still lower, if the fact that many unemployed Indian Tamil reported themselves as Sri Lankan Tamil had been taken into consideration.

that of the Low-country Sinhalese, while that of the Sinhalese in general was lower than that of the Sri Lanka Tamil. As many other studies have also established (e.g. SSA 1985, Oberst 1986, Wilson 1979), the conditions of the Sri Lanka Tamil community in terms of employment, education and income were better than those of the Sinhala community at Independence.

Education: the avenue for socio-economic advancement

It has been argued widely that the establishment of formal education in Sri Lanka in the colonial period reflected the requirement of colonial governments to secure indigenous manpower to serve in the colonial administrative system (Bastian 1984, Jayaweera 1986, Oberst 1986). It also made the imposition of Western and Christian culture on indigenous society possible (Silva 1974, 1977a). It was entirely different from pre-colonial traditional education. The modern education system gradually became the major avenue for socio-economic advancement for all social groups, and for low-income classes to escape poverty (Jayaweera 1986). Having seen the socio-economic advancement of those who first benefited from colonial education, society as a whole recognized the importance of education. The social expectations for education were, of course, fulfilled to a great extent by post-colonial national governments, which invested heavily in free education.

Education facilities were established in the colonial period mainly in the Jaffna peninsula of the North and the Western and the Southern maritime areas. As socio-economic advancement and the social value system of the country grew in association with the colonial education system, the traditional education system was absorbed into the colonial education system, but remained in close contact with local religions. From the late 19th century onwards, Buddhist and Hindu schools were founded in Colombo, Jaffna and other cities in response to the rise of Christian mission schools.

In 1879, according to Silva (1977a), the Northern, Eastern and Western provinces (in ascending order) reported the highest proportion of children enrolled in school. The Northern province remained in this dominant position for almost a century.[2] Missionary English education was available only in certain areas of the country initially, and the Western and the Northern provinces were the most important of these areas. The Western province, where the administrative and commercial capital of the country, Colombo, is located, developed an advantage over the rest of country. The Northern province, which has poor soil, was open to the colonial influence through missionary education. Thus, missionary education became 'land' to the Northern people (Sivanandan

2 According to Silva's estimates (1977a: 400), the highest proportion of children in school relative to the total population was 1:14 in the Northern province and 1:21 in the Western province in 1879. In 1930, the figure was 1:6 in the Northern province and 1:7 in the Western province. The proportion of school children to the population in all other provinces, except in the Southern province, where it was 1:8, was equal or over 1:10 in 1930. In 1971, the proportion of school children to the total population was 1:4.1 in the Northern province and 1:4.3 in the Western province.

1984: 4), and was welcomed in the North long before it became acceptable to
the Sinhalese majority. Some (Abeysekera 1985, Bastian 1985) maintain this was
a result of the 'divide and rule' principle of the colonial government, but whether or not colonial policy was deliberately divisive in Sri Lanka is a controversial
issue (Wickramasingha 1995). Education in Jaffna was better than that in the rest
of the country, particularly because of the presence of American missionary
schools, which were not accepted in the Western province by the British. Of
course, the Tamil population in the North could benefit from the presence of
these schools.

Table 7.3   *Literacy[a] rates of population over 5 years of
age by district in 1946*

District[b]	District literacy rates (%)	Percentage distribution of literate population			
		Literacy in mother tongue			Literacy in English
		Total	Sinhala	Tamil	
Colombo	72.8	27.1	30.3	14.2	45.6
Kalutara	63.8	7.6	9.5	2.6	5.5
Kandy	47.5	8.7	8.0	10.7	10.5
Matale	50.3	2.0	2.0	2.0	1.6
Nuwara Eliya	40.4	2.7	1.9	5.3	2.3
Galle	60.1	7.2	9.4	1.2	6.2
Matara	54.7	5.0	6.4	0.9	2.6
Hambantota	43.0	1.7	2.2	0.2	0.6
Jaffna	70.6	8.1	0.2	32.2	9.4
Mannar	64.8	0.5	0.0	2.1	0.3
Vavuniya	69.2	0.4	0.1	1.5	0.2
Batticaloa	43.1	2.3	0.2	8.6	1.3
Trincomalee	62.9	1.3	0.5	3.4	2.1
Kurunegala	57.5	7.3	9.3	1.6	2.1
Puttalam	58.4	0.7	0.5	1.1	0.3
Chilaw	73.5	2.7	3.2	1.1	1.1
Anuradhapura	51.6	1.9	2.2	1.2	0.9
Badulla	36.5	3.5	3.0	4.9	3.0
Ratnapura	46.4	4.1	4.7	2.4	2.2
Kegalle	52.2	5.4	6.3	2.8	2.2
All island	57.8	100	100	100	100

a. Literacy is defined in the original source as the ability to 'read and write'.
b. District classification regarding some of the districts differ from those reported in the
    surveys after 1946.
Source: DCS (1946).

Data regarding the regional distribution of literacy (defined as the ability of people over 5 years of age to read and write) is presented in Table 7.3. This information is an indication of the pattern of educational in 1946. However, these

data should be interpreted with care, because distortions may have resulted from the skewed distribution of the people of European and European-descendent (Burgher and Eurasian). In this community, which accounted for about 0.7 per cent of the total population (Table 7.6a), the literacy rate was high. The fact that the Tamil-speaking community includes the Sri Lanka Tamil, the Indian Tamil and the Moor communities should also be taken into account. The district literacy rates show that Colombo, Jaffna and Chilaw[3] were the most literate, with literacy rates exceeding 70 per cent. In terms of mother-tongue literacy, Jaffna, where 96.3 per cent of population was Sri Lanka Tamil, had the highest literacy rate (32.2 per cent). Colombo had the second highest level of mother-tongue literacy, namely 30.3 per cent literacy in Sinhala. In addition, the literacy rate in Tamil exceeded 10 per cent in Colombo and Kandy. In districts such as Kalutara, Galle, and Kurunegala, the literacy rate in Sinhala was close to 10 per cent. The highly unequal distribution of the literate population among the districts indicates the unequal distribution of colonial educational facilities. Colombo and Jaffna had the most literate populations. This is further explained by the unequal geographic distribution of the English-literate population.

Colombo had an exceptionally high number of English-literate people: 45.6 per cent of the total population. However, this figure should be treated with care, as the community of Europeans and people of European descent in Colombo was also 66.6 per cent of the total population of the community (Table 7.6b). The same distortion can also affect the figures for Kandy, where the English-literate population was 10.5 per cent, and where the community of Europeans and people of European descent accounted for 9.6 per cent. This distortion, however, hardly applies to Jaffna, where the community of Europeans and people of European descent accounted for only 0.9 per cent of the community total (Table 7.6b). But 9.4 percent of the population in Jaffna was literate in English. Therefore, in terms of literacy in English, Jaffna was in the leading position, given the smaller proportion of the community which had English as a mother-tongue.

University admissions and employment

The skewed regional distribution of educational facilities is reflected in the regional distribution of opportunities for university education and for employment. The distribution of opportunities favoured the Sri Lanka Tamil community and disadvantaged the Sinhala community (Abeysekera 1985, Bastian 1985, Oberst 1986, Wilson 1979). The pattern has changed after the 1950s, corresponding to a decrease in the share of the Tamil community in the total population and an increase in the share of the Sinhala community.

---

3 Chilaw appeared as a separate district only in the censuses of 1946 and 1953, because these surveys were based on ërevenue districtsí (DCS 1946, 1953). The population censuses after 1953 were based on 'administrative districts', and Chilaw was included in the administrative district of Puttalam (DCS 1963, 1971 & 1981).

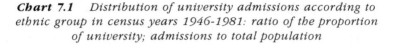

Chart 7.1   *Distribution of university admissions according to ethnic group in census years 1946-1981: ratio of the proportion of university; admissions to total population*

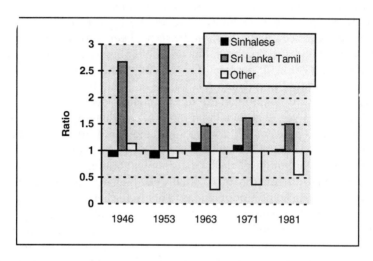

Note: Communities classified as Other do not include Indian Tamils.
Sources: UGC data for university admissions; Appendix I for population.

Chart 7.1 shows the distribution of university admissions according to ethnic group in the census years 1946681, as ratios of the proportion of university admissions to total population. If the ratio is unity, it means that university admissions are in proportion to the share of the community in the total population. If the ratio is above (or below) unity, it shows the disproportionate advantage or (disadvantage) of the community. Sri Lanka Tamil students enjoyed a disproportionate advantage over other communities until 1953, while the Sinhala students were at a disadvantage. However, since 1953, the disproportionate advantage of the Tamil community has declined, though the ratio remained above unity. In 1963 and 1971, the Sinhala community also acquired a disproportionate advantage, but in 1981 Sinhala university admissions were almost proportionate to the Sinhala share in the population.

Table 7.4 shows the percentages of different communities represented by university students and the total population in the census years 1946-81. The share of Sinhala students increased from 61.7 per cent in 1946 to 81.8 per cent in 1963, and declined to 76.4 per cent in 1981. The percentage of Tamil students, which was 29.4 per cent in 1946, increased to 33.7 per cent in 1953, but declined to 16.2 per cent in 1963. In 1981, it was 19.2 per cent. The Tamil community was over-represented in university admissions. The decline of its share in university admissions from the 1960s onwards is revealing. The factors underlying the rise of the Sinhala community are explored below. It should be noted that a sudden increase in the early 1960s in the number of students admitted to university benefited mainly the Sinhala community, as two of the Buddhist *pirivenas*[4] obtained university status in 1959. Due to the expansion of the university system, as I will discuss later (Table 7.8), the number of students admitted to the universities increased after the late 1950s.

Table 7.4 *University admissions according to ethnic group in the census years 1946-1981 (as a percentage of total)*

year	Sinhalese		Sri Lanka Tamil		Other[a]	
	University students	Population	University students	Population	University students	Population
1946	61.7	69.4	29.4	11.0	8.9	7.8
1953	60.2	69.4	33.7	11.2	6.1	7.0
1963	81.8	71.0	16.2	11.0	2.0	7.3
1971	79.0	72.0	18.2	11.2	2.8	7.5
1981	76.4	74.0	19.2	12.7	4.4	7.9

a.   Other does not include Indian Tamil.
Sources: UGC data for university admissions; Appendix I for population.

Chart 7.2 presents the distribution of employment according to ethnic group, relative to the share of the ethnic group in the total population. Ratios greater (or smaller) than unity indicate a disproportionate advantage (or disadvantage) of the group concerned. The ratio for the Indian Tamil community is much higher than unity, because the employment rate of this community, which is basically involved in tea plantations, is high. The 1953 and 1963 ratios show that the Sri Lanka Tamil community enjoyed a disproportionate advantage, and the Sinhala community was disproportionately disadvantaged. In 1973, both communities were disproportionate disadvantaged, while in 1981/82 the disadvantage of the Tamil community was higher than that of the Sinhala community.

Table 7.5 shows the employment rates of the ethnic groups as a percentage of the total population of each respective group. The employment rate of the Sinhala community declined from 29.5 per cent in 1953 to 24.2 per cent in 1973, while the 1981/82 figure in shows an increase to 29.7 per cent. Compared to all other communities except the Indian Tamil community, the Sri Lanka Tamil employment rate was the highest in 1953, at 34.9 per cent of This relative advantage remained unchanged even in 1963 and 1973, although employment on the whole declined in this period. However, although the 1981/82 Sri Lanka Tamil employment rate was higher than the 1973 level, it was lower than that of the Sinhala community.

---

4 Buddhist pirivenas were the traditional educational institutions, which had functioned since ancient times under the Buddhist monastic order. They still exist as free, semi-government educational institutions. According to DCS (Statistical Abstract 1995: 233), the number of pirivenas was 457 (out of 10382 schools in Sri Lanka) in 1990.

Chart 7.2   *Distribution of employment according to ethnic group in CFS years 1953-1981/82: ratio of the community proportion of employed to that of population*

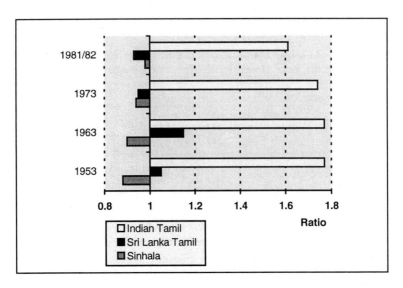

Source: Appendix VII.

The year 1973 shows the lowest employment ratios for all communities. As I discussed in detail in the previous chapter, the highest unemployment rate (almost one-fourth of the labour force) was recorded in 1973, and all communities were affected by the rapid increase in unemployment. However, the loss of advantage was more critical for the Tamil community than for the Sinhala community.

Table 7.5   *Distribution of employment according to ethnic group in CFS years 1953-1981/82, as percentages of population of the groups concerned*

Community	1953	1963	1973	1981/82
Sinhalese	29.5	24.6	24.2	29.7
Sri Lanka Tamil	34.9	31.4	24.5	28.3
Indian Tamil	59.1	48.4	44.8	48.7
Moor and Malay	28.9	24.4	20.0	22.2
Other	na	22.5	23.2	28.7
Total population	33.4	27.4	25.8	30.3

na Not available separately in the original source, but included in total.
Source: Appendix VII.

Analyses of the relative advantages and disadvantages of the Sinhala and Tamil communities generally postulate that the avenues for socio-economic advancement were more open to the Tamil community than to the Sinhala community. This situation mirrored the regional disparities in the distribution of education in the colonial period. However, the disproportionate privilege of the Sri Lanka Tamil community has declined since the 1960s, while the Sinhalese advantage has increased substantially. The increase in the Sinhala community's access to economic resources and opportunities is an important issue. Because the Sinhala community is the largest ethnic group in the country (over 70 per cent of the total population), the socio-economic advancement of the Sinhala community means a massive rise in absolute terms. The rise of the Sinhala, challenging the relatively small Sri Lankan Tamil community (about 11 per cent of total population) was of great weight.

The change in the distribution, since the 1960s, of socio-economic opportunities should be examined in the context of the development of ethnic conflict. As I analysed in Chapter V, the conflict between the Sinhala and the Tamil went through various stages, and gained momentum after the mid-1970s. From the point of view of Sinhala Buddhist nationalists, the change was a correction of the imbalance artificially created by the British. But for the Tamil nationalists, the change was a result of deliberate discrimination by the Sinhala- dominated government.

The challenge faced by previously privileged

I use the term 'privileged' to indicate the regions or social groups which were able to progress socio-economically through education and employment in the colonial period. As I have already discussed, the socio-economic advancement of these previously privileged regions and social groups was possible in a relatively uncompetitive society. As educational opportunities were limited to a minority group and located in certain areas of the country, until the 1960s the privileged social groups were not challenged by external forces.

However, there has been a remarkable expansion of education facilities throughout the island. Since 1946, the population of Sri Lanka has doubled, but school enrolment trebled. At Independence, higher education in particular was limited to the children of English-speaking, wealthy, high-caste families in both Sinhala and Tamil communities. After the 1950s, increasing numbers of youths from the rural peasantry and other lower level social groups obtained a university education. According to Jayaweera (1986: 53), the parents of 56 per cent of male and 70 per cent of female university students in 1950 were from professional and management categories, but by 1967, 58 per cent of all university students were from middle class families or from rural or urban working class groups. For these classes, education was more than an avenue for social mobility. It was the *only* way to enable the younger generations to escape poverty. The expansion of education resulted from a number of causes. The most important was the decision of the government to make education compulsory for children aged 5 to 14, accompanied by the introduction of free education, the increased role of the government in the provision of free education, and the shift from education in English to education in *swabhasha*, i.e. Sinhala and Tamil (Silva 1974). The important point is that the majority of the young people entering the formal education system were from the previously 'underdeveloped' regions.

The rapid expansion of school enrolment in the post-colonial period resulted in an increase in the competition for limited socio-economic resources. The island-wide expansion of education and school enrolment challenged the privileges enjoyed by a limited number of region. The rapid increase in school enrolment was further enhanced by the rapid increase in the proportion of population of school age due to the high population growth. Therefore, the opportunities for socio-economic advancement enjoyed by a minority were no longer unchallenged, as they had been in the colonial period.

Communities in the privileged and emerging regions

As the most privileged areas in terms of educational facilities, Colombo in the Western province and Jaffna in the Northern province should have been confronted by increasing competition more than other regions. Tables 7.6a and 7.6b show the regional ethnic distribution of the population in 1946. Some 24.9 per cent of the Sinhala community lived in the Colombo district, while 55.8 per cent of the Sri Lanka Tamil community lived in the Jaffna district (Table 7.6b). Moreover, Colombo and Jaffna together accounted for over one-fourth of the total population of the country facing the emerging competitive groups from other areas. In Colombo, 81.1 per cent of population was Sinhalese, while Sri Lanka Tamils accounted for 4.1 per cent. As the language of both Tamil and Moor communities is Tamil, the Tamil-speaking population in Colombo was approximately 13.9 per cent of the total.

Colombo, being the most rapidly developing region of Sri Lanka both before and after Independence had many advantages over the rest of the country. As a result of the centralization of administrative, commercial, trade and industrial activities, Colombo continued to provide better facilities and opportunities for education (both formal and informal) and employment, as well as business opportunities, than the other regions. Colombo developed the ability to cope with increased competition from the rest of the country. For the same reason, the population pressure in Colombo increased. Even in 1946, the Western province accounted for 27.9 per cent of total population in Sri Lanka, while Colombo district alone accounted for 21.3 per cent.[5] Moreover, a significant pro-

---

5 In 1981, according DCS (1981: 47), Colombo was the most densely populated district, with 2605 persons per square kilometre, followed by Gampaha with 994 persons. The population density of the Western province is 1072 persons per square kilometre; that of the Central province is 360, the second highest in the country. Another important change is that the population of Colombo population has become ethnically heterogeneous, as the proportion of Sri Lanka Tamils, Moors and Malays has increased (DCS 1981: 121).

Table 7.6a   *District distribution of population according to ethnic group in 1946 (percentage of total district population)*

District[a]	Sinhala	Sri Lanka Tamil	Indian Tamil	Moor[b]	European origins[c]	Other[d]
Colombo	81.1	4.1	4.3	5.5	2.2	2.8
Kalutara	86.8	0.8	6.4	5.5	0.2	0.3
Kandy	57.8	4.2	29.2	7.4	0.6	0.7
Matale	68.1	3.1	21.9	6.0	0.4	0.5
Nuwara Eliya	37.8	2.0	57.3	1.9	0.5	0.5
Galle	94.5	0.7	1.5	3.0	0.2	0.1
Matara	94.4	0.7	2.1	2.6	0.1	0.1
Hambantota	96.6	0.5	0.2	1.6	0.1	1.1
Jaffna	1.1	96.3	1.0	1.3	0.1	0.2
Mannar	3.8	51.0	11.2	33.0	0.2	0.8
Vavuniya	16.6	69.3	4.2	9.3	0.3	0.3
Batticaloa	5.8	49.7	0.6	42.2	0.6	1.0
Trincomalee	20.7	40.1	4.4	30.6	1.6	2.6
Kurunegala	92.2	1.5	1.6	4.2	0.2	0.3
Puttalam	52.0	12.8	2.1	31.6	0.2	1.2
Chilaw	87.0	5.2	3.3	3.2	0.2	1.1
Anuradhapura	79.7	6.7	2.2	10.7	0.2	0.6
Badulla	57.4	4.2	34.2	3.2	0.4	0.7
Ratnapura	75.8	1.2	20.6	1.7	0.2	0.5
Kegalle	82.1	0.8	12.9	3.7	0.1	0.3
All island	69.4	11.0	11.7	6.1	0.7	1.0

a. District categories in the DCS (1946) *Population Census 1946* are sometimes different from those in surveys carried out after 1953.
b. Moor refers to both Sri Lankan and Indian Moor community.
c. European origins includes Burgher, Eurasian and European communities.
d. Other includes Malay, Veddah and other.
Source: Appendix I.

portion of the upwardly mobile population migrated to Colombo regardless of ethnic background.[6]

In the Jaffna district, 96.3 per cent of population consisted of Sri Lanka Tamils, while the Tamil-speaking population was about 98.6 per cent of the population (Table 7.6a). Moreover, Jaffna accounted for only 6.4 per cent of the total population in Sri Lanka (Table 7.6b). Unlike Colombo, Jaffna obviously did not enjoy any comparative advantage except as regards education (Sivanandan

6 According to DCS (1981: 121), '...Colombo has changed towards an even more heterogeneous ethnic mix.... the proportion of Sri Lanka Tamils, Moors and Malays have all increased.' The Sri Lanka Tamil increased at the highest rate proportionate rate. Between 1946 and 1971), the percentage of the Colombo population consisting of Sri Lanka Tamils increased from 8 per cent to 12 per cent. The proportion of the community in Jaffna declined correspondingly from 56 per cent to 47 per cent, and further declined to 42 per cent in 1981.

Table 7.6b *District distribution of population according to ethnic group in 1946 (percentage of community total)*

District[a]	Sinhala	Sri Lanka Tamil	Indian Tamil	Moor[b]	European origins[c]	Other[d]
Colombo	24.9	8.0	7.8	19.1	66.6	60.0
Kalutara	8.6	0.5	3.8	6.1	1.6	2.0
Kandy	8.9	4.1	26.6	12.9	9.6	7.5
Matale	2.3	0.7	4.4	2.3	1.2	1.1
Nuwara Eliya	2.2	0.7	19.7	1.2	3.0	2.0
Galle	9.4	0.4	0.9	3.4	1.8	1.0
Matara	7.2	0.3	1.0	2.2	0.9	0.7
Hambantota	3.1	0.1	0.0	0.6	0.2	2.4
Jaffna	0.1	55.8	0.5	1.4	0.9	1.4
Mannar	0.0	2.2	0.5	2.5	0.1	0.4
Vavuniya	0.1	2.2	0.1	0.5	0.2	0.1
Batticaloa	0.3	13.8	0.2	21.0	2.6	3.1
Trincomalee	0.3	4.1	0.4	5.7	2.6	3.0
Kurunegala	9.7	1.0	1.0	5.0	1.6	2.3
Puttalam	0.5	0.8	0.1	3.3	0.2	0.8
Chilaw	2.6	1.0	0.6	1.1	0.5	2.4
Anuradhapura	2.4	1.3	0.4	3.7	0.5	1.2
Badulla	4.6	2.1	16.3	2.9	3.2	4.0
Ratnapura	5.6	0.6	9.1	1.4	1.4	2.7
Kegalle	7.1	0.4	6.7	3.7	1.2	1.8

a. District categories in the DCS (1946) *Population Census 1946* are sometimes different from those in surveys carried out after 1953.
b. Moor refers to both Sri Lankan and Indian Moor community.
c. European origins includes Burgher, Eurasian and European communities.
d. Other includes Malay, Veddah and other.
Source: Appendix I.

1984). Thus, Jaffna was more vulnerable to competition than Colombo, and lost its old privileges.

As we have already seen, some other regions also enjoyed disproportionate advantages. Among these, in the Southern province, Galle was an educationally privileged area for a long time in the colonial period. Galle, where 94.5 per cent of the total population in the district in 1946 was Sinhala(Table 7.6a), was one of the regions with the highest concentration of Sinhala people in its population. The total Sinhala population of Sri Lanka was 9.4 per cent (Table 7.6b). The old privileges of certain areas in the Western and Southern provinces, where the majority was Sinhala, as well in the Northern province, where the majority was Sri Lanka Tamil, were challenged by the rise of new generations from underdeveloped regions.

The Sinhala community, 69.4 per cent of the total population in Sri Lanka at the time, no doubt provided the majority of emerging competitors. The rising new generations came mainly from the provinces in the middle and south-east of the country. Anuradhapura, Moneragala and Hambantota show a high concentration of Sinhalese. In certain areas, however, the rising new generations entering the formal education system were ethnically mixed. In Nuwara Eliya and Badulla, the percentage of the Sinhala community is relatively small because of the presence of the Indian Tamil community in the tea plantation areas. Mannar, Vavuniya, Trincomalee, and Batticaloa were considered to be educationally 'underprivileged' in the 1970s, although they had had high literacy rates in 1946. In these districts, the Sinhalese communities were smaller than the Tamil-speaking communities in general, and the Sri Lanka Tamil community in particular.

Even though the expansion of free education benefited the underdeveloped areas in the country in general, its ultimate outcome was that these regions were confronted with competition to which they were unaccustomed. The newly emerging populations were disappointed by the limited opportunities to be gained from formal education. In Jaffna, people lost opportunities that they had previously had, since the colonial period. This was the case even for the new Sinhalese generations in the Southern province. In contrast, new generations in much of the rest of the country began to develop increasing expectations, but ended up losing to the old privileged areas and social groups.

The problems of underprivileged social groups and areas in the case of education escalated further, because they lacked the socio-economic foundation to benefit from free education: it has been established that children from affluent families benefit more than children from poor families do (Ranasinghe & Hartog 1997). Similarly, old privileged areas benefited more from free education than the rest of the country did, although this issue received much government attention. The important point is that previously established educational privileges were maintained in the face of rising competition. In addition, the qualitative disparity in education between the regions was an important factor.

Qualitative disparity: a defending force

The disproportionate privileges enjoyed by a few regions and by certain social gradually eroded with increasing competition, but the old privileges remained to a certain extent, in social, political and economic respects. Colombo was an exception in this respect. Despite the increased competition, substantial regional disparities remained throughout the post-colonial period in terms of the quality of education. These areas could, therefore, defend their 'old' privileges.

The quality of education can be assessed in many different ways. I use the disparities among districts in terms of the opportunities available in schools to study for the GCE (AL) in general and in science-based disciplines. Scientific educational programmes in general, and medicine and engineering in particular, are more highly valued than studies in social sciences ore humanities. The post-colonial expansion of free education pertained mostly to the latter type of education. Employment opportunities with high financial rewards and social status were guaranteed for those with an education in science. s Modern education in Sri Lanka has a strong academic bias (Silva 1977a), so professional training is highly valued and thus competitive. There are qualitative differences in the educational opportunities available to children in various districts.

Table 7.7 shows the 1973 district-wise distribution of government schools with GCE (AL) classes in general and those with classes in the science stream. The highest number of schools with GCE (AL) classes was reported for Colombo, and the second highest number in Jaffna. In Colombo, 49 out of 196 schools with GCE (AL) classes offer education in science at the GCE level (AL), while in Jaffna this is 33 out of 50. Jaffna has the lowest ratio of population per school with GCE (AL) classes in science, i.e. 21300. The second lowest ratio, 47300 people per school, was reported in Puttalam. In Colombo, this figure was 56900, about 2.7 times higher than the Jaffna level.

Table 7.7   *District distribution of schools with GCE (AL) classes 1973*

District	Number of schools[a] with GCE (AL) classes		Population[b] in 1000s per school with GCE (AL) classes	
	in science	all	in science	all
Colombo	47	196	56.9	13.6
Kalutara	15	65	48.6	11.2
Kandy	18	114	66.0	10.4
Matale	3	32	104.9	9.8
Nuwara Eliya	5	40	90.1	11.3
Galle	12	98	61.3	7.5
Matara	7	65	83.8	9.0
Hambantota	1	31	340.3	11.0
Jaffna	33	50	21.3	14.0
Mannar	1	3	77.8	25.9
Vavuniya	1	9	95.2	10.6
Batticaloa	5	12	51.3	21.4
Ampara	4	19	68.2	14.3
Trincomalee	1	9	188.2	20.9
Kurunegala	13	98	78.9	10.5
Puttalam	8	48	47.3	7.9
Anuradhapura	3	46	129.6	8.5
Polonnaruwa	0	12	–	13.6
Badulla	4	40	153.9	15.4
Moneragala	1	19	193.0	10.2
Ratnapura	6	59	110.2	11.2
Kegalle	9	75	72.8	8.7
All island	197	1140	64.4	11.1

a. Includes only government schools.
b. Population refers to 1971 census.
Source: For school data, DCS: *Statistical Abstract 1977*; For population data, DCS-PP10.XLS.

A substantial number of districts had a high population per school with GCE (AL) classes in science. In some districts that figure was well over 100,000. Hambantota, Mannar, Vavuniya, Trincomalee and Moneragala had only one school with GCE (AL) in science, while Polonnaruwa had no school of this type. The government labelled ten districts as educationally underprivileged in 1976 for the purpose of granting them special preference in university admissions, namely Nuwara Eliya, Hambantota, Mannar, Vavuniya, Ampara, Trincomalee, Anuradhapura, Polonnaruwa, Badulla and Moneragala. In 1978, Batticaloa, and in 1980 Puttalam, were added to this list.[7] Table 7.7 shows that of these disadvantaged districts, only Nuwara Eliya and Batticaloa had five schools with GCE (AL) in science, while all others had less than five schools and high ratios of population per school with GCE (AL) in science. However, Matale and Ratnapura, which were not considered 'underprivileged', also had over 100,000 people per school with GCE (AL) in science, but a low ratio of population per school with GCE (AL) in all curriculum streams.

Even though the opportunities of privileged regions were challenged by the increasing numbers of educated people from the newly emerging regions, their challenge did not result in a complete equalization of opportunities. Regional disparities in the quality of education were reflected in employment patterns and in university admissions. According to Wilson, '..disproportionate numbers of Ceylon [Sri Lanka] Tamils entered the employment-oriented faculties of science, medicine and engineering in the University of Ceylon compared to Sinhalese'(1979: 11). Regional or community representation in university admissions has become an important and controversial issue attracting attention in political and academic debates of the 1970s.

State intervention in university admissions

Regarding university education, two important factors appear to provide the rationale for government intervention. One is the inadequate expansion of the university system in relation to the rapid increase in demand. The second factor is the increasing failure of newcomers in the competition with the old privileged groups in terms of admission to university. The concept of demand means the social and political demand rather than the willingness to pay, as I have explained in Chapter V. The view widely held is that the expansion of university education in the post-colonial period was not demand-led, but supply-driven. Due to the expansion of free education throughout the island since the mid-1940s, a vast number of young people were emerging from secondary school in the 1960s. A significant proportion of the new generations consisted of Sinhalese youths. Table 7.8 shows the increase in the number of applicants for the GCE (AL) examination for selected years from 1943 to 1984/85. The number of applicants for the HSC, which was later replaced with the GCE (AL) exam-

---

7 The number of educationally 'underprivileged' districts was 13 by 1980. A new district of Mullaitive, which was already in the 'underprivileged' group, was distinguished in 1979 (UGC 1984).

ination increased from 3938 in 1959 to 31199 in 1965. However, the need to expand the university system did not receive due consideration. University admission, 30.0 per cent of candidates in 1959, dropped to 20.3 per cent in 1965 and to 10.9 in 1970. Since the end of 1970s, about 5 per cent of over 100 thousand applicants were granted university admission

Table 7.8   *University education: demand and supply;*
selected years 1946-1984/85

Year	GCE (AL) applicants number	Admitted to University	
		number	percentage
1943	350	197	56.3
1946	1171	372	31.7
1950	1443	438	30.3
1955	2096	658	31.3
1959	3938	1189	30.0
1965	31199	6359	20.3
1970	30973	3457	10.9
1975	48432	3482	8.4
1979	101015	5255	5.2
1984/85	105500	5630	5.3

Source: Jayaweera (1986: 52)

An inevitable consequence of this declining proportion of university admissions was a gradual increase in the minimum requirements. Thus, students with hopes of entering university have come under increasing pressure. The university system did not expand. As a result, the drop-out rate from the GCE (AL) examination increased. As was discussed in the previous chapter, a majority of these drop-outs faced a second disappointment on the labour market. In the 1960s, the marks obtained by Sinhala applicants were lower than those obtained by Tamil students of Jaffna, due to regional disparities in the quality of education. Allegations that Tamil teachers evaluated Tamil students too highly became an important issue in parliament.

Just as in the case of employment and education, the ethnic disparities with respect to university admissions were an important source of antagonism. Against this escalating ethnic antagonism, the period of 1970-77 was marked by the most controversial issues relating to the intervention of the government in university admissions. As discussed, the government of this period, formed by the United Front coalition of the SLFP and Marxist parties, was for redistribution and had a declared itself committed to achieving a socialist society. This was a period of vigorous debate on university admissions. A policy to eliminate the inequalities in the distribution of opportunities received due consideration. The best policy would have been to develop the underdeveloped regions, but this was a long-term project. Besides, growth performance was poor, while the economy was in a deep crisis. The attention of the government focused on the mechanism rather than on the problem (Jayaweera 1986: 45). Therefore, the government imposed quantitative controls on higher education in a discriminating manner.

Equalizing language disparity: 1970-1974

Prior to 1965, universities had had their own entrance examinations, while during the period of 1965-70, university admission was based entirely on the marks obtained at GCE (AL) examinations (UGC 1984).[8] Having recognized the high representation of the Tamil community in university admissions, and having noted the grievances of the Sinhala community, the government started a series of experiments to equalize the opportunities available.

The first of the experiments, which came into effect in 1970, was as a policy measure to reduce the number of students studying in Tamil.[9] The marks required for admission for students studying in Sinhala were lower than the marks required by students intending to study in Tamil. The same minimum mark levels were used for English students, depending on whether the student concerned was Sinhalese or Tamil. However, the policy was implemented only once, and was abandoned the very next year. In 1971, the government commenced the standardization of marks obtained at the GCE (AL) examination in terms of both the subject and the language, and these standardized marks were used for university admissions until 1974. From any point of view, the policy based on the *language* obviously was a 'racist one, because its objective was to assist Sinhala students at the expense of Tamil students.

Furthermore, the policy was ineffective, because it assumed that all Tamil students are equally competitive, and, by the same token, that all Sinhala language students are uncompetitive. As was already noted, education facilities were exceptionally high in Jaffna in the Northern province populated by the Sri Lanka Tamil community and in Colombo in the Western province. Even by the government's own standards in 1976, as I will discuss later, some districts inhabited mainly by the Tamil community were educationally underprivileged in terms of the educational facilities. As a result of the policy, the disadvantage of the Tamil students of these underprivileged areas was exacerbated. In contrast, the advantage enjoyed by the Sinhala students of privileged areas such as Colombo was increased. In a situation where many districts, including Colombo, were populated by both communities, the fortunes of Sinhala and Tamil students were affected unjustly by the policy.

8 All information in this section regarding the changes in government policy for university admission was obtained from UGC (1984), unless otherwise specified.

9 This policy was, however, developed by the Minister of Education in 1970, Alhaj Badi-uddin Mahmud, who was a Muslim and whose mother-tongue was Tamil. No doubt, the negative effects of the policy equally applied to his own Tamil-speaking community.

Table 7.9   *University admissions according to ethnic group, 1970-74 (percentage of total number of admissions)*

	1970	1971	1974	1977	1980
Engineering					
Sinhala	51.7	55.9	78.8	79.5	62.5
Tamil	48.3	40.8	16.3	19.1	32.2
Other	0.0	3.3	4.9	1.4	5.3
Total number	149	152	283	288	512
Medicine[a]					
Sinhala	48.9	53.4	70.0	68.0	76.3
Tamil	48.9	40.9	25.9	27.8	21.4
Other	2.2	5.7	4.2	4.1	2.2
Total number	229	247	263	241	401
Science faculties					
Sinhala	57.7	60.6	75.4	74.8	70.4
Tamil	39.8	35.3	21.0	22.1	25.7
Other	2.5	4.1	3.6	3.1	3.8
Total number	792	955	1403	1491	1905
All faculties					
Sinhala	80.6	81.1	81.9	82.4	77.4
Tamil	15.7	15.2	14.2	13.7	18.3
Other	3.7	3.7	3.9	3.9	4.3
Total number	3129	3457	3653	3902	4703

a. Students in Dental surgery and Veterinary science are not included in Medicine.
Source: UGC data.

As Table 7.9 shows, there was a disproportionately high representation of Tamil students in science faculties generally, and in faculties of medicine and engineering in particular. In 1970, the year in which the government's language-wise standardization was introduced, the representation of Tamil students in engineering and medicine was 48.3 per cent and 48.9 per cent respectively. In all science courses, 39.8 per cent of students were from the Tamil community. In the subsequent period, the proportion of Tamil students in science courses declined, with a corresponding increase in the proportion of Sinhala and other students. By 1974, Tamil students were only 16.3 per cent in engineering and 25.9 per cent in medicine, while 22.1 per cent in all science courses. However, their representation increased again in 1977 and further in 1980.

As Table 7.10 shows, in the period of 1970-74, the number of Tamil students has decreased annually by 5.4 per cent in engineering and by 10.8 per cent in medicine, although the total number of Tamil students admitted to the universities has increased by 1.6 per cent. In contrast, the total number of Sinhala students admitted to the universities increased annually by 4.5 per cent, but the increase in all courses was 23.0 per cent. The highest increase of students in all categories of study was, however, not for the Sinhala community, but for other communities.[10] For the 1977-81 period, again the admission of Tamil students increased annually by 17.0 per cent in all faculties and at high rates in science faculties, while that of the Sinhala students increased by only 4.9 per cent.

Table 7.10 *Annual average change in university admissions, 1970-1974 and 1977-1981 (percentages)*

	Sinhala	Tamil	Other	Total
1970-1974				
Engineering	35.0	-5.4	49.2a	21.4
Medicine	13.9	-10.8	40.4	4.0
All science faculties	23.0	-1.0	33.3	15.1
All faculties	4.5	1.6	8.6	4.1
1977-1981				
Engineering	11.2	30.7	91.3	13.8
Medicine	16.2	25.0	19.3	15.4
All science faculties	7.2	20.3	19.8	9.4
All faculties	4.9	17.0	11.5	6.7

a. Figure refers to the period 1971-1974
Source: UGC data.

The issue is whether the decline in the proportion and the number of Tamil students admitted to universities can be attributed to the policies of the government. Actually, this was not the case. Even without interventionist government policies, the proportion of Tamil students had already been declining. As was already discussed, the proportion of Tamil students in the universities declined from 33.7 per cent in 1953 to 16.2 per cent in 1963 (Table 7.4). As has been argued by others, (Silva 1974), the decline in the proportion of Tamil university students was not only due to the standardization of university admissions. Chart 7.3 shows the behaviour of the ratio of the proportion of provincial university admission to that of the provincial population in the period of 1967-74. When the ratio is unity, the proportion in provincial university admission equals that of the provincial population. The ratios for the Western, Southern and Northern provinces were well above unity, indicating a higher proportion of university students than the respective provincial population. The ratio for the rest of the country was below unity, indicating a lower proportion of university admission than the population. The ratio for the Northern province, which was the highest in 1967, was already declining, while that for the rest of the

10 The category of other, which consisted largely of Moor and Malay communities, actually shows a disproportionately low admission to university education since the 1960s (Table 7.4), see also Silva (1974).

country was increasing even before government intervention. The introduction of quantitative controls by the government was only one cause of the accelerated decline of the university admission of Tamil students and students of privileged areas.

Chart 7.3   *Provincial origin of university students 1967-1974: ratio of the proportion of university students to proportion of population*

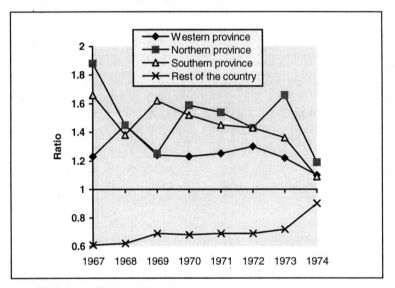

Note: Population data refer to 1971 census.
Source: UGC data for university admissions; Appendix I for population census.

Equilizing regional disparity: after 1974

The third government experiment was a district quota system introduced in 1974. Under this policy, the places in each course of university education were allocated to districts based on merit (raw marks) according to district population. Thus, the district-wise university admission ratio was kept equal to the district population ratio. This policy was changed in 1976, however. The new policy of 1976 included (a) the allocation of 70 per cent of university places on the basis of merit and (b) the allocation of the remaining 30 per cent on a district quota basis, of which 50 per cent was for educationally underprivileged districts. With occasional modifications, this system continued into the 1980s. One of the major modifications, which took place in 1979, was the change in the allocation formula. After 1979, 30 per cent of places was allocated on the basis of merit and 55 per cent on a district population basis, while the remaining 15 per cent was granted to underprivileged districts.

There were two important characteristics of the system of university admission adopted after 1974. The first was the introduction of district quotas, and second, the classification of certain educationally 'underprivileged' districts. These policies were not ethnically based. In terms of the outcome, there were implications for all communities, which could be interpreted in different ways.

The district quota system was originally applied to all university admissions, but due to revisions in 1976 and 1979, the percentage of university applicants affected by the system changed. The importance of the policy is, however, that the distribution of a share of the admissions was dependent on the district proportion of population. Therefore, if a certain district enjoyed any disproportionate advantage, the policy could have offset this to a certain extent. Table 7.11 shows the provincial distribution of university admissions and population in 1971. The proportion of university students in science courses from both the Western and the Northern provinces, which accounted for 45.3 per cent 24.1 per cent respectively, was markedly higher than the 19.2 per cent of students from the rest of the island, excluding the Southern province. The case of Northern province was exceptional. Its population proportion was only 6.9 per cent. But the share of university admissions for the population of that province was about one-fourth for science courses. This contrasts sharply with the less than one-fifth of the opportunities for science courses granted to over half of the population in the rest of the country other than the Western, Northern and Southern provinces.

If university admission was determined by population proportions, the students from the relatively privileged three provinces, where over three-fifths of the opportunities in science courses and over four-fifths of the opportunities in all university courses were granted, should have declined to match their popu-

Table 7.11   *University admissions and population by province 1971*

Province	University admission as a % of total		Population as a % of community total			
	Science course	Total	Total	Sinhala	Sri Lanka Tamil	Moor
Western province	45.3	33.6	26.8	31.2	12.4	25.2
Northern province	24.1	10.6	6.9	0.3	53.7	4.4
Southern province	11.4	19.0	13.1	17.2	0.5	6.2
Rest of the country	19.2	36.8	53.2	51.3	33.4	66.7
Central province	8.5	11.1	15.4	12.7	5.6	16.5
Eastern province	3.4	2.1	5.7	1.6	21.3	26.6
North western province	2.6	10.6	11.1	13.8	2.5	9.4
North central province	0.5	1.8	4.4	5.5	0.9	3.7
Uva province	1.2	2.7	6.4	5.9	1.6	2.9
Sabaragamuwa province	3.0	8.7	10.4	11.8	1.5	5.1

Source: UGC data for university admissions; Appendix I for population census.

Table 7.12   *Change in university admissions by district between 1969 and 1984: ratio of the proportion of university entrants to that of district population*[a]

District	1969[b] University Admission for		1984[c] University admission for	
	Science faculties	All faculties	Science faculties	All faculties
Privileged in terms of educational facilities[d]				
Jaffna	4.5	2.1	2.9	2.1
Colombo	2.3	1.1	1.9	1.4
Gampaha	ne	ne	0.7	0.8
Galle	1.1	1.4	1.1	1.0
Kandy	0.7	0.9	0.8	0.9
Kalutara	0.5	1.4	0.7	0.8
Matale	0.5	0.7	0.7	0.7
Matara	0.2	1.3	0.9	0.9
Kurunegala	0.2	1.0	0.6	0.8
Ratnapura	0.1	0.6	0.5	0.6
Kegalle	0.1	0.9	0.6	0.7
Underprivileged in terms of educational facilities[d]				
Batticaloa	0.5	0.0	1.1	1.1
Mannar	0.2	0.2	0.8	1.3
Hambantota	0.1	0.9	0.9	1.3
Trincomalee	0.1	0.6	0.8	0.9
Puttalam	0.1	0.6	0.8	1.0
Nuwara Eliya	0.0	0.3	0.4	0.7
Vavuniya	0.0	0.1	1.1	1.2
Mullaitive	ne	ne	0.6	1.3
Ampara	0.0	0.1	1.1	1.2
Anuradhapura	0.0	0.5	0.8	1.0
Polonnaruwa	0.0	0.1	0.5	0.9
Badulla	0.0	0.3	0.9	1.0
Moneragala	0.0	0.1	0.3	0.9

a.   Ratio of zero indicates the proportion of university entrants to that of district population is either nil or negligible (less than 0.05).
b.   Population refers to 1971 census.
c.   Population refers to 1981 census.
d.   Ten districts, except Batticaloa, Puttalam and Mullaitive, were considered educationally underprivileged in 1976. Batticaloa and Puttalam were included in this group in 1978 and in 1980, respectively. Mullaitive, was considered to be a separate underprivileged district in 1979.
ne. Gampaha and Mullaitive did not exist at the time as separate districts.
Source: UGC data for university admissions; Appendix I for population census.

lation proportions. If this was the case, according, the most affected province appeared to have been the Northern province. In terms of communities, the

Western province included for 31.2 per cent Sinhala, 31.2 per cent Tamil and 25.2 per cent Moor. In the Southern province, the most affected has been the Sinhalese community. In the Northern province, the most affected ethnic group has been the Sri Lanka Tamil community, which accounted for 53.7 per cent.

The benefits of the policy have been distributed among the communities. Particularly, the Eastern and the North Central provinces seem to have been the least-privileged, in terms of the proportion of the university admission for all the courses, which accounted for only 1.7 per cent and 1.8 per cent, respectively. Because the Eastern province is inhabited by 21.3 per cent of the Sri Lanka Tamil community, and 26.6 per cent of Moor community, both ethnic groups have benefited from the district quota system.

It can be suggested that the losses and the gains of the district quota system were shared by all communities. It is not possible, however, to indicate clearly the communities in each of the provinces which were affected, and the extent of the impact. It is possible that, due to the concentration of the Sinhala community in the Southern province and the concentration of the Tamil community in the Northern province, the negative impact of the policy was higher in these two provinces. Moreover, the weight given to the district quota system was reduced in 1976, and proportion of opportunities allocated on the basis of merit was raised. This has lessened the negative impact of the district quota system on the privileged areas. As a result, the consequences of the regional disparities in education were not eliminated entirely in the university admission systems adopted after 1976.

Table 7.13   *Population by community in 'underprivileged' districts, 1971 and 1981*

	Population census 1971			Population census 1981		
	Underprivileged districts as of 1976[a]		All island	Underprivileged districts as of 1980[a]		All island
Community	as a % of community population	as a % of district population	as a % of total population	as a % of community population	as a % of district population	as a % of total population
Sinhala	18.7	61.3	72.0	25.7	62.1	74.0
Sri Lanka Tamil	19.6	10.0	11.2	38.9	16.2	12.7
Indian Tamil	42.0	17.7	9.3	55.4	10.0	5.5
Moor	34.3	10.5	6.7	48.7	11.2	7.1
Other	12.3	0.5	0.8	21.2	0.5	0.8
Total	21.9	100	100	30.6	100	100

a. Population of educationally 'underprivileged' districts differs according to the changes in classification. With respect to classification in 1978-1980, populations of Batticaloa and Puttalam have been added.
Source: Appendix I.

In addition to the district quota system, the second important factor has been the special favour granted to educationally underprivileged districts. Table 7.12 shows the differences *between* and *within* educationally privileged and underprivileged districts in the case of university admission, and its changes between 1969 and 1984. The figures in the table show the ratios of the district proportion of university entrants to that of district population.

As the figures for 1969 indicate, there has been a significant difference between privileged and underprivileged districts in the case of university admissions. Jaffna ranks highest, according to university admission for all degrees (2.1) and for only science faculties (4.5). Colombo is in second position because the ratio for science faculties was 2.3. Nevertheless, judging from the ratio of 1.1 for all faculties, Colombo was not an exception. In the case of university entrants for all faculties, Kalutara of the Western province, and Galle and Matara of the Southern province were better off than Colombo. Other than Jaffna and Colombo, in the case of university entrants for science faculties, even among the privileged districts only Galle, has a ratio of 1.1. The ratios for all other districts were below unity. In contrast, in the group of underprivileged districts, the ratio for science faculties was zero, indicating either nil or a negligible number of university admissions. Even in the case of university admission for all faculties, the ratio was close to unity only in Hambantota, while all other districts show low ratios.

Table 7.13 shows the population composition in educationally underprivileged districts. Two levels of classifications are given in the table, according to changes in the system, while the populations of Batticaloa and Puttalam are also included in the group of underprivileged followed by classification changes during the period 1978-1980. I use population data of 1971 census for the first classification in 1976, and those of 1981 census for the second classification in 1978-1980. When both the changes in the classification system and the intercensal changes of the district composition of population are taken in to account, the population in the underprivileged districts has increased from 21.9 per cent of total to 30.6 per cent. This total population, however, consisted of all communities.

The Indian Tamil community is most largely represented in underprivileged districts, but their involvement in tea plantation activities has prevented them form benefiting from the policies regarding university admissions. If the Indian Tamil community is excluded from the analysis, in to both classifications, the community benefiting most, proportionately, was the Moor community, while the second beneficiary was the Sri Lanka Tamil community. In proportion to their ethnic representation, however, over 60 per cent of the population in underprivileged districts were Sinhala, nearly three-fourths of the total population in Sri Lanka. For the Sri Lanka Tamil community, which accounted for over one-tenth of the total population, the community proportion in underprivileged districts was 10.0 per cent in 1971, and increased to 16.2 per cent in 1981. Relative to the proportion of the total population, the Sri Lanka Tamil community in underprivileged districts was low in 1971, but increased significantly in 1981 because of the expansion of the underprivileged region to include Batticaloa and Puttalam. More than one-tenth of the Moor community, which accounted for about 7 per cent of total population, was from the underprivileged districts.

Table 7.14 shows the district distribution of communities as of 1981, which can be compared with the distribution of university admission in 1984 (Table 7.12). The university admission of people from communities in the privileged areas has substantially declined in favour of those of the underprivileged areas. The most affected region has been Jaffna. The ratio of university admission to science faculties declined from 4.5 in 1969 to 2.9 in 1981. Because 95.2 per cent of the population in Jaffna consisted of the Sri Lanka Tamil community, the rapid decline had a direct negative impact. The second-most privileged district was Colombo, where the ratio of the admission to science faculties declined from 2.3 in 1969 to 1.9 in 1984. In Colombo, the Sinhala community numbers

Table 7.14   *District population by community 1981 as a percentage of district total*

District	Sinhala	Sri Lanka Tamil	Indian Tamil	Moor	Other
Privileged in terms of educational facilities					
Jaffna	0.8	95.2	2.4	1.6	0.1
Colombo	77.6	10.0	1.2	8.2	3.0
Gampaha	92.0	3.5	0.4	2.7	1.4
Galle	94.5	0.9	1.4	3.2	0.1
Kandy	74.3	5.0	9.4	10.5	0.8
Kalutara	87.2	1.2	4.1	7.4	0.2
Matale	79.9	5.8	7.0	7.0	0.4
Matara	94.5	0.7	2.2	2.5	0.1
Kurunegala	92.9	1.2	0.5	5.0	0.3
Ratnapura	85.0	2.4	10.6	1.7	0.2
Kegalle	85.9	2.2	6.7	5.0	0.2
Underprivileged in terms of educational facilities					
Batticaloa	3.4	70.8	1.2	23.9	0.7
Mannar	8.2	51.3	13.0	26.1	1.4
Hambantota	97.1	0.6	0.1	1.2	1.1
Trincomalee	33.4	34.3	2.1	29.3	0.9
Puttalam	82.6	6.6	0.5	9.9	0.4
Nuwara Eliya	42.1	12.7	42.7	2.0	0.5
Vavuniya	16.6	56.8	19.6	6.8	0.2
Mullaitive	5.2	75.4	14.5	4.7	0.2
Ampara	37.8	20.0	0.4	41.5	0.3
Anuradhapura	91.1	1.4	0.1	7.1	0.3
Polonnaruwa	91.4	2.0	0.0	6.4	0.2
Badulla	69.1	5.9	20.2	4.2	0.7
Moneragala	92.7	2.0	3.2	1.9	0.2

Source: Appendix I.

77.6 per cent, while the Sri Lanka Tamil community is 10.0 per cent of the total population. However, the Tamil-speaking community in Colombo accounted for over 20 per cent of the total population. In Galle, where 94.5 per cent of the population is Sinhala, the ratio of admission to science faculties has not changed, but that of admission to arts faculties declined from 1.4 in 1969 to 1.0 in 1981. In fact, admission to science faculties in all of the less privileged districts in the privileged group improved, but remained below the population proportions. All these districts were largely populated by the Sinhala community.

In the underprivileged region, the district proportion of university admission to science faculties improved to a level *above* or *close* to district population proportions. The position of Nuwara Eliya, Mullaitive, Polonnaruwa and Moneragala remained unimproved. The district proportion of university admission to arts faculties in many underdeveloped districts improved *above* the level of their population proportions. In fact, districts such as Batticaloa, Mannar, Hambantota, Vavuniya, Mullaitive and Ampara have exceeded the position of privileged districts other than Jaffna and Colombo. The population in many districts which made significant improvements was ethnically mixed. Among these districts, in Mannar and Vavuniya the Sri Lanka Tamil community alone accounted for over 50 per cent of the population, while in Trincomalee and Ampara, the figures are 34.5 per cent and 20.0 per cent, respectively. The Tamil-speaking Moor community accounted for 26.1 per cent in Mannar, 29.3 per cent in Trincomalee, and 41.5 per cent in Ampara. In the other districts which have made significant improvements in university admission, the concentration of the Sinhala community was high in Hambantota (97.1 per cent) and in Anuradhapura (91.1 per cent). The Sri Lanka Tamil community is 70.8 per cent in Batticaloa, while the Sinhala community is 82.6 per cent in Puttalam.

The university admission policy based on language reduced significantly the number of Tamil-speaking people at university in the early 1970s. This has been acknowledged by some other studies as well (Bastian 1985, Silva 1974). Yet this argument does not appear to be valid for the period after 1974. The university admission policies adopted after 1974 did not have an ethnic character. Nevertheless, as the opportunities in the university system did not expand relative to the increase in demand, both the system of district quotas and the special allocations to underprivileged areas were unpleasant to the old privileged areas. These policies reduced the highly disproportionate advantages enjoyed by Jaffna and Colombo, and to some extent also by some other districts such as Galle. Due to the significant ethnic and regional differences in the case of university admissions which had existed since the colonial period, and due to the significant differences in regional ethnic concentration, it was inevitable that the outcome of these policies involved ethnically distinguishable features.

A positive outcome of the university admission policies adopted after 1974 was the government assistance extended to the new generations emerging from relatively underdeveloped areas of the country. What, then, is the source of the frustration of those groups? The answer is the rapid increase in the number of competitors vying for limited numbers of places at university. Whatever the policies adopted, the number of disappointed youths, regardless of ethnic background, increased drastically in the post-colonial period. The reasons were mainly the development of an acutely competitive society in the context of a deepening economic crisis.

Indian Tamils: an emerging group of competitors

In the preceding analysis, I paid little attention to the Indian Tamil community, because this community has not yet formed a significant part of the country's national political crisis. However, it is a matter of time before this will happen. The indigenous Sri Lanka and the Indian Tamil communities share language and religion, but they differ from each other in terms of social status, culture, caste, occupations, historical roots, political affiliation and geographical location (Devaraj 1985, Jayawardena 1985, Manor 1984, Peiris 1991). The Indian Tamil community was brought to Sri Lanka by British planters between the mid-19th and the early 20th century to work on the colonial tea plantations.[11] The term 'Indian Tamil', which was officially used in the census of 1911 for the first time, distinguished this community from the indigenous Sri Lankan Tamil community.[12]

Table 7.15   *Population of Indian Tamil community,*
census years 1946-1981

| Census year | Indian Tamil population | | Intercensal rate of increase: annual average in percentages | | |
	Number (in 1000s)	Percentage	Indian Tamil	Sri Lanka Tamil	Sinhala
1946	780.6	11.7	1.0[a]	1.4[a]	1.7[a]
1953	974.1	12.0	3.2	2.7	2.8
1963	1123.0	10.6	1.4	2.7	2.8
1971	1174.6	9.3	0.5	2.4	2.4
1981	818.7	5.5	-3.8	3.0	1.9

a. Figure refers to the period 1921-1946.
Source: DCS (1981).

From an economic point of view, the Indian Tamil community has been late in emerging as a group competing with other communities for socio-economic ad-

---

11 In 1833, the British colonial government attempted to extract labour from the indigenous Kandyan Sinhala community by abolishing the ancient Kandyan tenure system (*rajakariya*). The Kandyan Sinhalese refused to be plantation labourers (Jayawardena 1985, Snodgrass 1966: 24).
12 There are also some other Tamil-speaking South Indian migrants, a tiny proportion of the total population, who live mainly outside the plantation regions (Devaraj 1984). In the census, they are included in the Indian Tamil category.

vancement. A major cause of this delay was the denial of their citizenship and franchise rights through the Acts passed by the first national government (Chapter V). The domestic and international changes affecting the Sri Lankan economy have had little impact on the Indian Tamil community. As we have already seen (Chart 7.2), the employment rate of the Indian Tamil community is significantly higher than that of the Sinhala and Tamil communities. Housing, health care, education, other social services, consumer requirements and almost all daily needs satisfied at a minimum level within the tea estates.

Slowly, however, the world for the Indian Tamil community has also been changing. One indicator in this regard is the substantial decline of the Indian Tamil community during the last few decades, both in absolute and in relative terms. According to Table 7.15, the Indian Tamil community accounted for 11.7 per cent of total population in 1946, but declined to 9.3 per cent in 1971 and to 5.5 per cent in 1981. The population increased from 780.6 thousand in 1946 to 1174.6 thousand in 1971, but decreased to 818.7 in 1981. The reduction in the size and the proportion of the Indian Tamil community is a result of two causes. Part of the trend is explained by the repatriation of non-citizen Indian Tamils to India under the Sirima-Shastri pact of 1964. Between 1971 and 1981, 312 thousand Indian Tamils were repatriated (DCS 1981: 115). The rest of the Indian Tamil community has received Sri Lankan citizenship. The reduction of the non-citizen population in Sri Lanka by 42 per cent between 1971 and 1981 (DCS 1981: 128), was largely due to this.

The second reason for the reduction of the Indian Tamil community is their preference to identify themselves as Sri Lankan Tamils. This identity shift resulted in a statistical misrepresentation in the population census. This tendency was noted as early as the 1950s (DCS 1953: 11). After receiving citizenship, this tendency has intensified: 200 thousand Indian Tamils reported themselves as Sri Lanka Tamils in 1981 (DCS 1981: 115). The high percentage of the rate of average annual growth of the Sri Lankan Tamil population by 3 per cent along with the declining size of the Indian Tamil population (Table 7.15) was partly due to this. From an economic point of view, citizenship and ethnic identity should be assessed in the context of the rising competition for economic resources. Indian Tamils are increasingly investigating socio-economic opportunities outside the plantation economy.

Another important cause is the increased awareness of the new generations about the world outside the plantation economy. Education is largely responsible for this. Table 7.16 shows the changes in the levels of education of the Indian Tamil community over the CFS years 1953-81/82. The figures in the table should be interpreted with care, as the changes in population proportions in terms of education level can be affected by the changes in the age groups as a proportion to the total population. Also, the figures refer to the whole Indian Tamil community and not only to those in the plantation sector. The level of education in the Indian Tamil community was extremely low in 1953. The population with no education was 60.4 per cent, while secondary education was received by only 3.6 per cent. Furthermore, no Indian Tamils were reported to have received education above the secondary level. This situation has changed during the subsequent period. The percentage of the population with no education declined with a corresponding increase in population proportions at higher levels of education, even above the HSC or GCE (AL) level. The population proportion without education declined to 44.6 per cent by 1981/82. Some 1.6 per cent of the population reached SSC or GCE (OL), and 0.2 per cent had HSC or GCE (AL) or higher education levels.

Table 7.16 *Indian Tamil community by level of education, CFS years 1953-1981/82 as a percentage of Indian Tamil population*

Education level	1953	1963	1973	1978/79	1981/82
No schooling	60.4	60.8	51.5	45.0	44.6
Primary education	35.9	31.8	42.1	47.6	44.9
Secondary education	3.6	6.6	5.6	6.2	8.6
SSC or GCE (OL)	0.0	0.6	0.8	1.1	1.6
HSC or GCE (AL) & higher	0.0	0.1	0.0	0.1	0.2

Source: Appendix VIII.

The changes in the Indian Tamil community will have future implications in relation to political conflict. The increasing tendency for Indian Tamils to identify themselves as Sri Lankan Tamils points to the fact that the Indian Tamil community is already an emerging contender in Sri Lankan society. Also, if the new generations are becoming increasingly educated, there is little doubt that they will move away from the traditional estate economy. There are hardly any opportunities available for educated people in the estate sector. The educated youth population of the plantation sector will not remain tied to the plantation economy. What will likely to happen, and has already started, is the flight of labour from the plantation sector to the modern sector. Competition for economic resources will increase further. Hence, the escalation of political conflict, in which the Indian Tamil community is also playing a significant part, is actually a matter of time, if the slow generation of economic resources and opportunities persists.

Summary

The regional and communal inequalities in socio-economic advancement were already established in Sri Lanka in the colonial period due to the different patterns and levels of exposure to foreign influence through colonization. Regardless of ethnic differences, minorities from both the Sinhala and Tamil communities have acquired advantages in terms of access to modern of education and employment. Due to the importance of education, socio-economic advancement has been limited to certain urban areas of the Western, Northern and Southern provinces. In particular, Colombo and Jaffna occupied favourable positions. It was against this socio-economic background that the new generations of the Tamil community began to experience the losses of the means of the socio-economic advancement, at two levels.

First, during the post-colonial period, large numbers of young people from underdeveloped challenged the uncompetitive privilege of old elites. In the Tamil community, Jaffna elites were challenged by the new generations. The number of newcomers was exceptionally large, because they represented large groups of neglected society and regions of the country during the colonial period. This newly emerging generation has also become a proportionately large due to the population explosion of the 1940s to the 1960s. All ethnic groups are represented, but owing to the ethnic composition of the population, the majority is Sinhala. The Tamil representation in education and employment rapidly declined due to state intervention, with a corresponding increase in the upward social mobility of the Sinhala community.

Secondly, a new group of Tamil youth increasingly experienced the loss of the means for socio-economic advancement due to the increased scarcity of economic resources and opportunities. However, these emerging Tamil youth have come from the underprivileged areas of the Northern and Eastern provinces. Faced with a sluggish growth of the economy, Sri Lankan society continued to suffer from an increasing resource scarcity relative to the level of rising expectations. Consequently, the new generations of youth entering the competitive society experienced disappointment and frustration. The same situation was faced by the younger generations of the Sinhala majority as well.

Recognizing the unpleasant consequences of the ethnic and regional disparities based on educational opportunities, the government carried out a series of experiments in relation to university admission. Quantitative controls introduced during the period of 1970-74 accelerated the decline of the participation of Tamils in higher education, and has increased Sinhala representation in university education. Nevertheless, the district quotas introduced after 1974 were beneficial to both Sinhala and Tamil communities. Yet they helped only a tiny minority of newcomers. In contrast, the majority from both communities dropped out of the competition, facing they faced a second disappointment on the labour market.

The major problem was that less unequal distribution did not make sense when there was so little to distribute. This was the macroeconomic reality underlying the generation of economic resources in all spheres of socio-economic advancement. The social exclusion of the youth from socio-economic advancement became acute by the 1970s, providing a fertile basis for political conflict. At the same time, there are signs that new competitors from the Indian Tamil community are stepping in, though slowly. A further increase in the competition for scarce resources is to be expected. However, an analysis of the evolution of political conflict into civil war must incorporate many other fields besides the problem of the generation and distribution of economic resources and opportunities. With special reference to this issue, I will conclude the study in the next chapter.

Concluding Remarks: Development Paradoxes and Other Factors

VIII

The purpose of this study was to analyse the economic dimensions of intrastate political conflict in developing countries within a conceptual framework of development economics. In this concluding chapter, I summarize the conclusions of the preceding study on the concept of political conflict in developing countries, the theoretical analysis of such conflicts, and the empirical findings for Sri Lanka. Then, I focus on the importance of economic factors in explaining political conflict in developing countries, and the conditions for the outbreak of collective violence. Finally, I discuss areas for further research.

The concept of political conflicts

The expression 'political conflicts' refers to the formation of actual or potential collective violence to achieve a specified political objective. Thus, political conflict should be understood as a historical process of several formative stages, before it reaches the stage at which collective violence threatens the established political, social and economic system. I exclude from the analysis various individual violent activities and small-scale riots guided by personal or narrow objectives. Yet due consideration should be given to the fact that these violent activities and riots, though they are not sustainable, can sometimes be associated directly or indirectly with political conflict. This is particularly important in an analysis of economic factors underlying the *process* of the formation of political conflicts rather than the ultimate stage of collective violence.

Political conflicts during the period after the Second World War show two distinguishing characteristics. First, political conflicts in the modern world have been concentrated largely in the so-called developing regions of the world. Second, these conflicts have been intrastate in character. These two characteristics do not imply, however, that the so-called developed countries are not exposed to civil political conflicts, or that they have nothing to do with political conflicts in developing regions. No society in the world is free from political violence altogether. Some countries in the developed region are exposed to armed conflict, while not all countries in the developing region are. However, as far as the *intensity* of political conflict in terms of the human, physical, social and economic costs, generally, the developing region has been exposed more to political conflict than the developed region. In addition, even though most political conflicts have been located in the developing region, they are closely related to economic and political developments in the developed region.

The theoretical framework

The fact that political conflicts are highly concentrated in the developing region was the point of departure of this study in two respects. First, it casts doubt upon over-generalized theories, which attempt to explain the sources of political conflict within the context of *universal* and *timeless* conceptual frameworks. Second, it calls for a development economics perspective on modern political conflict. Mainstream economic thinking does not offer adequate scope to analyse the economic dimensions of political conflict. Depending on the concept of 'equilibrium', mainstream economics assumes that the interests of various economic agents are ultimately harmonious and non-contentious. To the extent that there is any scope within the field of economics for the analysis of political conflict, it has been in economic traditions developed outside mainstream economics.

Theoretical contributions

Theoretical contributions to the analysis of political conflict, based on an economic perspective, have come primarily from three economic traditions: classical Marxism, and neo-Marxist and modernization theories. Marxism presents an economic theory of political conflict within a framework of the 'class struggle'. In contrast to what Marx anticipated, modern political conflicts occur more in underdeveloped agrarian than in industrial capitalist countries, and are caused by a wide range of complex economic, political and cultural factors. The Marxist conceptual framework is too general and reductionist for the analysis modern political conflicts in developing countries, for it leaves aside many   political, social, cultural and economic features.

In contrast to classical Marxism, neo-Marxist and modernization theories focus on economic development or underdevelopment in developing countries. These two types of theories share the notion of unilinear economic change in developing countries, though they stand in contradiction to each other. The neo-Marxist paradigm presents a pessimistic view on economic change due to its prediction of increasing 'peripheralization' in underdeveloped countries. Peripheralization in underdeveloped countries is a result of the appropriation of economic surplus by Western capitalist economies. Thus, intrastate political conflicts in underdeveloped countries are an expression of the international exploitative relationship, and are expected to escalate, with deepening peripheralization. In contrast, modernization theories present an optimistic view of economic change. In that approach,developing countries are modernizing, moving towards the stage already reached by industrially developed Western economies. Thus, political conflicts in developing countries are an 'intermediate' phenomenon accompanying the transition of these societies from traditional to modern stages. Political conflicts are, therefore, an expression of the social disorder created by, or the social objection to change resulting from, modernization. This means that political conflicts, which are a by-product of the modernization process, are expected to disappear once the change is completed, and the stage of a 'modernized' society has been attained.

Modernization theory focuses on internal forces underlying political conflicts in underdeveloped countries, and the neo-Marxist theory shifts the focus of analysis to external forces. The neo-Marxist and modernization theories provide valuable guidelines in any conceptualization of political conflict in developing countries, particularly because the focus of analysis of both theories is on underdeveloped countries. Yet the fundamental assumptions and the conclusions of the theories are opposed to each other. These contradictions limit the scope to evaluate the importance of both internal and external forces of political conflicts within a single theoretical framework. In addition, economic change in underdeveloped countries, as a whole, is not uniform or unilinear, as these theories posit. Evidently, economic change has shown divergent patterns in different countries and in different regions of the world, and in different periods of time. A conceptual framework based exclusively on any of these theories of economic change will, therefore, be problematic.

A development perspective

The conceptual framework developed in this study to analyse political conflict in developing countries is based on a development economics perspective. It uses the existing ideas of both neo-Marxist and modernization theories. Nevertheless, the framework of analysis was not restricted by strict theoretical boundaries of these theories. The conceptual framework rejects the idea of uniform or unilinear economic change in developing countries. It assumed that both internal and external factors are important in varying degrees in conditioning economic change in developing countries. Thus, modern political conflicts were approached as a phenomenon associated strongly with the 'problem of development', after the Second World War.

What was the 'development problem' of developing countries in the past few decades? The term development implies an ideal normative status of human society that is expected to be achieved by an increased creation of wealth and its distribution throughout society. In development economics, the problem of development is analysed in terms of 'growth plus distribution', or the ability to provide 'basic needs' to the masses. What the term development means depends first on personal value judgements, and secondly on the 'types of changes' that are included in, or excluded from, the term. Economies in the world are transforming anyway. Whether this transformation is development or not is an analytically separate issue, and is subject to different interpretations.

The context in which economic transformation in developing countries takes place is important. Economic transformation in developing countries takes place later than in Western Europe, and in a globalized economic environment. Within this context, development problems and development goals are introduced to developing countries, while the development aspirations of society in terms of personal socio-economic advancement are conditioned. The term 'socio-economic advancement' is used here to explain the achievement of socially valued patterns and levels of lifestyles in obtaining access to such economic resources and opportunities as income, consumer goods, education and career prospects. Therefore, the strategic development problem faced by developing countries is that of generating economic resources and opportunities to meet escalating social aspirations, rather than providing a set of pre-defined basic needs.

Development can possibly lead to a paradox. This paradox arises because, on the one hand, the term development implies creating *abundance*. On the other hand, development creates *scarcity*. Developmental performance is, indeed, rationalized in development thinking in terms of *equity* and *efficiency*. It is widely accepted that to raise living standards, the masses should have access to the economic resources and opportunities enjoyed by affluent social classes. In an international perspective, underdeveloped societies should have access to economic resources and opportunities, enjoyed by developed societies. In regard to efficiency, it is accepted that delivering social services to fulfil the basic needs of the poor improves the productivity, leading to acceleration of development.

Development achievement expands the range of choices at an aggregate level. But it can also contract the range of choice *aspired* by society. The social aspirations escalate in relation to the social context, conditioned by both local and global forces, and by the development achievements themselves. As relative deprivation exists at different levels locally and globally, development solves the problems only at a certain level, but contributes to more problems at higher levels of deprivation. Thus, development solves problems and creates more problems to be solved by development itself.

Contradiction in growth

Economic growth is considered a major component of development performances, because all other achievements relating to distribution or the availability of basic needs are subservient to economic growth. The source of economic growth is *commoditization*, which is the production of more and new exchange values in less time. In principle, commoditization produces material abundance, and therefore commoditization is justified in development thinking. Yet it also creates material scarcity in societies exposed to global commoditization. Commoditization is uneven in the world owing to economic, political and institutional factors, but the effects of commoditization are transmitted across the world, producing homogeneity in social aspirations for material consumption.

The interaction between globalizing exchange values, expressed in terms of monetary values or 'prices', and localizing 'income' patterns, produces a major problem of underdevelopment, leading to international and internal inequalities in income and consumption of developing countries. Therefore, commoditization is a source of rising social aspirations for material consumption, which cannot be permitted in developing countries by the income patterns determined locally. Thus, the modern consumption patterns in developing countries, similar to those in developed countries, are sustained by excluding large social segments in the same society from material consumption. Of course, the state can have the ability to create a fair distribution pattern, reducing domestic income and consumption inequalities. Nevertheless, the state cannot influence the international income and consumption inequality in low-income developing countries, which are exposed to global commoditization. Therefore, such state redistribution policies compel society to share scarcity rather than abundance.

Contradiction in basic needs

Modern states are considered to have the *responsibility* to provide basic needs to the poor on the one hand, and the poor are considered to have the *right* to these on the other hand. The provision of social services such as education, health and nutrition to the masses in the modern welfare states depends not only on economic capacity but also on the policy commitment of governments. It is true that programmes of social services for the poor solve some problems of underdevelopment at one level, relieving certain symptoms of poverty. Yet at the same time, they contribute to the rise of social expectations that could not possibly be met in developing societies with an underdeveloped economic capacity.

Development theorists and planners have defined a set of 'basic needs' to be delivered to society. They decide that what should be given to people, on the basis of dogmatic and permanent standards and specifications of basic needs. As people's needs are determined socially, the question arises as to whether the provision of pre-defined basic needs solves the problem of development. Welfare systems liberate people from their traditional socio-economic ties and certain conditions of underdevelopment, and qualify them to seek socio-economic advancement in a modern socio-economic environment. Thus, the welfare states should anticipate that the welfare systems create a single competitive society, characterized by a decline in the share of population in traditional society. Welfare systems stimulate the growth of population, quantitatively as the population grows, and qualitatively as social preferences change. Therefore, welfare systems bring together divergent populations of traditional societies into a competitive modern society that is politically and economically unified. They compete for economic resources and opportunities for socio-economic advancement in terms of higher income, consumption patterns, education and career prospects, of the types that are socially valued by modern standards. The result will be an increase in the scarcity of economic resources and opportunities *relative* to rising social expectations. In the face of the growing relative scarcity of economic resources and opportunities for socio-economic advancement of individuals and social groups in the competitive society, on individual's achievements necessarily exclude those of others.

Welfare systems create the problems of *irreversibility* and *sustainability* particularly in developing countries. This is one of the major contradictions in welfare states. It is easy to begin a programme of welfare provision when it is financially feasible, but difficult to terminate it when it is found financially unfeasible. Moreover, the state should not only continue the welfare programmes, but also expand them with the quantitative and qualitative expansion of population. Then, economic capacity must increase, to sustain the welfare level. In addition, when the populations that were brought up within a welfare system face the scarcity of economic resources and opportunities for socio-economic advancement, they will still be dependent on the assistance of the government, which used to act as a provider. Therefore, the governments cannot ignore the social pressure for welfare despite the economic difficulties..

The political commitment and the capacity of the state and of society are of prime importance in enabling the nation to achieve the long-term growth objectives. Economic growth is necessary either to sustain the welfare state or to reduce the dependence of the population on welfare measures. Even though democratic political systems are rationalized in development and modernization thinking as being a prerequisite of or complementary to economic development, it has not been proved that they establish the required political commitment and capacity for maintaining the balance between welfare and economic growth. The most important point is not whether a country can achieve growth through the democratic political system or the authoritarian political system, but the *political discipline* that needs to be established under any political system.

Paradox of development and political conflicts

Contradictions in *growth* and *distribution* form a paradox of development, which has received little attention in development analysis or development planning. The development paradox explains that the economic transformation in developing countries produces a mix of contradictory processes. Economic growth and its distribution or the provision of basic needs are considered to be associated positively with development in attacking the problems of underdevelopment, on the one hand. These development achievements contribute, on the other hand, to more problems in society to be solved by development itself.

The contradiction between the two processes, i.e. those of *solving* and *creating* development problems, arises from the escalation of social expectations. The escalation of social expectations, as was mentioned above, is a process conditioned by both local and global forces of economic change. Developing societies experience an enlargement of, and a contraction of, the range of choices at the same time, but in different contexts. The range of choices available to people may be expanding in an absolute sense only if the social expectations are assumed to be constant. Yet, social expectations are not given, and hence cannot be assumed to be constant. Development results in the contraction of the range of choices, thus reflecting a growing scarcity of economic resources and opportunities in relation to rising social expectations.

The development paradox leads to social exclusion, by which individuals and social groups are prevented from obtaining access to economic resources and opportunities by formal and informal criteria. Evidently, social exclusion is to be understood as a relative concept, indicating how some individuals or social groups are denied access to the means of socio-economic advancement in relation to what others have achieved. There are different forms of economic, social, cultural, political and legal factors in operation formally and informally for social exclusion, and by contrast, for social inclusion. In the face of the growing scarcity of economic resources and opportunities relative to rising social expectations in the expanding competitive society, the problem of social exclusion is exacerbated..

Regarding social exclusion and its link to political conflict, knowledge is also important. Individuals and social groups have integrated increasingly into a larger society locally and globally through globalization. The term globalization stands for the formation of a global society. In this context, individuals and social groups realize their social exclusion and experience frustration due to a high degree of awareness of and exposure to the visible growth in the rest of society. The realization of social exclusion and the right to social inclusion results in the formation of group identities of frustrated social groups. This is localization in developing societies that are increasingly exposed to globalization. Social exclusion results from the paradox of development, and political conflict are connected processes in the sense that the development paradox creates and develops fertile ground for the emergence and the sustenance of political conflict. The main issue for the study was to understand under what *economic* circumstances, the *situation* for political conflict is created and sustained.

The case of Sri Lanka

The empirical study of Sri Lanka was based primarily on macroeconomic data for the post-colonial development period. The focus was on the contradictions in the country's economic change regarding declining economic capacity *relative* to rising social expectations. A number of secondary data sources, such as regular macroeconomic data reports, consumer finance surveys, demographic and labour force surveys and other institutional databases, were used to obtain historical information. A basic issue confronted in the empirical analysis was the identification and analysis of the complex issue of the development paradox and its link to political conflict. This led to a substantial simplification of data to a manageable level to analyse contradictions in the country's development process and the growth of political conflict. A major problem was that historical data have not been collected and recorded to match the type of analysis in the study. Due to this problem, the analysis was limited to some of the key areas for which macroeconomic and demographic data are available. Moreover, in some cases, historical data are not available for the early periods covered by the study. Other studies had to be consulted for relevant information. There are also problems of data classification and comparison. The study was carried out while attempting to minimize the consequences of these date limitations. Nevertheless, as the key issues in relation to the development paradox and political conflicts were addressed extensively in the analysis, the impact of data limitations on the overall analysis and conclusions is expected to be minimal.

Economic crisis and political conflict: simultaneous processes

At least aspects of the socio-economic and political conditions of Sri Lanka prevalent at the time of independence in 1948 are acknowledged in the social science development literature of the country:

1. Relative economic prosperity based on favourable market conditions for primary exports enabling development of consumerism and welfare;

2. High welfare level largely in the form of free health care, free education and consumer subsidies for the whole population; and

3. A pluralistic and competitive democratic political system enabling a high degree of popular political participation in decision-making.

It was within this socio-economic and political context that the country encountered the growth of political conflict, which ultimately turned into a twin civil war in the early 1980s. The war in the South is the insurrection of sections of the youth population among the Sinhala community, organized as *Janatha Vimukthi Peramuna* (JVP). The JVP launched its first insurrection in 1971. This movement aimed to overthrow the existing political order and establish its own government. The Northern civil war is waged by youth groups of the Tamil community. This conflict was dominated by a guerrilla organization known as the Liberation Tigers of Tamil Eelam (LTTE). The LTTE, which acted as the sole representative of the Tamil community of the country, aimed to carve out a separate Tamil state in Sri Lanka in the northern and eastern provinces of the country.

These two segments of the political conflict are logically separate from each other, but historically connected. The political conflict in Sri Lanka, though it came to the stage of a twin civil war in the early 1980s, was a historical process that evolved through various stages before becoming a full-scale civil war. In its evolution, the political conflict revealed two important characteristics.

1. In the post-colonial period, the political conflict developed *between* and *within* the communities. The former was reflected by the conflict between the country's majority community, the Sinhala, and the largest minority community, the Sri Lanka Tamil. This does not mean, however, that the two eth-

nic groups are totally hostile to each other at the individual or macro level. The conflict within the communities was reflected by the fact that the political conflict developed between social groups of the same communities. This reflected the non-homogenous character of *both* the Sinhala and Tamil communities, resulting from the cultural, social, economic and political differences.

2. Particularly in the 1970s, it was clear that the struggle for political power developed between *established* and *non-established* political groups. This was seen as a sharp split in both Sinhala and Tamil communities. Established groups were represented by the traditional political parties, which remained in parliamentary politics sharing political power. Non-established groups were represented by the radical youth who believed not in parliamentary politics, but in collective violence to achieve their political goals.

It is interesting to inquire why political conflict of such magnitude emerged in a country with such admirable socio-economic and political conditions at Independence. The post-colonial economic development of the country in these conditions clearly reflected the escalation of a development paradox due to contradictions within the development process. The contradictions developed as a result of the rising social and political demand for economic resources and opportunities in relation to the decline in economic capacity.

Sri Lanka has witnessed the gradual emergence of a consumer-oriented competitive society, which joined independent and divergent individuals, social classes, communal groups and regions in a unified economy and polity. In fact, this process started in colonial times, and has accelerated under the regimes after political independence. The three initial conditions, i.e. the relative economic prosperity, the high welfare level, and the democratic political system, provided the foundation of the competitive society. The economic prosperity enabled consumer-orientation and the expansion of the welfare level. The high welfare level enabled the growth of the competitive society, quantitatively (with high population growth from the 1940s to the 1960s), and qualitatively (with rising social aspirations). The highly competitive and pluralistic political system coupled with a high degree of political consciousness in society provided instruments for the political, semi-political, other national and local institutions, pressure groups and the national press to influence decision-making. Under this political system, the traditional political parties competed with each other to be more *welfare-oriented*, and to be more *nationalist* than others for political power. Thus consumerism and nationalism were promoted in the competitive society, and were expressed via democratic politics.

An unsustainable paradox of the Sri Lankan welfare democracy was created by the continuous decline in economic capacity. This was reflected in the growing scarcity of economic resources and opportunities relative to the rising social and political demand for them. On the one hand, the country's sound economic position deteriorated through the financing of the expansion of the welfare system, demanded by the country's specific political system. On the other hand, the economy could not achieve the growth momentum needed to generate economic resources and opportunities to sustain the competitive society. This was the result of economic mismanagement, guided by specific economic and political ideological positions of not only the governments but also society, manipulated by the pluralistic and competitive political system.

The social segments that faced the harsh consequences of the development paradox comprised the country's new generations, the youth that was brought up within a post-colonial democratic welfare state. The younger generation was proportionately large, and relatively healthy, educated, politically conscious, and ambitious. Yet, they were confronted by a competitive society characterized by an increasing scarcity of economic resources and opportunities.

The economic crisis deepened in the 1960s, hand in hand with increasing *economic control* and *political liberalism*. The government's emphasis on distribution rather than growth produced an episode of sharing poverty rather than growth. Thus the economic capacity to provide resources and opportunities to meet rising social and political demands for socio-economic advancement fell far short of the expectations of society. Radical youth groups, brought up within a post-colonial welfare democratic regime, began to organize in the South in the mid 1960s and in the North in the early 1970s. In the post- 1977 regime, the country's anti-growth economic and political ideology made a radical shift towards one of *economic liberalism* with *political control*, and the country's twin political conflict gained momentum. The government emphasis was on growth rather than distribution, within a supportive authoritarian political structure, to ensure the political power of the ruling party over a long period. In the context of widespread political turmoil in the post-1977 regime, the government got itself entangled in a twin civil war, one in the South and the other in the North, which emerged in the first half of the 1980s.

Distribution under conditions of scarcity

In the post-colonial development history of Sri Lanka, it was evident that the strategic development problem was not one of providing basic needs to the masses, but that of generating economic resources and opportunities to sustain rising social aspirations. The blame was naturally placed on the government, which was viewed as both the 'provider' of the means for socio-economic advancement and the 'facilitator' of the escalation of social expectations. It failed to play the role society expected of it. With the growth of an acute contradiction between the means for and the expectations of socio-economic advancement, distribution became unequal and unfair.

Social inequality, associated with the distribution of economic resources and opportunities, was discussed in terms of material consumption, income, employment and education. From generation to generation, people in modernizing societies integrating with the global economy through such forces of globalization as transactions, transportation and information, have developed aspirations for socially valued patterns of socio-economic advancement. The development of social aspirations is guided not only by global forces, but also by domestic conditions. In the context of Sri Lanka's development model, the formation of a competitive society against a high welfare level and political pluralism was important. The visible improvement of socio-economic conditions of affluent social classes in the same society conditioned the social aspirations in the rest of society.

The empirical analysis carried out in this study showed that the development of social aspirations for socio-economic advancement to achieve socially valued consumption patterns, income levels, employment and education in Sri Lanka has exceeded the country's economic capacity. In terms of material consumption, nevertheless, the consumption pattern was changing towards that of high-income countries in the face of global commoditization. Thus, at a macro level, the range of new commodities was expanding and the share of consumption expenditure was changing in favour of non-food and consumer durable sectors, even without a sufficient generation of income. This tendency has not been a socially neutral process, as the increase in material consumption absorbed an increasing share of national income. This, in turn, marginalized social groups in the population by excluding them from advancing material consumption.

If the consumption capacity depends basically on income, its generation and distribution should be in line with the quantitative and qualitative changes in consumption patterns. Prior to the late 1970s, income growth was relatively slow, but there was a relatively fair redistribution of income. The basic problem in this system was that in the absence of sufficient economic growth, there was so little to distribute. The outcome was one of shared poverty. In the late 1970s, economic growth was relatively high, but its distribution became relatively unequal and unfair. The relatively high economic growth was not shared adequately by lower income classes. In addition, distribution was in favour of the urban sector in general, and the capital Colombo in particular. In terms of regional income generation, the growth of income occurred at different rates in different regions in a discriminating manner. The disadvantage of the Northern and Eastern provinces was a clear example in this respect.

Generating the opportunities to match the expectations of the expanding youth population was another aspect of the development problem. There was a flight of youth from the traditional to the modern economy. But the latter does not have the capacity to productively absorb them. This led to the growth of a modern type of unemployment. This problem had two distinguishing features. It affected the 'youth' on the one hand, and the 'educated' on the other. In the post-colonial development history, every year increasing numbers of youths emerged from formal education system with qualifications and high aspirations for socio-economic advancement. But many experienced social exclusion and frustration. It is misleading to view the majority of those who were able to find employment as being better off. In the advancing consumer society, locally and globally, socio-economic advancement turned out to be a quite distant objective for the majority of income earners, who struggled to provide basic everyday needs out of their small incomes.

Regional and communal competition

The foundations for regional and communal inequality in socio-economic advancement were already laid in Sri Lanka in the colonial period. As a result, at the time of Independence, access to means of socio-economic advancement was limited in several respects:

1. A minority group in both the Sinhala and the Tamil communities had privileged socio-economic positions through access to economic resources and opportunities, thus producing an acute inequality within those communities.

2. The distribution of the means of socio-economic advancement was largely in favour of the Western and Southern provinces, populated largely by the Sinhala community, and of the Northern province populated by the Tamil community. In these provinces, the capital of Colombo in the Western province and the Jaffna city in the Northern province enjoyed the highest advantage.

3. In relation to communal population shares, there was a disproportionate distribution of economic resources and opportunities in favour of the Tamil, and against the Sinhala communities.

In the post-colonial period, particularly through the expansion of education, new generations with higher achievement levels in education emerged from the provinces and the social segments that previously were neglected. These new generations of competitors, which challenged the position of the 'old' privileged regions and social groups, were significantly large for two reasons. First, they came from large social segments and regions of the country. Secondly, owing to the population explosion from the 1940s to the 1960s, the proportion of this young generation in the total population was large. This group of new competitors belonged to all communities. Nevertheless, naturally owing to the differences in community shares of the population and to the initial differences between the communities in terms of socio-economic advancement, the numbers among these new generations were overwhelmingly large among the Sinhala community.

In the competitive society characterized by the scarcity of economic resources and opportunities, a dual social exclusion emerged *between* and *within* communities:

1. Tamil representation in employment and higher education declined in the post-colonial period. This change, from a Sinhala point of view, was a correction of the imbalance created in colonial times. In contrast, from a Tamil point of view, the change was a result of the denial of their position in favour of the Sinhala community. This change, therefore, established the economic basis for conflict between the two communities.

2. The 'old' privileged classes of *both* Sinhala and Tamil communities confront new acute competition. In contrast, the emerging new generations from *both* Sinhala and Tamil communities confronted the scarcity of economic resources and opportunities. Therefore, young people in the communities experienced the loss of the means of socio-economic advancement due to the overall decline of economic capacity in the competitive society.

Given this background, it is necessary comment on the general claim regarding the so-called 'ethnic conflict' that 'the Sinhalese gained and the Tamil lost' in the post-colonial history of the country. An analysis of socio-economic exclusion in Sri Lanka revealed three important points:

1. If there was a distribution of economic resources and opportunities initially in favour of the Tamil community against the Sinhala community, the rising competition from the previously neglected populations and regions has resulted in a decline of the 'old' privileges enjoyed by the Tamil community. Obviously, owing to the fact that about three—fourths of the population in the country comprised the Sinhala, the majority of the rising populations and regions were Sinhala.

2. The post-colonial governments adopted constitutional reforms to define Sri Lanka as a 'Sinhala-Buddhist' country, and policies to correct the initial imbalance regarding the distribution of economic resources and opportunities between the Sinhala and the Tamil. Consequently, the natural decline of the share of the Tamil community in employment and higher education has been stimulated by the governments. Yet, it should be noted that government actions to equalize opportunities for university admission among the regions has been beneficial to both the 'underprivileged' Sinhala community and the 'underprivileged' Tamil community.

3. The most important observation was the decline in economic possibilities in relation to the rising social and political demand. This resulted in a growing social exclusion in both Sinhala and Tamil communities. Therefore, a major macroeconomic problem observed in the preceding study was that attempts to lessen unequal distribution did not make sense in Sri Lanka, when there was so little to distribute.

These facts revealed that the growth of social exclusion was a common problem throughout Sri Lankan society. Yet, the Tamil communities were additionally disadvantaged, for being the minority but enjoying privileges initially against the majority Sinhala, and for being 'Tamil' in a country defined as Sinhala-Buddhist. The increase of acute social exclusion of the youth from both the Sinhala and the Tamil communities constituted fertile ground for political conflict. At the same time, the emergence of new competitors from the youth generations of the Indian Tamil community were also evident. Thus, the participation of the Indian Tamil community in political conflict is obviously a matter of time, given the country's development paradox.

The conditions for collective violence

Clearly, the development paradox does not trigger collective violence. The development paradox and political conflicts are connected processes. Social exclusion, resulting from the development paradox, forms fertile ground for the emergence and the sustenance of political conflicts, which *can* lead to an outbreak of collective violence. Therefore, the main issue was not why people resort to collective violence, but, rather, under what *economic* circumstances the *situation* for political conflicts is created and sustained. The question that remains to be answered is what the link between social exclusion and collective violence is.

If the development paradox is important in creating and sustaining political conflict, rather than in triggering collective violence, there should be some other forces to link the conflict situation with collective violence. Lenin pointed out that a revolution is impossible without a revolutionary situation, while not every revolutionary situation leads to revolution (Possony 1966: 358). The same thesis can be applied to political conflict. Thus, collective violence are born out of the situation of political conflicts. In addition, it is possible that every situation of political conflict does not necessarily lead to collective violence. Then the question at issue is under what conditions political conflicts can escalate into sustainable collective violence.

It is generally believed that democratic political systems are characterized by institutions in which decision-making is based on the majority's will. Therefore, it is argued that the scope for non-violent means of achieving the goals is larger in such democratic systems than in authoritarian political systems. Yet, there are a few problems, as was the case in Sri Lanka. Democratic systems permit the expression of grievances, but for a number of reasons the grievances of at least part of society are left unattended tot. The problem is acute in the face of widening gap between the rising social expectations and declining economic possibilities. This results in distortions in the pattern of distribution based on formal and informal criteria in a sense that the pattern of distribution is not acceptable by each and every individual or social group of society. Thus, those who were socially excluded begin to recognize that the system is ineffective in addressing their grievances.

In addition, there is no guarantee that the majority's will is always rational, while rationality is also subject to value judgements by individuals or social groups. It is also true that the majority's will can be manipulated in the pluralistic and competitive democratic system, as was the case in post-colonial Sri Lanka. Thus every democratic political party, to attain political power, had to be more welfare-oriented and more nationalist than others. In theory, the voice of the excluded can be heard in a democratic system, but their social and political lobby may not by effective. This eventually erodes the possibilities for non-violent means of achieving the goals, and enlarges those for violent means.

For the outbreak of collective violence, of course, there has to be a substantially large human resource, which could be used for collective violence by a charismatic political leadership. In economies where economic resources and opportunities are growing in relation to rising social and political demand, *time* is becoming valuable for every member of society. Yet, in economies experiencing a widening gap between the two processes, i.e. economic resources and opportunities, and social and political demand, individuals or social groups confront the loss of expectations, and time cannot be used for improving socio-economic conditions. With respect to the formation of human resources for collective violence, the *degree of awareness* of the excluded and frustrated social groups serves is important. The degree of awareness becomes a valuable input in collective violence, when social groups can judge their position against other groups in their own society or against the rest of the world, and understand their capacity and right to change the system according to their own specifications and standards. In the advancement of the degree of awareness, education and the degree of exposure to information play a major role.

The twin political conflict in Sri Lanka has met these conditions regarding the formation of human resources for collective violence. Generally, unemployed or underemployed and educated youths provided the required human resources for both the JVP insurgency in the South and the LTTE separatist war in the North. Even the majority of the employed were unable to advance socio-economically due to the declining economic capacity of the country. Thus, time was not economically valuable for the growing youth population, as there were no resources and opportunities for them to obtain access to. Due to the high degree of education and exposure to information, their recognition of their social exclusion from socio-economic advancement was high. This situation could easily be exploited by charismatic leader seeking political power.

A vital condition for collective violence is the emergence of leadership, which can channel the widespread social exclusion and frustration into an anti-state armed struggle. Leadership may not necessarily emerge within the social groups, which feel excluded. It can also emerge outside these social groups. When the development paradox comes to a critical stage in a sense that the excluded lose their confidence in the existing political system, and when the rulers are unable to find solutions to contain social agitation, the political conflicts require leadership. This is true not only for an outbreak of collective violence but also for other types of political change, as in Sri Lanka in 1956 and in 1994.

In Sri Lanka, where the existing political system failed to contain the escalation of the development paradox, the widespread youth agitation received the required leadership on time. The democratic system offered the youths little reason to hope that their goals would be achieved in parliament. Thus, the country's widespread youth agitation was organized by Sinhala and Tamil rebel leaders, and divided itself into two militant organizations, i.e. the JVP and the LTTE, which became far more nationalist than the rest of the communities.

Without leadership, the political conflict of the country could have been potential rather than actual.

The sustainability of collective violence depends on the availability of financial, military and other physical resources. In this respect, both the JVP and the LTTE had resources, but the LTTE was far more effective than the JVP. Through its world-wide international network, the LTTE became a 'transnational enterprise' to maintain its war in Sri Lanka (Kloos 1996b). One major difference between the JVP and the LTTE is their ability to obtain access to these 'war resources'. The government was able to repress the JVP war by the end of the 1980s, and to destroy its leadership. Yet, the war between the LTTE and government forces has continued for well over a decade. The sustainability of the LTTE and its war is due mainly to the fact that it has developed as a transnational company.

It should be noted that there is also no linear relationship between social exclusion and collective violence, because political conflicts and their escalation into collective violence encompass many other factors than those explained in economics. In addition, political conflicts emerge not only for economic reasons, but also for political, cultural or other reasons. Nevertheless, economic factors can play a major role covertly or openly as either destabilizing or stabilizing forces of political conflicts. Perhaps in this regard, the experience of Malaysia, which shares many similarities with Sri Lanka in terms of political, economic and cultural factors, can be compared to that of Sri Lanka (Ali 1991, Lee 1991). Malaysia is a multi-ethnic society in which the government was dominated by the majority organized and referred to as *Bumiputhra*, which literally means 'sons of the soil'. Initially, under colonialism the socio-economic advancement of society was in favour of the minority Chinese community. In the post-colonial development history, the majority *Bumiputhra* emerged into a competitive society, advancing socio-economic conditions leading to a decline in the share of the minority in economic resources and opportunities. Thus, as in Sri Lanka, the potential for political conflict emerged in Malaysia too. But it did not create a sustainable political conflict evolving into collective violence. One major reason was that the economic capacity of the country expanded, generating resources and opportunities to meet the rising social and political demand from all communities. Thus, unlike in Sri Lanka, at least on economic grounds Malaysia was able to prevent the development paradox. This is not to say, however, that economic growth necessarily diminishes the chance that the development paradox will occur. The possibilities for a development paradox are created not by the lack of economic expansion, but by the widening gap between the social and political demand for economic resources and opportunities, and the economic capacity to provide them on a large scale.

An economic analysis of political conflicts confines itself to the boundaries of the discipline. Therefore, this study focused on political, social and cultural factors, which also play a vital role in political conflicts. In fact, the issue of political conflicts has been addressed widely in political science, sociology, psychology and anthropology. Therefore, this study was intended to provide a complementary analysis to a variety of social science perspectives on political conflicts with reference to the case of developing countries.

From an economic point of view, given the limited scope of the study, many other issues relating to political conflicts in developing countries were not addressed. There are two important research areas to which an economic analysis should be extended. One is the economic cost of political conflicts. Some studies have attempted to estimate the actual economic cost of the civil war in Sri Lanka (Richardson & Samarasinghe 1991). The economic cost of political conflicts cannot be limited only to its actual cost, however. There are potential economic costs of political conflicts, as they undermine the development in an economy that could otherwise have gained. In addition, aspects such as militarization involve not only negative but also positive impacts on economic growth. The second area of research is related to the economic and political management of the economy in the face of a civil war to minimize its development costs (Stewart 1993). Developing economies are exposed more to political conflicts than developed economies, so there are additional considerations for governing the economy. These additional considerations are related to the fact that the economy should not only achieve its economic goals, but also achieve them in the face of political conflicts. Therefore, government actions should minimize the development costs of political conflicts and minimize the potential for political conflicts. The research on these areas should provide valuable insights into development processes in developing economies.

References

Abeykoon, A.T.P.L. (1993) 'Population, Environment and Sustainable Development', *Sri Lanka Journal of Social Sciences* 16 (1/2): 57-64.

Abeyratne, S. (1997) 'Trade Strategy and Industrialisation', in W.D. Lakshman (ed.) *Dilemmas of Development: Fifty Years of Economic Change in Sri Lanka*. Colombo: Sri Lanka Association of Economists.

Abeyratne, S. (1993) *Anti-Export Bias in the 'Export-Oriented' Economy of Sri Lanka*. Amsterdam: VU University Press.

Abeyratne, S. (1989) 'Industrialisation in the NICs and in Sri Lanka: Why the NICs Succeeded and Sri Lanka Failed', *Upanathi* 4 (1/2): 45-72.

Abeysekera, C. (1985) 'Ethnic Representation in the Higher Satate Services' in SSA (Social Scientists' Association) *Ethnicity and Social Change in Sri Lanka*. Colombo: SSA.

Abeysekera, C. & N. Gunasinghe (eds) (1987) *Facets of Ethnicity in Sri Lanka*. Colombo: Social Scientists' Association of Sri Lanka.

Abraham, W.I. (1948) 'The Comparability of National Income Statistics of English-Speaking Countries', *Review of Economics & Statistics* 30 (3): 207-214.

Agarwala, A.A. & S.P. Singh (eds) (1958) *The Economics of Underdevelopment*. London: Oxford University Press.

Alailima, P.J. (1997) 'Social Policy in Sri Lanka', in W.D. Lakshman (ed.) *Dilemmas of Development: Fifty Years of Economic Change in Sri Lanka*. Colombo: Sri Lanka Association of Economists.

Alvares, C. (1992) *Science, Development and Violence: The Revolt Against Modernity*. New Delhi: Oxford University Press.

Amin, S. (1977) *Imperialism and Unequal Development*. Sussex: Harvester Press.

Amin, S. (1976) *Unequal Development: An Essay on the Social Formulation of Peripheral Capitalism*. Sussex: Harvester Press.

Appadurai, A. (ed.) (1986) *The Social Life of Things: Commodities in Cultural Perspective*. Cambridge: Cambridge University Press.

Apter, D.E. (1987) *Rethinking Development: Modernization, Dependancy, and Postmodern Politics*. Newbury Park: Sage Publications.

Athukorala, P. (1987) 'Industrialisation: Its Policies and Achievements', in D. Dunham & C. Abeysekera (eds) *Essays on the Sri Lankan Economy 1977-83*. Colombo: Social Scientists' Association of Sri Lanka.

Athukorala, P. (1986) 'The Impact of 1977 Policy Reforms on Domestic Industry', *Upanathi* 1 (1): 69-105

Aya, R. (1990) *Rethinking Revolutions and Collective Violence: Studies on Concept, Theory and Method*. Amsterdam. Het Spinhuis.

Ayoob, M. (1991) 'The Security Problematic of the Third World', (a review article), *World Politics* 43 (2): 257-283.

Banerjee, D. (ed.) (1985) *Marxian Theory and the Third World*. New Delhi: Sage Publications.

Banuri, T. (1990a) 'Development and the Politics of Knowledge: A Critical Interpretation of the Social Role of Modernization Theories in the Development of the Third World', in Marglin & Marglin [pp?]

Banuri, T. (1990b): 'Modernization and its Discontents: a Cultural Perspective on the Theories of Development', in F.A. Marglin & S.A. Marglin (eds) *Dominating Knowledge: Development, Culture and Resistance.* Oxford: Clarendon Press.

Baran, P. (1957) *The Political Economy of Growth.* New York: Monthly Review Press.

Bastian, S. (1985) 'University Admission and the National Question', in SSA (Social Scientists' Association) *Ethnicity and Social Change in Sri Lanka.* Colombo: SSA.

Baxter, J.L. (1988) *Social and Psychological Foundations of Economic Analysis.* New York: Harvester-Wheatsheaf.

Becker, G.S. (1974) *Human Capital: A Theoretical and Empirical Analysis, with Special Reference to Education.* New York: National Bureau of Economic Research.

Bellah, R.N. (1964) 'Religious Evolution,' *American Sociological Review* 29 (3): 358-374.

Bhalla, S.S. (1988) 'Is Sri Lanka an Exception? A Comparative Study of Living Standard,' in T.N. Srinivasan & P.K. Bardhan (eds) *Rural Poverty in South Asia.* New York: Columbia University Press.

Blaug, M. (1974) *Education and Employment Problem in Developing Countries.* Geneva: ILO.

Block, F. (1990) *Post-industrial Possibilities: a Critique of Economic Discourse.* Berkeley: University of California Press.

Brozoska, M. (1983) 'Research Communication: The Military Related External Debt of Third World Countries', *Journal of Peace Research* 20 (3): 271-77.

Buarque, C. (1993) *The End of Economics: Ethics and the Disorder of Progress,* translated from Portuguese by M. Ridd. London: Zed Books.

Campbell, C. (1995) 'The Sociology of Consumption', in D. Miller (ed.) *Acknowledging Consumption.* London: Routledge.

CBSL (Central Bank of Sri Lanka) (1993) *Report on Consumer Finances and Socio-Economic Survey 1986/87,* Part I. Colombo: CBSL.

CBSL (CFS 1986/87) *Report on Consumer Finances and Socio-Economic Survey 1986/87,* Part II. Colombo: CBSL.

CBSL (CFS 1984) *Report on Consumer Finances and Socio-Economic Survey 1981/82,* Part I. Colombo: CBSL.

CBSL (CFS 1981/82) *Report on Consumer Finances and SocioEconomic Survey 1981/82,* Part II. Colombo: CBSL.

CBSL (CFS 1978/79) *Consumer Finances and Socio Economic-Survey 1978/79.* Colombo: CBSL.

CBSL (CFS 1973) *Survey of Sri Lanka's Consumer Finances 1973.* Colombo: CBSL.

CBSL (CFS 1963) *Survey of Ceylon's Consumer Finances 1963.* Colombo: Central Bank of Ceylon.

CBSL (CFS 1953) *Report on the Sample Survey of Ceylon's Consumer Finances 1953.* Colombo: Central Bank of Ceylon.

CBSL (ROE annual issues) *Review of the Economy.* Colombo: CBSL.

Chandraprema, C.A. (1991) *Sri Lanka: The Tears of Terror. The JVP Insurrection 1987-1989.* Colombo: Lakehouse Investment Ltd.

Chandraratna, D. (1993) *Sri Lanka: Perspectives on the Resolution of Conflict.* Nedlands: The Indian Ocean Centre for Peace Studies, University of Western Australia.

Chenery, H., M.S. Ahluwalia, C.L.G. Bell, J.H. Duloy, & R. Jolly (1974) *Redistribution with Growth: Policies to Improve Income Distribution in Developing Countries in the Context of Economic Growth*. London: Oxford University Press.

Connerton, P. (ed.) (1976) *Critical Sociology: Selected Readings*. Harmondsworth: Penguin Books.

Connor, W. (1972) 'Nation-Building or Nation-Destroying?', *World Politics* 24 (3): 319-355.

Cooper, R. & M. Berdal (1993) 'Outside Intervention in Ethnic Conflicts', *Survival* 35 (1): 118-42.

Cuthbertson, A.G. & P. Athukorala (1991) 'Sri Lanka,' in D. Papageorgiou, M. Michaely & A.M. Choksi (eds) (1991) *Liberalizing Foreign Trade: The Experience of Indonesia, Pakistan and Sri Lanka*. Cambridge: Basil Blackwell.

Davies, J.C. (1962) 'Towards a Theory of Revolution,' *American Sociological Review*. 6 (1): 5-19.

DCS (Department of Census & Statistics of Sri Lanka) (1992) *Sri Lanka Labour Force Survey 1992. Final Report*. Colombo: DCS.

DCS (1985/86) *Labour Force and Socio-Economic Survey - 1985/86. Preliminary Report*. Colombo: DCS.

DCS (1981) *Census of Population and Housing 1981. General Report*, Vol. 3. Colombo: DCS.

DCS (1971) *Census of Population - Ceylon 1971*. Colombo: DCS.

DCS (1963) *Census of Population - Ceylon 1963*. Colombo: DCS.

DCS (1953) *Census of Ceylon 1953*. Colombo: DCS.

DCS (1946) *Census of Ceylon 1946*. Colombo: DCS.

DCS (Annual issues) *Statistical Abstract*. Colombo. DCS..

Devaraj, P. (1985) 'Indian Tamils of Sri Lanka - Identity Stabilisation and Inter-Ethnic Interaction,' in SSA (Social Scientists' Association) *Ethnicity and Social Change in Sri Lanka*. Colombo: SSA.

Dewaraja, L.S. (1988) *The Kandyan Kingdom of Sri Lanka 1707-1782*. Colombo: Lakehouse Investment Ltd.

Dharmasena, K. & H.W. Karunaratne (1993) 'Poverty as a Cause of Social Unrest in Sri Lanka - A Historical Overview', in D. Chandraratna (1993) *Sri Lanka: Perspectives on the Resolution of Conflict*. Nedlands: The Indian Ocean Centre for Peace Studies, University of Western Australia.

Dissanayake, W., P. Fernando, S. de Silva & R. Kumara (1995) [in Sinhala] *Javipe: Prabhawaya, Vikashaya ha Deshapalanaya*. (JVP: Origin, Evolution and Politics). Colombo: Diyasa Publications.

Dunham, D. & C. Abeysekera (eds) (1987) *Essays on the Sri Lankan Economy 1977-83*. Colombo: Social Scientists' Association of Sri Lanka.

Durkheim, E. (1964) [1893] *The Division of Labour in Society*. New York: Free Press.

ECLA (1950) *The Economic Development of Latin America and its Principle Problems*. New York: United Nations.

Eisenstadt, S.N. (1966) *Modernization, Protest, and Change*. Englewood Cliffs, NJ: Prentice-Hall.

Eisenstadt, S.N. (1964a) 'Institutionalization and Change,' *American Sociological Review* 29 (2): 235-247.

Eisenstadt, S.N. (1964b) 'Social Differentiation, Integration and Evolution,' *American Sociological Review* 29 (3): 375-386.

Eisenstadt, S.N. (1961) *Essays on Sociological Aspects of Political and Economic Development*. The Hague: Mouton & Co.

Eisenstadt, S.N. (1957) 'Sociological Aspects of Political Development in Underdeveloped Countries,' *Economic Development & Cultural Change* 5 (3): 289-307.

Emmanuel, A. (1972) *Unequal Exchange: A Study of the Imperialism of Trade*. New York: Monthly Review Press.

Esteva, G. (1992) 'Development,' in W. Sachs (ed.) *The Development Dictionary; A Guide to Knowledge as Power*. London: Zed Books.

Finer, S.E. (1975) 'State- and Nation-building in Europe: The Role of the Military,' in C. Tilly (ed.) *The Formation of National States in Western Europe*. Princeton: Princeton University Press.

Frank, A.G. (1978) *Dependent Accumulation and Underdevelopment*. London: Macmillan.

Frank, A.G. (1969) *Latin America: Underdevelopment or Revolution: Essays on the Development of Underdevelopment and the Immediate Enemy*. New York: Monthly Review Press.

Furtado, C. (1970) *Economic Development in Latin America*. London: Cambridge University Press.

Ginsberg, M. (1961) *Essays in Sociology and Social Philosophy*. Vol. III. London: Heinemann.

Goldblat, J. (1987) 'Demilitarization in the Developing World,' *Journal of Peace Research* 24 (1): 1-4.

Goor, L.L.P. van der (1994) 'Conflict and Development: The Causes of Conflict in Developing Countries,' paper presented at the Netherlands Institute of International Relations, March 22-24, The Hague.

Gourevitch, P. (1978) 'The Second Image Reversed: The International Sources of Domestic Politics,' *International Organization* 32 (4): 881-911.

Griffin, K. & A.R. Khan (1992) *Globalization and the Developing World: An Essay on the International Dimensions of Development in the Post-Cold War Era*. Geneva: UNRISD.

Gunaratne, R. (1990) *Sri Lanka, a Lost Revolution? The Inside Story of the JVP*. Colombo: Institute of Fundamental Studies.

Gunasinghe, N. (1986) 'Open Economic Policy and Peasant Production', *Upanathi*. 1 (1): 37-67.

Gunasinghe, N. (1984) 'The Open Economy and its Impact on Ethnic Relations in Sri Lanka', *Lanka Guardian*. Issues of 07, 14 and 21 January.

Gurr, T.D. (1993) *Minorities at Risk: A Global View of Ethnopolitical Conflicts*. Washington DC: Institute of Peace Press.

Gurr, T.R. & R. Duvall (1973) 'Civil Conflict in the 1960s: A Reciprocal Theoretical System with Parameter Estimates,' *Comparative Political Studies* 6 (2): 135-169.

Gurr, T.R. (1970) *Why Men Rebel*. Princeton NJ: Princeton University Press.

Hall, R.H. (1994) *Sociology of Work: Perspectives, Analyses, and Issues*. Thousand Oaks, CA: Pine Forge Press.

Harrison, D. (1988) *The Sociology of Modernization and Development*. London: Unwin Hyman.

Heilbroner, R.L. (1963) *The Great Ascent: The Struggle for Economic Development in Our Time*. New York: Harper & Row.

Heldt, B., P. Wallensteen & K. Nordquist (1992) 'Major Armed Conflicts in 1991,' in SIPRI, *SIPRI Yearbook 1992: World Armaments and Disarmament*. Oxford: Oxford University Press.

Hennayake, S.K. (1993) 'Symbolic Ownership of Sri Lanka and Ethnonationalist Solution,' in D. Chandraratna (1993) *Sri Lanka: Perspectives on the Resolution of*

Conflict. Nedlands: The Indian Ocean Centre for Peace Studies, University of Western Australia.

Hennayake, S.K. (1992) 'Interactive Ethnonationalism: An Alternative Explanation of Minority Ethnonationalism,' *Political Geography* 11 (6): 526-549.

Hettige, S. (forthcoming) *Social Implications of Economic Liberalization.* Colombo: University of Colombo.

Hettige, S. (1995) 'Economic Liberalization and the Emerging Patterns of Social Inequality in Sri Lanka,' *Sri Lanka Journal of Social Sciences* 18 (1/2): 89-115.

Hettige, S. (1992) 'Youth Unrest in Sri Lanka: A Sociological Perspective', in S. Hettige (ed.) *Unrest or Revolt: Some Aspect of Youth Unrest in Sri Lanka.* Colombo: Goethe-Institut.

Hettige, S. (ed.) (1992) *Unrest or Revolt: Some Aspect of Youth Unrest in Sri Lanka.* Colombo: Goethe-Institut.

Hicks, J.R. (1940) 'The Valuation of the Social Income,' *Economica*, new series, 7 (May issue): 105-124.

Hill, K.Q. (1978) 'Domestic Politics, International Linkages, and Military Expenditures,' *Studies in Comparative International Development* 13 (1): 38-59.

Hirschman, A.O. (1981) *Essays in Trespassing: Economics to Politics and Beyond.* Cambridge: Cambridge University Press.

Holsti, K.J. (1991) *Peace and War: Armed Conflicts and International Order 1648-1989.* Cambridge: Cambridge University Press.

Hoogvelt, A.M. (1976) *The Sociology of Developing Societies.* London: Macmillan.

Hoselitz, B.F. (1960) *Sociological Aspects of Economic Growth.* Illinois: Free Press of Glencoe.

Hoselitz, B.F. (ed.) (1952) *The Progress of Underdeveloped Areas* Chicago: University of Chicago Press

Hoselitz, B.F. & W.E. Moore (eds) (1963) *Industrialization and Society.* UNESCO: Mouton.

Hubbell, L.K. (1990) 'Political and Economic Discrimination in Sri Lanka', in M.L. Wyzan (ed.) *The Political Economy of Ethnic Discrimination and Affirmative Action: A Comparative Perspective.* New York: Praeger Publishers.

Hunt, D. (1989) *Economic Theories of Development: An Analysis of Competing Paradigms.* New York: Harvester Wheatsheaf.

Huntington, S.P. (1968) *Political Order in Changing Societies.* New Haven: Yale University Press.

IBRD (1953) *The Economic Development of Ceylon.* Baltimore: Johns Hopkins Press.

ILO (1978) *Employment, Growth and Basic Needs: A One-World Problem.* Geneva: ILO.

ILO (1971) *Matching Employment Opportunities and Expectations: A Programme of Action for Ceylon.* Geneva: ILO.

Indraratna, A.D.V. de S. (ed.) (1986) *Increasing Efficiency of Management of Higher Education Resources.* Colombo: Division of Planning and Research, University Grants Commission.

Isard, W. & E.W. Schooler (1963) 'An Economic Analysis of Local and Regional Impacts of Reduction of Military Expenditures,' *Papers*, 1, Peace Research Society, Chicago Conference.

Isenman, P. (1980) 'Basic Needs: The Case of Sri Lanka,' *World Development* 8 (3): 237-258.

Islam, R. (ed.) (1987) *Rural Industrialisation and Employment in Asia.* New Delhi: ILO.

Ivan, V. (1989) *Sri Lanka in Crisis: Road to Conflict.* Ratmalana: Sarvodaya Book Publishing Services.

Jackson, S., B. Russett, D. Snidal & D. Sylvan (1978) 'Conflict and Coercion in Dependent States" *Journal of Conflict Resolution* 22 (4): 627-657.

James, J. (1993) *Consumption and Development.* New York: St. Martin's Press.

Jayasekara, P.V.J. & Y. R. Amarasinghe (1987) 'The Economy, Society and Polity from Independence to 1977,' in D. Dunham & C. Abeysekera (eds) *Essays on the Sri Lankan Economy 1977-83.* Colombo: Social Scientists' Association of Sri Lanka.

Jayawardena, K. (1990) *Ethnic and Class Conflicts in Sri Lanka.* Colombo: Sanjiva Books.

Jayawardena, K. (1987) 'The National Question and the Left Movement in Sri Lanka,' in C. Abeysekera & N. Gunasinghe (eds) *Facets of Ethnicity in Sri Lanka.* Colombo: Social Scientists' Association of Sri Lanka.

Jayawardena, K. (1985) 'Some Aspects of Class and Ethnic Consciousness in Sri Lanka in the Late 19th and Early 20th Centuries,' in SSA (Social Scientists' Association) Ethnicity and Social Change in Sri Lanka. Colombo: SSA.

Jayawardena, K. (1984) 'Class Formation and Communalism', *Race & Class* 26 (1): 51-62.

Jayewardene, J.R. (1951) *Economic and Social Development in Ceylon 1926-1950: A Survey.* Colombo: Ministry of Finance.

Jayaweera, S. (1986) 'Socio-Economic Needs and Higher Education Planning,' in A.D.V. de S. Indraratna (ed.) (1986) *Increasing Efficiency of Management of Higher Education Resources.* Colombo: Division of Planning and Research, University Grants Commission.

Jongman, A.J. & A.P. Schmid (1994) 'Wars, Low-intensity Conflicts and Serious Disputes: A Global Inventory of Current Confrontations,' paper presented at the Netherlands Institute of International Relations, March 22-24, The Hague.

Jongman, B. (1983) *War, Armed Conflict and Political Violence: A Pilot Study: Data Concerning the Year 1980 According to the International Herald Tribune.* Polemological Institute, University of Groningen.

Jupp, J. (1978) *Sri Lanka: Third World Democracy.* London: Frank Cass.

Karunatilake, H.N.S. (1987) *The Economy of Sri Lanka.* Colombo: Centre for Demographic and Socio-Economic Studies.

Kearney, R.W. (1973) *The Politics of Ceylon (Sri Lanka).* London: Cornell University Press

Keynes, J.M. (1936) *The General Theory of Employment Interest and Money.* London: Macmillan.

King, J.E. (ed.) (1990) *Marxian Economics.* Vol. I. Aldershot: Edward Elgar.

Kiribanda, B.M. (1997) 'Population and Employment,' in W.D. Lakshman (ed.) *Dilemmas of Development: Fifty Years of Economic Change in Sri Lanka.* Colombo: Sri Lanka Association of Economists.

Klein, P.A. (1988) [1977] 'An Institutionalist View of Development Economics,' in W.J. Samuels (ed.) (1988) *Institutional Economics.* Vols I, II and III. Aldershot: Edward Elgar.

Kloos, P. (1996a) 'Anthropology of Violence. A one-day conference,' Vrije Universiteit Amsterdam, 15 November.

Kloos, P. (1996b) 'The Liberation Tigers of Tamil Eelam in Sri Lanka as a Transnational Regime,' paper presented at the staff seminar of the Centre for Asian Studies, Amsterdam, 16 April.

Kloos, P. (1995) 'The Paradox of Sri Lanka: Civil War and the Demise of the Trias Politica,' paper presented at the IIAS/NIAS International Workshop on Democracy in Asia, 26-29 October, Copenhagen.

Kloos, P. (1993) 'Globalization and Localized Violence,' *Folk* 35: 5-16.

Kopytoff, I. (1986) 'The Cultural Biography of Things: Commoditization as a Process,' in Appadurai, A. (ed.) *The Social Life of Things: Commodities in Cultural Perspective.* Cambridge: Cambridge University Press.

Kumaraswamy, R. (1987) 'Myths without Conscience: Tamil and Sinhalese Nationalist Writings of the 1980s,' in C. Abeysekera & N. Gunasinghe (eds) *Facets of Ethnicity in Sri Lanka.* Colombo: Social Scientists' Association of Sri Lanka.

Krader, L. (1975) *The Asiatic Mode of Production: Sources, Development and Critique in the Writings of Karl Marx.* Assen: Van Gorcum.

Kuznets, S. (1968) *Toward a Theory of Economic Growth.* New York: W.W. Norton.

Kuznets, S. (1955) 'Economic Growth and Income Inequality,' *American Economic Review* 45 (1): 1-28.

Kuznets, S. (1953) 'International Differences in Income Levels: Reflections on Their Causes,' *Economic Development & Cultural Change* 2 (1): 3-26.

Kuznets, S. (1951) 'The State as a Unit in Study of Economic Growth,' *Journal of Economic History* 11 (winter issue): 25-41

Kuznets, S. (1948a) 'On the Valuation of Social Income - Reflections on Professor Hicks' Article,' *Economica*, new series, 15 (February issue): 1-16

Kuznets, S. (1948b) 'National Income: A New Version,' *Review of Economics & Statistics* 30 (3): 151-179.

Lakshman, W.D. (1992) 'The Macro-Economic Policy Framework and its Implications for Youth Unrest,' in S. Hettige (ed.) *Unrest or Revolt: Some Aspect of Youth Unrest in Sri Lanka.* Colombo: Goethe-Institut.

Lakshman, W.D. (1986) 'State Policy in Sri Lanka and its Economic Impact 1970-85: Selected Themes with Special Reference to Distributive Implications of Policy', *Upanathi* 1 (1): 5-36

Lakshman, W.D. (ed.) (1997) *Dilemmas of Development: Fifty Years of Economic Change in Sri Lanka.* Colombo: Sri Lanka Association of Economists.

Lakshman, W.D. (ed.) (1979) *Public Enterprise in the Economic Development in Sri Lanka.* Colombo: National Institute of Business Management.

Lal, D. & S. Rajapathirana (1989) *Impediments to Trade Liberalization in Sri Lanka.* Thames essay no. 51. Aldershot: Gower.

Lenin, V.I. (1975) [1917] *Imperialism: The Highest Stage of Capitalism: A Popular Outline.* Peking: Foreign Languages Press.

Lerner, D. (1958) *The Passing of Traditional Society.* New York: Free Press.

Lewis, A. (1955) *The Theory of Economic Growth.* London: Allen & Unwin.

Lewis, W.A. (1985) *Racial Conflict and Economic Development.* Cambridge: Harvard University Press.

Lewis, W.A. (1958) 'Economic Development with Unlimited Supplies of Labour', in A.A. Agarwala & S.P. Singh (eds) (1958) *The Economics of Underdevelopment.* London: Oxford University Press.

Little, I.M.D. (1949) 'The Valuation of the Social Income,' *Economica*, new series, 16 (February issue): 11-26.

Manor, J. (ed.) (1984) *Sri Lanka in Change and Crisis.* London: Croom Helm.

Marglin, S.A. (1990) 'Towards the Decolonization of the Mind', in F.A. Marglin & S.A. Marglin (eds) (1990) *Dominating Knowledge: Development, Culture and Resistance.* Oxford: Clarendon Press.

Marglin, F.A. & S.A. Marglin (eds) (1990) *Dominating Knowledge: Development, Culture and Resistance.* Oxford: Clarendon Press.

Marx, K. (1976) [1844] 'The Critique of Hegelian Philosophy,' in P. Connerton (ed.) *Critical Sociology: Selected Readings.* Harmondsworth: Penguin Books.

Marx, K. (1954) *Capital: A Critical Analysis of Capitalist Production*, Vol. I. (English edition (1887) by F. Engels; reprinted version (1974)) London: Lawrence & Wishart.

Marx, K. & F. Engels (1950) *Selected Works.* Vol. I. London: Lawrence & Wishart.

McGowan, W. (1992) *Only Man is Vile: The Tragedy of Sri Lanka.* Calcutta: Rupa & Company.

Mehmet, O. (1995) *Westernizing the Third Worl:; The Eurocentricity of Economic Development Theories.* London: Routledge.

Melotti, U. (1977) *Marx and the Third World.* Translated from the Italian by P. Ransford and edited by M. Caldwell. London: Macmillan Press.

Meyer, E. (1984) 'Seeking the Roots of the Tragedy,' in J. Manor, J. (ed.) *Sri Lanka in Change and Crisis.* London: Croom Helm.

Miliband, R. (1991) *Divided Societies: Class Struggle in Contemporary Capitalism.* Oxford: Oxford University Press.

Miller, D. (ed.) (1995) *Acknowledging Consumption.* London: Routledge.

Minister of Finance (1970) *Budget Speech 1970-1971.* Colombo: Ministry of Finance.

Mintz, A. (1986) 'Arms Imports as an Action-Reaction Process: An Empirical Test of Six Pairs of Developing Nations,' *International Interactions* 12 (3): 229-243.

Moaddel, M. (1994) 'Political Conflict in the World Economy: A Cross-National Analysis of Modernization and World-System Theories,' *American Sociological Review* 59 (2): 276-303.

Moore, M. (1993) 'Thoroughly Modern Revolutionaries: The JVP in Sri Lanka,' *Modern Asian Studies* 27 (3): 593-642.

Moore, M. (1992): 'Retreat from Democracy in Sri Lanka,' *Journal of Commonwealth & Comparative Politics* 30 (1): 64-84.

Moore, M. (1990) 'Economic Liberalization versus Political Pluralism,' *Modern Asian Studies* 24 (2): 341-383.

Moore, W.E. (1964) 'Predicting Discontinuities in Social Change,' *American Economic Review* 29 (3): 331-338.

Mörner, M. & T. Svensson (eds) (1991) *The Transformation of Rural Society in Third World.* London: Routledge.

Morris, D.M. (1979) *Measuring the Conditions of the World's Poor: The Physical Quality of Life Index.* London: Frank Cass.

MPE (Ministry of Planning & Employment) (1971) *The Five Year Plan 1972-1976.* Colombo: MPE.

Mullins, A.F. (1987) *Born Arming: Development and Military Power in New States.* Stanford: Stanford University Press.

Nevitte, N. & C.H. Kennedy (eds) (1986) *Ethnic Preference and Public Policy in Developing States.* Boulder: Lynne Rienner Publication Inc.

Nithiyanandan, V. (1987) 'An Analysis of Economic Factors Behind the Origin and Development of Tamil Nationalism in Sri Lanka,' in C. Abeysekera & N. Gunasinghe (eds) *Facets of Ethnicity in Sri Lanka.* Colombo: Social Scientists' Association of Sri Lanka.

NPC (National Planning Council) (1959) *The Ten Year Plan 1959-1968.* Colombo: NPC.

Nurkse, R. (1958) 'Some International Aspects of the Problem of Economic Development,' in A.A. Agarwala & S.P. Singh (eds) *The Economics of Underdevelopment.* London: Oxford University Press.

Nutter, G.W. (1957) 'On Measuring Economic Growth,' *Journal of Political Economy* 65 (1): 51-63.

O'Ballance, E. (1989) *The Cyanide War: Tamil Insurrection in Sri Lanka 1973-88.* London: Brassey's.

Oberst, R.C. (1991) 'Youth Movements and the Persistence of Violence in Sri Lanka.' 3rd Sri Lanka Conference, 2-5 April, Vrije Universiteit Amsterdam. Amsterdam: Department of Cultural Anthropology/Sociology of Development.

Oberst, R. (1986) 'Policies of Ethnic Preference in Sri Lanka,' in N. Nevitte & C.H. Kennedy (eds) *Ethnic Preference and Public Policy in Developing States.* Boulder: Lynne Rienner Publication Inc.

Obeyesekere, G. (1974) 'Some Comments on the Social Backgrounds of the April 1971 Insurgency in Sri Lanka (Ceylon),' *Journal of Asian Studies* 33 (3): 367-384.

Oliver, H.M. Jr. (1957) *Economic Opinion and Policy in Ceylon.* Durham: Duke University Press.

Olson, M. Jr. (1965) *The Logic of Collective Action.* Cambridge MA: Harvard University Press.

Olson, M. Jr.(1963) 'Rapid Growth as a Destabilizing Force,' *Journal of Economic History* 23: 529-552.

Osmani, S.R. (1987) 'The Impact of Economic Liberalisation on the Small-Scale and Rural Industries of Sri Lanka', in R. Islam, R. (ed.) *Rural Industrialisation and Employment in Asia.* New Delhi: ILO.

Papageorgiou, D., M. Michaely & A.M. Choksi (eds) (1991) *Liberalizing Foreign Trade: The Experience of Indonesia, Pakistan and Sri Lanka.* Cambridge: Basil Blackwell.

Parsons, T. (1971) *The System of Modern Societies.* Englewood Cliff NJ: Prentice Hall.

Parsons, T. (1966) *Societies.* Englewood Cliff NJ: Prentice Hall.

Parsons, T. (1964) 'Evolutionary Universals in Society,' *American Sociological Review* 29 (3): 339-357.

Parsons, T. (1951) *The Social System.* Glencoe IL: Free Press.

PCY (1990) *Report of Presidential Commission on Youth.* Sri Lanka Session Reports. Colombo: PCY.

Peiris, G.H. (1991) 'Changing Prospects of the Plantation Workers of Sri Lanka,' in S.W.R. de A. Samarasinghe & R. Coughlan (eds) *Economic Dimensions of Ethnic Conflict: International Perspectives.* London: Pinter Publishers.

Pieris, R. (1956) *Sinhalese Social Organization: The Kandyan Period.* Colombo: Ceylon University Press.

Piyadasa, L. (1984) *Sri Lanka: The Holocaust and After.* London: Mrram Books.

Polachek, S.W. & W.S. Seibert (1993) *The Economics of Earnings.* Cambridge: Cambridge University Press.

Polanyi, K. (1957) [1944] *The Great Transformation.* Boston: Beacon Press.

Ponnambalam, S. (1983) *Sri Lanka: The National Question and the Tamil Liberation Struggle.* London: Zed Books.

Ponnambalm, S. (1980) *Dependent Capitalism in Crisis: The Sri Lankan Economy, 1948-1980.* London: Zed Press.

Popper, K.R. (1952) *The Open Society and its Enemies.* Vol. II. London: Routledge & Kegan Paul.

Possony, S.T. (ed.) (1966) *The Lenin Reader: The Outstanding Works of V.I. Lenin.* Chicago: Henry Regnery Company.

Prebisch, R. (1959: 'Commercial Policy in Underdeveloped Countries,' *American Economic Review* 49 (2): 251-273.

Preteceille, E. & J.P. Terrail (1985) *Capitalism, Consumption and Needs.* Translated from the French by S. Matthews. New York: Basil Blackwell.

Pryor, F.L. (1990) [1980] 'The Asian Mode of Production as an Economic System' in J.E. King (ed.) (1990) *Marxian Economics.* Vol. I. Aldershot: Edward Elgar.

Rajapathirana, S. (1988) 'Foreign Trade and Economic Development: Sri Lanka's Experience,' *World Development* 16 (10): 1143-1156.

Ram, M. (1989) *Sri Lanka: The Fractured Island.* New Delhi: Penguin Books.

Ranasinghe, A. & J. Hartog (1997) 'Investment in Post-Compulsory Education in Sri Lanka,' Discussion Paper TI 97-021/3, Tinbergen Institute, Amsterdam.

Richardson, J.M. Jr. & S.W.R. de A. Samarasinghe (1991) 'Measuring the Economic Dimensions of Sri Lanka's Ethnic Conflict', in S.W.R. de A. Samarasinghe & R. Coughlan (eds) *Economic Dimensions of Ethnic Conflict: International Perspectives.* London: Pinter Publishers.

Roberts, M. (1982) *Caste Conflict and Elite Formation.* Cambridge: Cambridge University Press.

Rodgers, G., C. Gore, & J.B. Figueiredo (eds) (1995) *Social Exclusion: Rhetoric, Reality, Responses.* Geneva: ILO.

Rodrigo, C. & N. Attanayake (1988) *The Employment Consequences of Alternative Development Strategies in Sri Lanka.* Colombo: Institute of Policy Studies.

Roemer, J.E. (1990) [1978] 'Neoclassicism, Marxism, and Collective Action', in J.E. King (ed.) *Marxian Economics.* Vol. I. Aldershot: Edward Elgar.

Rogers, J.D. (1994) 'Post-Orientalism and the Interpretation of Premodern and Modern Political Identities: The Case of Sri Lanka,' *Journal of Asian Studies* 53 (1):10-23.

Rosh, R.M. (1990) 'Third World Arms Production and the Evolving Interstate System,' *Journal of Conflict Resolution* 34 (1): 57-73.

Rosh, R.M. (1987) 'Ethnic Cleavage as a Component of Global Military Expenditures,' *Journal of Peace Research* 24 (1): 21-31.

Rostow, W.W. (1960) *The Stages of Economic Growth: A Non-Communist Manifesto.* Cambridge: Cambridge University Press.

Rule, J.B. (1988) *Theories of Civil Violence.* Berkeley: University of California Press.

Sachs, W. (ed.) (1992) *The Development Dictionary; A Guide to Knowledge as Power.* London: Zed Books.

Sahlins, M.D. & E.R. Service (eds) (1960) *Evolution and Culture.* Ann Arbor: University of Michigan Press.

Salmi, J. (1993) *Violence and Democratic Society: New Approaches to Human Rights.* London: Zed Books.

Samarasinghe, S.W.R. de A. & R. Coughlan (eds) (1991) *Economic Dimensions of Ethnic Conflict: International Perspectives.* London: Pinter Publishers.

Samuels, W.J. (ed.) (1988) *Institutional Economics.* Vols I, II and III. Aldershot: Edward Elgar.

Samuelson, P. (1976) *Economics.* 10th edn. New York: McGraw-Hill.

Schlichte, K. (1994) 'Research on Causes of War at the University of Hamburg,' paper presented at the Netherlands Institute of International Relations, March 22-24, The Hague.

Schrijvers, J. (1993) *The Violence of 'Development'.* Utrecht: International Books; New Delhi: Kali for Women.

Seers, D. (1972) 'What are We Trying to Measure?,' *Journal of Development Studies* 8 (3): 21-36.

Sen, A. (1988) 'Freedom of Choice,' *European Economic Review.* 32: 269-94.

Sen, A. (1983) 'Development: Which Way Now?,' *Economic Journal* 93: 745-762.

Sen, A.K. (1977) 'Rational Fools: A Critique of the Behavioral Foundations of Economic Theory,' *Philosophy & Public Affairs* 6 (4): 317-344.

Shiozawa, K. (1990) [1966] 'Marx's View of the Asiatic Society and His Asiatic Mode of Production,' in J.E. King (ed.) *Marxian Economics.* Vol. I. Aldershot: Edward Elgar.

Siddhisena, K.A.P. (1994) 'Sri Lanka Population in Historical Perspective,' *Economic Review* 20 (8): 6-10, Colombo: People's Bank.

Silva, C.R. de (1977a) 'Education,' in C.R. de Silva (ed.) *Sri Lanka: A Survey.* Honolulu: University Press of Hawaii.

Silva, C.R. de (ed.) (1977b) *Sri Lanka: A Survey.* Honolulu: University Press of Hawaii.

Silva, C.R. de (1974) 'Weightage in University Admission: Standardisation and District Quotas in Sri Lanka 1970-1975,' *Modern Ceylon Studies* 5 (2): 151-178.

Silva, K.M. de (1986) *Managing Ethnic Tensions in Multi-Ethnic Societies, Sri Lanka 1880-1985.* Lanham: University Press of America.

Silva, N. de (1995) [in Sinhala] *Prabakaran, ohuge Seeyala, Bappala ha Massinala* (Prabakaran, his Grandfathers, Uncles and Cousins). Maharagama (Sri Lanka): Chinthana Parshadaya.

Singer, H.W. (1950) 'The Distribution of Gains between Investing and Borrowing Countries,' *American Economic Review* 40 (2): 473-485.

Singer, J.D. (1994) 'Armed Conflict in the Ex-colonial Regions: From Classification to Explanation,' paper presented at the Netherlands Institute of International Relations, March 22-24, The Hague.

SIPRI (1992) *SIPRI Yearbook 1992: World Armaments and Disarmament.* Oxford: Oxford University Press.

Sivanandan, A. (1984) 'Sri Lanka: Racism and the Politics of Underdevelopment,' *Race & Class* 26 (1): 1-37.

Smelser, N.J. (1963a) 'Mechanisms of Change and Adjustment to Changes', in B.F. Hoselitz & W.E. Moore (eds) (1963) *Industrialization and Society.* UNESCO: Mouton.

Smelser, N.J. (1963b) *Theory of Collective Behavior.* New York: Free Press.

Smith, A. (1910) [1776] *The Wealth of Nations.* London: J.M. Dent & Sons Ltd.

Snodgrass, D.R. (1966) *Ceylon: An Export Economy in Transition.* Illinois: Richard D. Irwin, Inc.

Spencer, J. (ed.) (1990) *Sri Lanka: History and the Roots of the Conflict.* London: Routledge.

Srinivasan, T.N. & P.K. Bardhan (eds) (1988) *Rural Poverty in South Asia.* New York: Columbia University Press.

SSA (Social Scientists' Association) (1985) *Ethnicity and Social Change in Sri Lanka.* Colombo: SSA.

Stewart, F. (1993) 'War and Underdevelopment: Can Economic Analysis Help Reduce the Cost?,' *Journal of International Development* 5 (4): 357-380.

Svensson, T. (1991) 'Prologue: Theories and Mythologies in the Third World', in M. Mörner & T. Svensson (eds) (1991) *The Transformation of Rural Society in Third World.* London: Routledge.

Tambiah, S.J. (1992) *Buddhism Betrayed? Religion, Politics, and Violence in Sri Lanka.* Chicago: University of Chicago Press.

Tambiah, S.J. (1986) *Sri Lanka: Ethnic Fratricide and the Dismantling of Democracy.* London: I.B. Tauris & Co.

Terhal, P. (1992) *Economic Growth and Political Insecurity: Towards a Multidisciplinary Approach.* Series Development and Security No. 36. Rotterdam: Centre for Development Planning, Erasmus University.

Terrel, L.M. (1971) 'Societal Stress, Political Instability, and Levels of Military Effort,' *Journal of Conflict Resolution* 15 (3): 329-346.

Tilly, C. (1993) *European Revolutions, 1492-1992.* Oxford: Blackwell.

Tilly, C. (1990) *Coercion, Capital, and European States, AD 990-1990.* Cambridge: Basil Blackwell.

Tilly, C. (1978) *From Mobilization to Revolution.* Reading MA: Addison-Wesley.

Tilly, C. (1973) 'Does Modernization Breed Revolutions?,' *Comparative Politics* 5 (3): 425-447.

Tilly, C. (ed.) (1975) *The Formation of National States in Western Europe.* Princeton: Princeton University Press.

Tilly, L.A. & C. Tilly (1981) *Class, Conflict and Collective Action.* Beverly Hills: Sage Publications.

Todaro, M.P. (1985) *Economic Development in the Third World.* New York: Longman Inc.

Tsetung, M. (1971) *Selected Readings from the Works of Mao Tsetung.* Peking: Foreign Languages Press.

UGC (University Grants Commission) (1984) *Report of the Committee Appointed to Review University Admissions Policy.* Colombo: UGC.

UNDP (HDR annual issues) *Human Development Report.* New York: Oxford University Press.

UNHCR (1993) *The State of the World's Refugees: The Challenge of Protection.* New York: Penguin Books.

UTHR (1994) *Someone Else's War.* Colombo: University Teachers for Human Rights (Jaffna), Movement for Inter Racial Justice and Equality.

Uyangoda, J. (1992) 'Political Dimensions of Youth Unrest,' in S. Hettige (ed.) *Unrest or Revolt: Some Aspect of Youth Unrest in Sri Lanka.* Colombo: Goethe-Institut.

Veblen, T. (1992) [1899] *The Theory of the Leisure Class.* With an introduction by C.W. Wright. New Jersey: Transaction Publishers.

Vittachi, V.P. (1995) *Sri Lanka: What Went Wrong?* New Delhi: Navrang Publishers.

Wallerstein, I. (1979) *The Capitalist World Economy.* Cambridge: Cambridge University Press.

Watnick, M. (1952) 'The Appeal of Communism to the Underdeveloped People', in B.F. Hoselitz (ed.) *The Progress of Underdeveloped Areas.* Chicago: University of Chicago Press.

Weber, M. (1946) *From Max Weber: Essays in Sociology.* Translation by H. Gerth & C.W. Mills. New York: Oxford University Press.

Webster, A. (1990) *Introduction to the Sociology of Development.* Hampshire: Macmillan.

Wells, J. (1977) 'The Diffusion of Durables in Brazil and Its Implications for Recent Controversies Concerning Brazilian Development,' *Cambridge Journal of Economics* 1 (3): 259-279.

Wickramasingha, N. (1995) *Ethnic Politics in Colonial Sri Lanka 1927-1947.* New Delhi: Vikas Publishing House.

Wickremeratne, L.A. (1977) 'The Economy in 1948', in C.R. de Silva (ed.) (1977b) *Sri Lanka: A Survey.* Honolulu: University Press of Hawaii.

Wilson, A.J. (1988) *The Break-up of Sri Lanka: The Sinhalese-Tamil Conflict.* Honolulu: University of Hawaii Press.

Wilson, A.J. (1979) *Politics in Sri Lanka, 1947-1979.* London: Macmillan.

World Bank (WDR annual issues) *World Development Report*. Washington DC: World Bank.

World Bank (1983) *World Tables*. Vol. II. Baltimore: Johns Hopkins University Press.

Wriggins, W.H. & J.F. Guyot (eds) (1973) *Population, Politics and the Future of Southern Asia*. New York: Cambridge University Press.

Wriggins, W.H. & C.H.S. Jayewardene (1973) 'Youth Protest in Sri Lanka (Ceylon),' in W.H. Wriggins & J.F. Guyot (eds) *Population, Politics and the Future of Southern Asia*. New York: Cambridge University Press.

Wyzan, M.L. (ed.) (1990) *The Political Economy of Ethnic Discrimination and Affirmative Action: A Comparative Perspective*. New York: Praeger Publishers.

Zimmerman, W. & G. Palmer (1983) 'Words and Deeds in Soviet Foreign Policy: The Case of Soviet Military Expenditures,' *American Political Science Review* 77 (2): 358-367.

Zolberg, A.R., A. Suhrke, & S. Aguayo (eds) (1989) *Escape from Violence: Conflict and the Refugee Crisis in the Developing World*. Oxford: Oxford University Press.

Appendix I

Population in Sri Lanka by Area and Community, Census Years 1946-1981

1.1 Population by district and province as a percentages of community totals

Population Census 1946

District and Province	Sinhala	Sri Lanka Tamil	Indian Tamil	Sri Lanka Moor	Indian Moor	Other[a]	Total
Colombo	24.9	8.0	7.8	16.1	49.9	62.7	21.3
Gampaha[b]							
Kalutara	8.6	0.5	3.8	6.6	1.1	1.9	6.9
Western province	33.5	8.5	11.6	22.7	51.0	64.6	28.2
Kandy	8.9	4.1	26.6	12.9	13.0	8.4	10.7
Matale	2.3	0.7	4.4	2.2	2.9	1.1	2.3
Nuwara Eliya	2.2	0.7	19.7	1.0	3.5	2.5	4.0
Central province	13.4	5.5	50.7	16.2	19.3	12.0	17.1
Galle	9.4	0.4	0.9	3.7	0.4	1.3	6.9
Matara	7.2	0.3	1.0	2.4	0.1	0.8	5.3
Hambantota	3.1	0.1	0.0	0.6	0.0	1.5	2.2
Southern province	19.7	0.9	1.9	6.7	0.6	3.6	14.4
Jaffna	0.0	55.8	0.5	1.4	1.3	1.2	6.4
Mannar	0.0	2.2	0.5	2.5	2.5	0.3	0.5
Vavuniya	0.0	2.2	0.1	0.5	0.4	0.1	0.3
Mullaitive[b]							
Northern province	0.2	60.1	1.1	4.5	4.2	1.6	7.2
Batticaloa	0.3	13.8	0.2	22.9	1.2	2.9	3.1
Ampara[c]							
Trincomalee	0.3	4.1	0.4	5.9	3.0	2.8	1.1
Eastern province	0.6	17.9	0.6	28.8	4.2	5.7	4.2
Kurunegala	9.7	1.0	1.0	5.0	4.9	2.0	7.3
Puttalam	0.5	0.8	0.1	3.5	1.0	0.6	0.6
Chilaw[d]	2.6	1.0	0.6	1.1	1.3	1.6	2.1
North western province	12.8	2.7	1.7	9.6	7.1	4.1	10.0
Anuradhapura	2.4	1.3	0.4	3.8	2.5	0.9	2.1
Polonnaruwa[c]							
North central province	2.4	1.3	0.4	3.8	2.5	0.9	2.1
Badulla	4.6	2.1	16.3	2.7	4.9	3.7	5.6
Moneragala[c]							
Uva province	4.6	2.1	16.3	2.7	4.9	3.7	5.6
Ratnapura	5.6	0.6	9.1	1.3	3.3	2.2	5.2
Kegalle	7.1	0.4	6.7	3.8	2.7	1.6	6.0
Sabaragamuwa province	12.8	1.0	15.7	5.0	6.0	3.7	11.2
Total population (1000s)	4620.5	733.7	780.6	373.6	35.6	113.3	6657.3

Population Census 1953[e]

District and Province	Sinhala	Sri Lanka Tamil	Indian Tamil	Sri Lanka Moor	Indian Moor	Other[a]	Total
Colombo	24.5	10.1		17.2		60.3	21.1
Gampaha[b]							
Kalutara	8.1	0.7		6.1		2.1	6.5
Western province	32.5	10.7		23.3		62.4	27.6
Kandy	8.6	3.6		12.3		8.8	10.4
Matale	2.5	1.0		2.4		1.1	2.5
Nuwara Eliya	2.1	1.0		1.0		2.1	4.0
Central province	13.2	5.6		15.8		12.1	16.9
Galle	8.8	0.4		3.1		1.5	6.5
Matara	6.9	0.3		2.2		0.6	5.1
Hambantota	3.3	0.1		0.7		1.7	2.4
Southern province	19.0	0.9		6.0		3.7	14.0
Jaffna	0.1	51.7		1.4		1.1	6.1
Mannar	0.0	2.2		2.3		0.0	0.5
Vavuniya	0.1	2.6		0.6		0.2	0.4
Mullaitive[b]							
Northern province	0.3	56.5		4.3		1.4	7.1
Batticaloa	0.6	14.3		22.5		2.2	3.3
Ampara[c]							
Trincomalee	0.3	3.9		6.0		1.7	1.0
Eastern province	0.8	18.2		28.5		4.0	4.4
Kurunegala	10.3	1.1		5.4		4.2	7.7
Puttalam	0.6	0.9		3.7		0.6	0.7
Chilaw[d]	2.6	1.0		1.1		1.0	2.1
North western province	13.4	3.0		10.1		5.8	10.6
Anuradhapura	3.4	1.6		4.0		1.3	2.8
Polonnaruwa[c]							
North central province	3.4	1.6		4.0		1.3	2.8
Badulla	4.8	2.1		3.0		5.1	5.8
Moneragala[c]							
Uva province	4.8	2.1		3.0		5.1	5.8
Ratnapura	5.7	0.9		1.1		2.4	5.2
Kegalle	6.9	0.7		3.9		1.9	5.8
Sabaragamuwa province	12.5	1.5		5.0		4.2	11.0
Total population *(1000s)*	5621.3	908.7		468.1		93.3	8098.6

Population Census 1963

District and Province	Sinhala	Sri Lanka Tamil	Indian Tamil	Sri Lanka Moor	Indian Moor	Other[a]	Total
Colombo	24.3	11.4	5.1	17.1	42.4	65.9	20.4
Gampaha[b]							
Kalutara	7.3	0.4	3.4	5.8	1.2	1.7	6.0
Western province	31.6	11.7	8.4	22.9	43.6	67.6	26.4
Kandy	8.3	2.8	26.2	12.4	13.5	8.2	9.9
Matale	2.5	0.8	3.9	2.3	3.5	0.9	2.4
Nuwara Eliya	2.0	0.9	20.1	0.8	3.3	2.1	3.8
Central province	12.8	4.4	50.2	15.6	20.3	11.2	16.1
Galle	8.0	0.3	1.1	3.0	0.5	1.3	6.1
Matara	6.4	0.2	1.4	2.0	0.2	0.5	4.9
Hambantota	3.5	0.0	0.0	0.6	0.1	2.8	2.6
Southern province	18.0	0.6	2.6	5.6	0.8	4.6	13.6
Jaffna	0.1	50.1	1.0	1.3	1.9	1.0	5.8
Mannar	0.0	2.6	0.9	2.3	5.4	0.2	0.6
Vavuniya	0.2	3.7	0.7	0.7	0.5	0.2	0.7
Mullaitive[b]							
Northern province	0.3	56.5	2.6	4.3	7.7	1.4	7.1
Batticaloa	0.0	12.0	0.1	7.3	0.6	2.0	1.9
Ampara	0.8	4.2	0.1	15.6	1.2	0.9	2.0
Trincomalee	0.5	4.4	0.3	6.5	2.3	2.1	1.3
Eastern province	1.4	20.6	0.6	29.4	4.1	5.1	5.2
Kurunegala	10.5	0.9	1.0	5.5	6.3	2.2	8.1
Puttalam	3.2	1.9	0.7	4.5	2.9	1.3	2.9
North western province	13.8	2.7	1.7	10.1	9.1	3.5	11.0
Anuradhapura	3.3	0.6	0.2	3.1	1.6	0.5	2.7
Polonnaruwa	1.3	0.4	0.0	1.5	0.8	0.3	1.1
North central province	4.7	1.0	0.2	4.6	2.4	0.8	3.7
Badulla	3.8	1.3	17.6	2.5	3.8	3.2	4.9
Moneragala	1.5	0.1	1.1	0.4	0.7	0.5	1.3
Uva province	5.4	1.5	18.6	3.0	4.5	3.7	6.2
Ratnapura	5.6	0.6	9.3	1.0	3.9	1.2	5.2
Kegalle	6.4	0.4	5.9	3.6	3.6	0.9	5.5
Sabaragamuwa province	12.1	1.0	15.2	4.6	7.4	2.1	10.7
Total population (1000s)	7512.7	1164.7	1123.0	626.8	55.4	99.3	10482.6

Population Census 1971

District and Province	Sinhala	Sri Lanka Tamil	Indian Tamil	Sri Lanka Moor	Indian Moor	Other[a]	Total
Colombo	24.3	11.9	5.1	17.9	23.1	66.6	20.7
Gampaha[b]							
Kalutara	6.9	0.5	3.3	6.0	1.9	1.3	5.8
Western province	31.2	12.4	8.4	23.9	24.9	67.9	26.5
Kandy	8.1	3.6	24.4	11.7	16.2	8.1	9.4
Matale	2.6	0.8	4.0	2.4	4.2	1.1	2.5
Nuwara Eliya	2.0	1.3	20.0	0.9	4.5	1.8	3.6
Central province	12.7	5.6	48.4	15.0	25.0	10.9	15.4
Galle	7.6	0.3	1.3	2.7	1.1	0.9	5.8
Matara	6.0	0.1	1.6	1.8	0.4	0.4	4.7
Hambantota	3.6	0.1	0.0	0.5	0.0	3.3	2.7
Southern province	17.2	0.5	2.9	4.9	1.6	4.5	13.2
Jaffna	0.0	46.8	1.5	1.2	2.1	0.6	5.6
Mannar	0.0	2.8	1.1	2.4	6.9	0.0	0.6
Vavuniya	0.2	4.1	1.2	0.8	1.1	0.3	0.8
Mullaitive[b]							
Northern province	0.3	53.7	3.8	4.3	10.2	1.1	6.9
Batticaloa	0.1	12.4	0.4	7.4	2.3	2.0	2.0
Ampara	0.9	4.2	0.2	15.3	2.7	0.9	2.2
Trincomalee	0.6	4.6	0.4	7.3	1.8	1.8	1.5
Eastern province	1.6	21.3	0.9	29.9	6.8	4.7	5.7
Kurunegala	10.4	0.7	1.1	5.6	5.8	2.5	8.1
Puttalam	3.4	1.8	0.5	4.5	2.5	1.7	3.0
North western province	13.8	2.5	1.6	10.1	8.3	4.2	11.1
Anuradhapura	3.9	0.5	0.2	3.1	3.1	0.7	3.1
Polonnaruwa	1.6	0.3	0.0	1.4	0.4	0.1	1.3
North central province	5.5	0.9	0.2	4.5	3.5	0.8	4.4
Badulla	4.0	1.4	17.8	2.4	7.9	3.0	4.9
Moneragala	1.9	0.2	1.0	0.5	0.3	0.4	1.5
Uva province	5.9	1.6	18.8	2.9	8.2	3.3	6.4
Ratnapura	5.8	0.7	9.6	1.0	6.6	1.3	5.2
Kegalle	6.0	0.8	5.3	3.5	4.8	1.2	5.2
Sabaragamuwa province	11.8	1.5	14.9	4.5	11.4	2.5	10.4
Total population *(1000s)*	9131.2	1424.0	1174.6	828.3	27.4	104.3	12585.6

Population Census 1981

District and Province	Sinhala	Sri Lanka Tamil	Indian Tamil	Sri Lanka Moor	Indian Moor	Other[a]	Total
Colombo	12.0	9.0	2.4	13.3		43.8	11.2
Gampaha	11.7	2.6	0.7	3.6		16.9	9.3
Kalutara	6.6	0.5	4.1	5.8		1.4	5.6
Western province	30.3	12.1	7.3	22.8		62.2	26.1
Kandy	7.1	2.8	12.0	10.5		7.4	7.1
Matale	2.6	1.1	3.0	2.4		1.3	2.4
Nuwara Eliya	2.3	4.1	31.5	1.2		2.7	4.1
Central province	12.0	7.9	46.5	14.0		11.4	13.5
Galle	7.0	0.4	1.4	2.5		1.0	5.5
Matara	5.5	0.2	1.7	1.5		0.5	4.4
Hambantota	3.8	0.1	0.0	0.5		4.0	2.8
Southern province	16.3	0.8	3.1	4.5		5.6	12.7
Jaffna	0.0	41.9	2.4	1.2		0.5	5.6
Mannar	0.0	2.9	1.7	2.6		1.3	0.7
Vavuniya	0.1	2.9	2.3	0.6		0.2	0.6
Mullaitive	0.0	3.1	1.4	0.3		0.1	0.5
Northern province	0.3	50.7	7.8	4.9		2.1	7.5
Batticaloa	0.1	12.4	0.5	7.5		2.1	2.2
Ampara	1.3	4.1	0.2	15.4		1.1	2.6
Trincomalee	0.8	4.7	0.7	7.2		2.0	1.7
Eastern province	2.2	21.2	1.3	30.1		5.2	6.6
Kurunegala	10.3	0.8	0.8	5.8		3.1	8.2
Puttalam	3.7	1.7	0.3	4.7		1.7	3.3
North western province	14.0	2.5	1.1	10.5		4.8	11.5
Anuradhapura	4.9	0.4	0.0	4.0		1.4	4.0
Polonnaruwa	2.2	0.3	0.0	1.6		0.5	1.8
North central province	7.1	0.7	0.1	5.6		1.9	5.8
Badulla	4.0	2.0	15.8	2.5		3.8	4.3
Moneragala	2.3	0.3	1.1	0.5		0.4	1.9
Uva province	6.3	2.3	16.9	3.0		4.2	6.2
Ratnapura	6.2	1.0	10.4	1.3		1.7	5.4
Kegalle	5.4	0.8	5.6	3.3		1.0	4.6
Sabaragamuwa province	11.5	1.8	15.9	4.6		2.7	10.0
Total population *(1000s)*	10979.6	1886.9	818.7	1046.9		114.7	14732.0

1.2   Population by community as a percentages of district and provincial totals

Population Census 1946

District and Province	Sinhala	Sri Lanka Tamil	Indian Tamil	Sri Lanka Moor	Indian Moor	Other[a]	Popul. (1000s)
Colombo	81.1	4.1	4.3	4.2	1.3	5.0	1420.3
Gampaha[b]							
Kalutara	86.8	0.8	6.4	5.4	0.0	0.5	456.6
Western province	82.5	3.3	4.8	4.5	1.0	3.9	1876.9
Kandy	57.8	4.2	29.2	6.8	0.6	1.3	711.4
Matale	68.1	3.1	21.9	5.3	0.7	0.8	155.7
Nuwara Eliya	37.8	2.0	57.3	1.4	0.5	1.0	268.1
Central province	54.5	3.5	34.9	5.3	0.6	1.2	1135.3
Galle	94.5	0.7	1.5	3.0	0.0	0.3	459.8
Matara	94.4	0.7	2.1	2.5	0.0	0.2	351.9
Hambantota	96.6	0.5	0.2	1.6	0.0	1.1	149.7
Southern province	94.8	0.6	1.5	2.6	0.0	0.4	961.4
Jaffna	1.1	96.3	1.0	1.2	0.1	0.3	424.8
Mannar	3.8	51.0	11.2	30.1	2.9	1.0	31.5
Vavuniya	16.6	69.3	4.2	8.7	0.5	0.7	23.2
Mullaitiveb							
Northern province	2.0	92.0	1.8	3.5	0.3	0.4	479.6
Batticaloa	5.8	49.7	0.6	42.0	0.2	1.6	203.2
Ampara[c]							
Trincomalee	20.7	40.1	4.4	29.2	1.4	4.2	75.9
Eastern province	9.9	47.1	1.6	38.5	0.5	2.3	279.1
Kurunegala	92.2	1.5	1.6	3.8	0.4	0.5	485.0
Puttalam	52.0	12.8	2.1	30.8	0.8	1.5	43.1
Chilaw[d]	87.0	5.2	3.3	2.9	0.3	1.3	139.8
North western province	88.5	3.0	2.0	5.4	0.4	0.7	667.9
Anuradhapura	79.7	6.7	2.2	10.1	0.6	0.7	139.5
Polonnaruwa[c]							
North central province	79.7	6.7	2.2	10.1	0.6	0.7	139.5
Badulla	57.4	4.2	34.2	2.7	0.5	1.1	372.2
Moneragala[c]							
Uva province	57.4	4.2	34.2	2.7	0.5	1.1	372.2
Ratnapura	75.8	1.2	20.6	1.4	0.3	0.7	343.6
Kegalle	82.1	0.8	12.9	3.5	0.2	0.4	401.8
Sabaragamuwa province	79.2	1.0	16.5	2.5	0.3	0.6	745.4
Sri Lanka	69.4	11.0	11.7	5.6	0.5	1.7	6657.3

Population Census 1953[c]

District and Province	Sinhala	Sri Lanka Tamil	Indian Tamil[f]	Sri Lanka Moor	Indian Moor[f]	Other[a]	Popul. (1000s)
Colombo	80.6	5.4		4.7		3.3	1707.9
Gampaha[b]							
Kalutara	86.4	1.2		5.5		0.4	523.9
Western province	82.0	4.4		4.9		2.6	2231.8
Kandy	57.7	3.8		6.9		1.0	840.4
Matale	69.2	4.6		5.7		0.5	201.1
Nuwara Eliya	35.9	2.8		1.5		0.6	325.0
Central province	54.2	3.7		5.4		0.8	1366.6
Galle	94.2	0.7		2.8		0.3	524.4
Matara	94.0	0.7		2.5		0.1	413.9
Hambantota	96.7	0.6		1.7		0.8	191.7
Southern province	94.5	0.7		2.5		0.3	1130.0
Jaffna	1.3	95.4		1.3		0.2	492.4
Mannar	4.8	46.3		25.1		0.2	43.7
Vavuniya	16.8	67.3		8.2		0.5	35.1
Mullaitive[h]							
Northern province	2.5	89.9		3.6		0.2	571.2
Batticaloa	11.5	48.0		38.9		0.8	270.7
Ampara[c]							
Trincomalee	17.9	41.6		33.2		1.9	84.5
Eastern province	13.0	46.5		37.5		1.0	355.2
Kurunegala	92.1	1.6		4.0		0.6	626.1
Puttalam	53.5	13.7		29.1		1.0	58.9
Chilaw[d]	87.0	5.2		2.9		0.5	170.0
North western province	88.4	3.2		5.6		0.6	854.9
Anuradhapura	83.4	6.2		8.1		0.5	229.2
Polonnaruwa[c]							
North central province	83.4	6.2		8.1		0.5	229.2
Badulla	57.5	4.0		3.0		1.0	468.8
Moneragala[c]							
Uva province	57.5	4.0		3.0		1.0	468.8
Ratnapura	75.7	1.9		1.2		0.5	420.3
Kegalle	82.3	1.3		3.8		0.4	470.5
Sabaragamuwa province	79.2	1.6		2.6		0.4	890.8
Sri Lanka	69.4	11.2		5.8		1.2	8098.6

Population Census 1963

District and Province	Sinhala	Sri Lanka Tamil	Indian Tamil	Sri Lanka Moor	Indian Moor	Other[a]	Popul. (1000s)
Colombo	85.1	6.2	2.7	5.0	1.1	3.1	2142.0
Gampaha[b]							
Kalutara	87.4	0.7	6.0	5.8	0.1	0.3	629.8
Western province	85.6	4.9	3.4	5.2	0.9	2.4	2771.8
Kandy	60.3	3.1	28.4	7.5	0.7	0.8	1035.5
Matale	72.6	3.6	17.4	5.8	0.8	0.4	254.7
Nuwara Eliya	38.6	2.5	57.1	1.3	0.5	0.5	395.7
Central province	57.1	3.0	33.4	5.8	0.7	0.7	1685.9
Galle	94.4	0.6	2.0	2.9	0.0	0.2	640.2
Matara	94.0	0.4	3.1	2.4	0.0	0.1	514.4
Hambantota	98.0	0.4	0.1	1.5	0.0	1.0	271.5
Southern province	95.0	0.5	2.0	2.5	0.0	0.3	1426.2
Jaffna	1.2	95.4	1.9	1.3	0.2	0.2	611.6
Mannar	4.2	50.9	16.1	23.8	4.9	0.3	59.9
Vavuniya	17.8	63.7	11.3	6.8	0.4	0.4	68.4
Mullaitive[b]							
Northern province	3.0	88.9	3.9	3.6	0.6	0.2	739.9
Batticaloa	3.5	71.8	0.9	23.7	0.2	1.0	194.2
Ampara	29.3	23.4	0.6	46.3	0.3	0.4	210.6
Trincomalee	29.3	37.4	2.5	29.9	0.9	1.6	136.4
Eastern province	20.0	44.3	1.2	34.1	0.4	0.9	541.2
Kurunegala	93.0	1.2	1.3	4.1	0.4	0.3	850.5
Puttalam	80.3	7.3	2.4	9.4	0.5	0.4	301.3
North western province	89.7	2.8	1.6	5.5	0.4	0.3	1151.8
Anuradhapura	89.6	2.5	0.6	7.0	0.3	0.2	279.3
Polonnaruwa	87.4	3.8	0.2	8.2	0.4	0.2	113.7
North central province	89.0	2.9	0.5	7.3	0.3	0.2	393.0
Badulla	55.5	3.0	38.0	3.1	0.4	0.6	518.6
Moneragala	87.4	1.1	9.1	2.1	0.3	0.4	131.8
Uva province	62.0	2.6	32.2	2.9	0.4	0.6	650.4
Ratnapura	77.9	1.4	19.2	1.1	0.4	0.2	544.9
Kegalle	83.6	0.7	11.4	3.9	0.3	0.2	577.6
Sabaragamuwa province	80.8	1.1	15.2	2.5	0.4	0.2	1122.4
Sri Lanka	71.7	11.1	10.7	6.0	0.5	0.9	10482.6

Population Census 1971

District and Province	Sinhala	Sri Lanka Tamil	Indian Tamil	Sri Lanka Moor	Indian Moor	Other[a]	Popul. (1000s)
Colombo	85.3	6.5	2.3	5.7	0.2	2.7	2602.8
Gampaha[b]							
Kalutara	86.7	1.0	5.3	6.9	0.0	0.2	728.1
Western province	85.6	5.3	2.9	5.9	0.2	2.1	3330.9
Kandy	62.8	4.3	24.3	8.2	0.4	0.7	1179.5
Matale	74.8	3.5	14.9	6.4	0.4	0.4	313.7
Nuwara Eliya	41.5	4.1	52.5	1.6	0.3	0.4	448.4
Central province	59.8	4.1	29.3	6.4	0.4	0.6	1941.6
Galle	94.4	0.5	2.1	3.0	0.0	0.1	734.3
Matara	94.0	0.4	3.2	2.5	0.0	0.0	586.0
Hambantota	98.1	0.5	0.0	1.3	0.0	1.0	336.9
Southern province	95.0	0.4	2.1	2.5	0.0	0.3	1657.1
Jaffna	1.0	95.0	2.6	1.4	0.0	0.0	701.0
Mannar	4.1	51.5	16.7	25.3	2.4	0.1	77.7
Vavuniya	16.8	61.6	14.6	6.7	0.3	0.4	94.9
Mullaitive[b]							
Northern province	3.0	87.5	5.1	4.1	0.3	0.1	873.5
Batticaloa	4.5	69.6	1.7	23.9	0.2	0.8	254.6
Ampara	30.3	22.3	0.7	46.5	0.3	0.3	271.7
Trincomalee	29.4	35.4	2.7	32.3	0.3	1.0	186.4
Eastern province	20.8	42.6	1.6	34.7	0.3	0.7	712.7
Kurunegala	93.1	0.9	1.3	4.5	0.2	0.3	1023.0
Puttalam	81.5	6.8	1.6	9.9	0.2	0.5	376.6
North western province	90.0	2.5	1.4	6.0	0.2	0.3	1399.6
Anuradhapura	90.6	2.0	0.5	6.7	0.2	0.2	388.1
Polonnaruwa	89.9	3.0	0.2	6.9	0.0	0.0	163.5
North central province	90.4	2.3	0.4	6.7	0.2	0.2	551.6
Badulla	59.0	3.2	34.2	3.3	0.4	0.5	612.3
Moneragala	90.2	1.6	6.0	2.1	0.0	0.2	192.6
Uva province	66.5	2.8	27.5	3.0	0.3	0.4	804.9
Ratnapura	79.9	1.4	17.2	1.2	0.3	0.2	660.0
Kegalle	84.2	1.7	9.4	4.4	0.2	0.2	653.5
Sabaragamuwa province	82.0	1.6	13.3	2.8	0.2	0.2	1313.5
Sri Lanka	72.6	11.3	9.3	6.6	0.2	0.8	12585.6

Population Census 1981

District and Province	Sinhala	Sri Lanka Tamil	Indian Tamil	Sri Lanka Moor	Indian Moor[g]	Other[a]	Popul. (1000s)
Colombo	80.0	10.3	1.2	8.5		3.0	1649.0
Gampaha	93.3	3.5	0.4	2.8		1.4	1371.4
Kalutara	87.4	1.2	4.1	7.4		0.2	828.0
Western province	86.3	5.9	1.5	6.2		1.9	3848.5
Kandy	74.9	5.1	9.5	10.6		0.8	1039.8
Matale	80.2	5.8	7.0	7.0		0.4	355.8
Nuwara Eliya	42.4	12.7	42.9	2.0		0.5	600.5
Central province	66.1	7.5	19.1	7.4		0.7	1996.1
Galle	94.6	0.9	1.4	3.2		0.1	813.3
Matara	94.6	0.7	2.2	2.5		0.0	643.2
Hambantota	98.2	0.6	0.0	1.2		1.1	419.7
Southern province	95.4	0.8	1.3	2.5		0.3	1876.3
Jaffna	0.8	95.2	2.4	1.6		0.0	830.0
Mannar	8.3	52.0	13.2	26.5		1.4	104.7
Vavuniya	16.6	56.9	19.7	6.8		0.2	95.2
Mullaitive	5.2	75.5	14.6	4.7		0.2	77.1
Northern province	3.2	86.5	5.8	4.6		0.2	1107.0
Batticaloa	3.4	71.3	1.2	24.0		0.8	327.9
Ampara	37.9	20.1	0.4	41.7		0.3	387.7
Trincomalee	33.7	34.6	2.1	29.6		0.9	253.7
Eastern province	25.1	41.2	1.1	32.5		0.6	969.3
Kurunegala	93.2	1.2	0.5	5.0		0.3	1208.2
Puttalam	83.0	6.6	0.5	10.0		0.4	490.6
North western province	90.2	2.8	0.5	6.5		0.3	1698.9
Anuradhapura	91.4	1.4	0.1	7.1		0.3	586.4
Polonnaruwa	91.6	2.0	0.0	6.4		0.2	261.0
North central province	91.4	1.6	0.0	6.9		0.3	847.3
Badulla	69.6	5.9	20.3	4.2		0.7	636.6
Moneragala	92.9	2.0	3.2	1.9		0.2	273.1
Uva province	76.6	4.7	15.2	3.5		0.5	909.7
Ratnapura	85.2	2.4	10.7	1.7		0.2	795.1
Kegalle	86.1	2.2	6.7	5.0		0.2	683.8
Sabaragamuwa province	85.6	2.3	8.8	3.3		0.2	1478.9
Sri Lanka	74.5	12.8	5.6	7.1		0.8	14732.0

a. This category includes Burgher, Eurasian, European, Malay, Veddah and other ethnic categories, except for the year 1981, which includes Indian Moor as well.
b. Gampaha and Mullaitive were not separate districts. Gamapaha was part of Colombo, and Mullaitive was part of Vavuniya until the enumeration in 1981.
c. Ampara, Polonnaruwa and Moneragala were not enumerated separately in 1946 and 1953. They were included respectively in Batticaloa, Anuradhapura and Badulla.
d. In 1946 and 1953, Chilaw was reported as a separate district. For these years, population censuses were based on 'revenue districts', which were different from 'administrative districts', on which the population census in the latter periods were based. In the classification according to 'administrative districts' Chilaw is included in Puttalam.
e. In 1953, only 'Citizens of Ceylon' were enumerated, but the row total includes the whole population.
f. The Indian Tamil and Indian Moor categories were not reported separately, but were included in the total population.
g. The Indian Moor category, which was included in 'other', was not reported separately in the population census of 1981.

Source: DCS (Population Census).

Trade Indices for Imports of Consumer Goods 1950-1990: Volume, Value and Price

(1950 = 100)

Year	Food and drinks			Other consumer goods[a]		
	Volume	Value	Price	Volume	Value	Price
1950	100	100	100	100	100	100
1951	101	120	107	163	216	140
1952	101	140	129	151	208	140
1953	105	133	129	151	188	160
1954	101	113	114	113	136	160
1955	101	100	107	166	196	160
1956	114	120	107	190	232	160
1957	115	127	107	204	260	160
1958	122	120	100	227	300	160
1959	136	140	100	293	376	160
1960	127	127	100	335	420	160
1961	117	113	100	111	136	160
1962	110	107	100	102	112	160
1963	105	107	107	56	56	220
1964	144	160	129	118	64	180
1965	94	100	114	74	48	240
1966	153	160	107	102	72	240
1967	126	133	107	79	60	220
1968	123	167	143	77	56	320
1969	117	160	143	85	68	320
1970	135	180	143	95	84	340
1971	105	153	157	71	52	340
1972	149	153	186	96	76	280
1973	121	213	250	94	48	400
1974	73	347	486	118	64	340
1975	84	440	607	106	88	400
1976	75	280	414	211	116	640
1977	131	380	450	104	64	960
1978	97	667	714	122	400	2000
1979	90	749	935	102	471	3215
1980	75	956	1429	141	644	3181
1981	46	713	1764	122	596	3420
1982	35	478	1535	151	876	4036

Year	Food and drinks			Other consumer goods[a]		
	Volume	Value	Price	Volume	Value	Price
1983	62	778	1411	184	1061	4036
1984	61	713	1323	138	918	4685
1985	80	934	1323	140	1120	5609
1986	82	1067	1466	144	1355	6607
1987	81	1180	1654	151	1562	7258
1988	82	1616	2236	137	1777	9092
1989	83	2078	2828	118	1925	11431
1990	85	2399	3209	149	3147	14852
1991	92	2651	3273	162	3840	16649
1992	85	2912	3879	123	3393	19397
1993	114	3176	3161	142	4255	20986
1994	140	3783	3052	175	5429	21847
1995	107	4229	4457	176	5801	23080

a. Other consumer goods includes consumer durables and others, excluding textiles, which are considered intermediate goods in the source.
Source: CBSL (*ROE* annual issues).

Appendix III

Monthly Expenditure per Spending Unit[a], CFS Years 1953–1986/87

as a percentage of total expenditure[b]

Consumption categories[c]	1953	1963	1973	1978/79	1981/82	1986/87
Food consumption						
Rice	17.8	11.0	15.0	15.1	16.3	12.6
own production/rationed	–	5.5	10.3	5.9	4.2	2.7
bought/ not rationed	–	5.6	4.7	9.2	12.2	9.9
Flour	3.6	2.0	2.2	2.7	2.3	1.2
Bread	2.5	2.2	2.2	3.1	2.9	2.5
Other cereals	0.4	0.3	0.3	0.2	0.3	0.2
Consumed outside residence	1.6	–	–	1.2	–	0.7
Consumed at residence	–	–	–	–	–	0.5
Sugar	4.4	5.6	3.5	2.8	3.7	3.5
Sweets/bakery products	0.3	1.5	0.7	0.6	0.5	0.5
Meat	1.4	3.1	1.0	1.1	1.0	1.0
Meat products	–	–	–	–	–	0.1
Fish	4.7	4.8	4.3	4.7	4.7	5.0
Eggs	0.6	1.1	0.6	0.5	0.4	0.6
Starchy food	–	2.0	1.5	1.5	1.8	1.3
Vegetables	6.9	6.0	4.3	3.7	3.8	3.1
Leafy vegetables	–	–	–	–	–	0.5
Pulses	–	2.2	0.9	1.2	1.1	1.7
Condiments	5.5	3.0	7.9	5.2	4.7	4.6
Coconut	3.7	4.0	3.8	3.9	3.8	3.2
Palmyrah products	–	–	–	0.0	–	0.0
Cooking oil/fat	1.5	1.2	0.9	0.9	1.7	0.8
Jaggery and treacle	0.2	–	–	0.5	–	0.0
Milk	1.9	2.4	1.5	1.7	1.9	2.4
Milk products	0.4	0.4	0.2	0.2	0.1	0.3
Fresh fruits	0.8	1.0	0.5	0.8	0.8	1.1
Dried fruits	–	–	–	–	–	0.0
Tinned fruits	–	–	–	–	–	0.0
Oil seeds/nuts	–	–	–	–	–	0.0
Preserved food	0.0	–	–	0.0	–	0.1
Beverage (non-alcoholic)	2.0	2.5	1.3	1.1	1.1	1.4
Beverage (alcoholic)	2.6	3.9	1.3	1.3	0.9	1.1
Narcotics	–	–	–	0.0		0.0
Miscellaneous	4.0	4.6	6.3	3.4	2.9	2.9
Total	66.8	64.9	60.2	57.5	57.7	52.7

Consumption categories[c]	1953	1963	1973	1978/79	1981/82	1986/87
Non-food consumption						
Housing	3.6	7.4	6.8	5.6	5.8	7.9
Clothing	8.0	9.6	7.6	10.4	7.1	7.6
Fuel and electricity	2.0	4.5	4.2	3.9	5.2	4.6
Water	–	–	–	–	–	0.0
Transport and communications	2.6	2.2	3.4	4.5	3.9	5.0
Education	2.0	1.8	2.2	1.7	1.6	2.1
Recreation	1.3	0.7	0.8	1.4	1.2	2.0
Social and religious functions	1.9	1.6	2.2	3.1	3.1	3.9
Laundry and cleaning	1.4	1.5	1.2	1.1	1.3	1.1
Litigation	0.4	0.0	0.4	0.2	0.4	0.4
Gifts and donations	1.8	1.1	1.3	1.9	1.7	1.9
Personal expenditure	2.0	0.2	1.4	1.9	2.3	2.3
Servants/drivers	–	1.3	0.7	0.6	0.5	0.7
Medical	1.3	2.9	1.6	1.7	1.6	2.2
Infant requirements	–	–	–	0.0	0.0	0.0
Insurance	–	–	–	–	–	0.0
Miscellaneous	1.6	–	–	–	–	0.1
Total	30.0	34.7	33.8	37.9	35.8	42.1
Consumer durables						
Jewelry	1.2	0.1	0.6	0.6	1.6	1.1
Other	2.0	0.3	5.5	4.0	4.9	4.1
Total	3.2	0.4	6.1	4.6	6.5	5.2
Grand total	100	100	100	100	100	100

a. In the source, a 'spending unit' is one or more persons who take independent decisions with respect to spending, with their dependents.
b. Total expenditure does not include interest payments on loans and tax payments, as they were not recorded in some of the surveys.
c. The classification of consumption categories differs from survey to survey.
Source: CBSL (*CFSs*).

Monthly Income of Consumer Units, CFS Years 1963–1986/87

Appendix IV

4.1 Income per average consumer units

	1963	1973	1978/79	1981/82	1986/87
Number of:					
Households	4984	5088	7617	7927	7065
Spending units	5399	5363	8384	8388	7617
Income receivers	7781	7326	12524	12344	11434
Persons	28668	28587	41564	41451	36013
Monthly income (Rs.)					
in current values	1040272	1666733	7725472	13712606	20779185
in constant values	1061502	986232	2302674	2500019	2400830
GNP deflator (1960=100)[a]	98	169	335.5	548.5	865.5
Monthly real income per:					
Household	213.0	193.8	302.3	315.4	339.8
Spending unit	196.6	183.9	274.7	298.0	315.2
Income receiver	136.4	134.6	183.9	202.5	210.0
Person	37.0	34.5	55.4	60.3	66.7

a. GNP deflator for 1978/79, 1981/82 and 1986/87 is the average of annual deflators for the respective years.
Source: CBSL (*CFSs*).

4.2 Income disparity of income receivers by zones and sectors[a]

Sample population: number of income receivers and persons

Zones & Sectors	Sample population				
	1963	1973	1978/79	1981/82	1986/87
Zone 1	10094	9017	14278	12873	12464
Zone 2	3056	4256	4984	7074	7007
Zone 3	3004	2905	3902	4516	–
Zone 4	12514	11358	16555	15461	15176
Zone 5	–	1051	1845	1527	1366
Urban	4590	5378	9544	7943	6511
Rural	20916	20432	28424	30766	26634
Estate	3162	2777	3596	2742	2868
All island	28668	28587	41564	41451	36013

Sample population: number of income receivers and persons (continued)

Zones & Sectors	Income receivers				
	1963	1973	1978/79	1981/82	1986/87
Zone 1	2700	2430	4342	3963	4087
Zone 2	701	882	1262	1774	1916
Zone 3	713	610	994	1202	–
Zone 4	3667	3159	5358	4924	4952
Zone 5	–	245	568	481	479
Urban	1152	1285	2740	2381	2244
Rural	5102	4746	7958	8558	7873
Estate	1527	1295	1826	1405	1317
All island	7781	7326	12524	12344	11434

Total and average monthly income of income receivers

Zones & Sectors	Total monthly income (Rs)				
	1963	1973	1978/79	1981/82	1986/87
Zone 1	451663	637647	2721257	4462375	8201214
Zone 2	97853	231411	899724	2098612	3807437
Zone 3	112227	166693	737276	1361427	–
Zone 4	378530	563504	2722944	4838184	6930055
Zone 5	–	67480	644271	952008	1840479
Urban	293865	406495	2267389	3868354	6539434
Rural	647972	1106948	4909288	9213728	13180344
Estate	98435	153290	548795	630524	1059407
All island	1040272	1666733	7725472	13712606	20779185

Zones & Sectors	Average monthly income (Rs)				
	1963	1973	1978/79	1981/82	1986/87
Zone 1	167	262	627	1126	2007
Zone 2	140	262	713	1183	1987
Zone 3	157	273	742	1133	–
Zone 4	103	178	508	983	1399
Zone 5	–	275	1134	1979	3842
Urban	255	316	828	1625	2914
Rural	127	233	617	1077	1674
Estate	64	118	301	449	804
All island	134	228	617	1111	1817

Indice for average monthly income per income receiver

Zones & Sectors	GNP deflator (1960 = 100)[b]				
	1963	1973	1978/79	1981/82	1986/87
Zone 1	171	155	187	205	232
Zone 2	142	155	212	215	229
Zone 3	161	162	221	206	–
Zone 4	105	106	151	179	162
Zone 5	–	163	338	361	444
Urban	260	187	246	296	337
Rural	130	138	184	196	193
Estate	66	70	89	82	93
All island	136	135	184	202	210

Zones & Sectors	GNP deflator (1960 = 100)[b]				
	1963	1973	1978/79	1981/82	1986/87
Zone 1	125	115	102	101	110
Zone 2	104	115	116	106	109
Zone 3	118	120	120	102	–
Zone 4	77	78	82	88	77
Zone 5	–	121	184	178	211
Urban	191	139	134	146	160
Rural	95	103	100	97	92
Estate	48	52	49	40	44
All island	100	100	100	100	100

a. Zones refer to the agro-climatic divisions adopted in the CFSs, while the sectors refer to urban, rural and estate sectors. The zone classification of the island is as follows:

Zone 1: Districts of Colombo excluding the Colombo Municipality, Gampaha, Kalutara, Galle and Matara.

Zone 2: Districts of Hambantota, Monaragala, Ampara, Polonnaruwa, Anuradhapura and Puttalam.

Zone 3: Districts of Jaffna, Mannar, Vavuniya, Mullative, Trincomalee and Batticaloa.

Zone 4: Districts of Kandy, Matale, Nuwara Eliya, Badulla, Ratnapura, Kegalle and Kurunegala.

Zone 5: Colombo Municipality.

Zone 5 was notdid not exist as a separate zone in survey year 1963, but was included in zone 1. Data for Zone 3 are not available for 1986/87, as the survey in this zone was not carried out due to the Tamil separatist war in this area.

b. GNP deflator is used as of Appendix table 4.1 above.

Source: CBSL (*CFSs*).

5.1 Rate of unemployment, as a percentage of labour force in each age group[a]

Year	Age group	14-18	19-25	26-35	36-45	46-55	over 55	Total
'63	Rate of unemployment	47.5	30.3	7.8	2.4	2.7	1.9	13.8
	Labour force:							
	number in the sample	939	1789	2153	1854	1397	894	9097
	as % of the sample							
	population	28.5	57.2	60.8	64.0	67.1	43.0	31.8
'73	Rate of unemployment	65.8	47.5	15.2	3.9	1.2	0.8	24.0
	Labour force:							
	number in the sample	1131	2419	2260	1824	1114	929	9695
	as % of the sample							
	population	34.3	64.5	64.4	64.4	60.9	38.7	33.9
'78/79	Rate of unemployment	29.6	30.0	12.5	2.6	0.6	0.2	14.1
	Labour force:							
	number in the sample	1587	3828	3988	2784	1991	1401	15678
	as % of the sample							
	population	31.1	67.2	69.9	69.5	63.1	38.1	37.7
'81/82	Rate of unemployment	30.1	28.8	8.8	1.7	0.5	0.1	11.7
	Labour force:							
	number in the sample	1074	3271	3833	2664	1967	1343	14205
	as % of the sample							
	population	22.9	58.4	64.1	65.3	59.5	36.3	34.3
'86/87	Rate of unemployment	48.0	35.3	10.6	3.2	0.7	0.6	15.5
	Labour force:							
	number in the sample	1173	3070	3502	2780	1889	1281	13734
	as % of the sample							
	population	27.9	68.4	68.2	69.0	62.0	32.0	38.1

a. Labour force is the sum of unemployed and employed people over the age 14. For working definitions of employed and employed population, see notes to Appendix table 5.2.

5.2 Employment,[a] unemployment,[b] labour force and sample population, as a percentage of population in each category

Year	Age group	14-18	19-25	26-35	36-45	46-55	over 55	Total[c]
'63	Employed	6.3	16.0	25.5	23.3	17.5	11.3	7842
	Unemployed	35.5	43.2	13.4	3.5	3.0	1.4	1255
	Labour force	10.4	19.8	23.9	20.5	15.5	9.9	9097
	Sample population	19.4	18.4	20.8	17.0	12.2	12.2	28646
'73	Employed	5.3	17.3	26.1	23.8	15.0	12.5	7369
	Unemployed	32.0	49.4	14.7	3.1	0.6	0.3	2326
	Labour force	11.7	25.0	23.4	18.8	11.5	9.6	9695
	Sample population	18.7	21.3	19.9	16.1	10.4	13.6	28587
'78/79	Employed	8.4	20.0	26.1	20.3	14.8	10.5	13473
	Unemployed	21.3	52.2	22.6	3.2	0.5	0.1	2205
	Labour force	10.2	24.6	25.6	17.9	12.8	9.0	15678
	Sample population	18.6	20.8	20.9	14.7	11.5	13.5	41564
'81/82	Employed	6.0	18.6	28.0	21.0	15.7	10.7	12547
	Unemployed	19.5	56.8	20.4	2.7	0.5	0.1	1658
	Labour force	7.6	23.1	27.1	18.8	13.9	9.5	14205
	Sample population	17.2	20.5	21.8	14.9	12.1	13.5	41451
'86/87	Employed	5.3	17.2	27.1	23.3	16.2	11.0	11604
	Unemployed	26.4	50.9	17.4	4.2	0.7	0.4	2130
	Labour force	8.6	22.4	25.6	20.3	13.8	9.4	13734
	Sample population	16.9	18.0	20.6	16.2	12.2	16.1	36013

a. Employed includes (a) self-employed, (b) employer (c) employee and, (d) unpaid family worker.
b. Unemployed does not include (a) juniors under 14 years old, (b) people infirm and unable to work and, (c) people who have not been seeking work (voluntarily unemployed).
c. Totals, except the category of unemployed, include the population in the age group below 14 years as well. Therefore, the total employed and the total labour force include a few persons under 14 years of age who were reported in the surveys as 'employed'.

Unemployment by Education Level, CFS Years 1953–1986/87

Appendix VI

6.1 Rate of unemployment, as a percentage of labour force in each education group[a]

Year		Illiterate	Literate	No schooling[b] Total	primary	secundary	SSC or GCE (OL)	HSC or GCE (AL)	degree	Total[d]
		No schooling[b]			Education		Passed[c]			
'53	Unemployed	—	—	190	264	71	14	2	—	540
	Labour force	—	—	1144	1606	394	57	53	—	3254
	Unemployment rate	—	—	16.6	16.4	17.9	25.0	3.0	—	16.6
'63e	Unemployed	116	44	160	387	468	212	26	—	1254
	Labour force	1851	770	2621	3671	2038	540	187	—	9083
	Unemployment rate	6.3	5.7	6.1	10.5	23.0	39.3	13.9	—	13.8
'73	Unemployed	112	33	145	523	1040	576	36	6	2326
	Labour force	1328	487	1815	3709	2803	1215	81	37	9695
	Unemployment rate	8.4	6.8	8.0	14.1	37.1	47.4	44.4	16.2	24.0
'81/82f	Unemployed	42	2	44	237	664	543	154	16	1658
	Labour force	1753	108	1861	4974	4549	2216	440	165	14205
	Unemployment rate	2.4	1.9	2.4	4.8	14.6	24.5	35.0	9.7	11.7
'86/87f	Unemployed	1	40	41	215	939	685	236	14	2130
	Labour force	75	-349	1424	4325	4753	2406	641	185	13734
	Unemployment rate	1.3	3.0	2.9	5.0	19.8	28.5	36.8	7.6	15.5

(See for explanation next page)

Explanation of the table on page 225:

a. For working definitions of employment, unemployment and labour force, refer to Appendix V.
b. For 1953 no distinction has been made between 'illiterate' and 'literate' in the 'No schooling' category.
c. In the CFSs of 1953 and 1963, all education levels higher than the SSC fall into a single category of 'Higher Education'. Therefore, the education level Passed HSC for these two years refers to any level of education higher than SSC, i.e. Passed HSC and Degree.
d. 'Other' includes vocational and other types of educational qualifications, and is provide in the CFS years 1963 and 1973 but not in other CFS years. This category is included in the totals for the respective CFS years.
e. In the CFSs of 1963, there is also a group with education level 'Not stated'. This group was excluded from estimates.
f. For 1981/82 and 1986/87 an education level of Undergraduate is given separately. This was included in the category of Passed HSC/GCE(AL).

Source: CBSL (*CFSs*).

6.2   Employment, unemployment, and labour force by education level, as a percentage of population in each category[a]

Explanation of the table on page 227:

a. For working definitions of employment, unemployment and labour force, refer to Appendix V.
b. For 1953 no distinction has been made between 'illiterate' and 'literate' in the 'No schooling' category.
c. In the CFSs of 1953 and 1963, all education levels higher than the SSC fall into a single category of 'Higher Education'. Therefore, the education level Passed HSC for these two years refers to any level of education higher than SSC, i.e. Passed HSC and Degree.
d. 'Other' includes vocational and other types of educational qualifications, and is provided in the CFS years 1963 and 1973 but not in other CFS years. This category is included in the totals for the respective CFS years.
e. In the CFSs of 1963, there is also a group with education level 'Not stated'. This group was excluded from estimates.
f. For 1981/82 and 1986/87 an education level of Undergraduate is given separately. This was included in the category of Passed HSC/GCE(AL).

Source: CBSL (*CFSs*).

Year	Educational level				Education		Passed[c]			Total[d]
	No schooling[b]									
	Illiterate	Literate	Total	primary	secundary	SSC or GCE (OL)	HSC or GCE (AL)	degree		
'53 Employed	–	–	35.2	49.5	11.9	1.6	1.9	–		2714
Unemployed	–	–	35.2	48.9	13.1	2.6	0.3	–		540
Labour force	–	–	35.2	49.4	12.1	1.7	1.6	–		3254
'63[e] Employed	22.2	9.3	31.4	41.9	20.1	4.2	2.1	–		7829
Unemployed	9.3	3.5	12.8	30.9	37.3	16.9	2.1	–		1254
Labour force	20.4	8.5	28.9	40.4	22.4	5.9	2.1	–		9083
'73 Employed	16.5	6.2	22.7	43.2	23.9	8.7	0.6	0.4		7369
Unemployed	4.8	1.4	6.2	22.5	44.7	24.8	1.5	0.3		2326
Labour force	13.7	5.0	18.7	38.3	28.9	12.5	0.8	0.4		9695
'81/82[f] Employed	13.6	0.8	14.5	37.8	31.0	13.3	2.3	1.2		12547
Unemployed	2.5	0.1	2.7	14.3	40.0	32.8	9.3	1.0		1658
Labour force	12.3	0.8	13.1	35.0	32.0	15.6	3.1	1.2		14205
'86/87[f] Employed	0.6	11.3	11.9	35.4	32.9	14.8	3.5	1.5		11604
Unemployed	0.0	1.9	1.9	10.1	44.1	32.2	11.1	0.7		2130
Labour force	0.5	9.8	10.4	31.5	34.6	17.5	4.7	1.3		13734

Sampled Population by Employment and Ethnicity, Selected CFS Years 1953–1981/82[a]

Sample data on employment and population[b]

Community	Employed labour force				Population			
	1953	1963	1973	1981/82	1953	1963	1973	1981/82
Sinhala	1661000	5185	4949	9160	5631000	21068	20424	30839
Sri Lanka Tamil	358000	934	812	1308	1025000	2972	3310	4626
Indian Tamil	537000	1200	1144	1364	909000	2477	2555	2802
Moor and Malay	141000	492	428	680	488000	2013	2143	3062
Other[c]	–	31	36	35	–	138	155	122
Total	2714000	7842	7369	12547	8130000	28668	28587	41451

Employment and population as a percentage of totals

Community	Employed labour force				Population			
	1953	1963	1973	1981/82	1953	1963	1973	1981/82
Sinhalese	61.2	66.1	67.2	73.0	69.3	73.5	71.4	74.4
Ceylon Tamil	13.2	11.9	11.0	10.4	12.6	10.4	11.6	11.2
Indian Tamil	19.8	15.3	15.5	10.9	11.2	8.6	8.9	6.8
Moor and Malay	5.2	6.3	5.8	5.4	6.0	7.0	7.5	7.4
Other[c]	–	0.4	0.5	0.3	–	0.5	0.5	0.3
Total	100	100	100	100	100	100	100	100

Ratio of community shares in employment and population, and employment rate

Community	Employed labour force				Population			
	1953	1963	1973	1981/82	1953	1963	1973	1981/82
Sinhalese	0.88	0.90	0.94	0.98	29.5	24.6	24.2	29.7
Ceylon Tamil	1.05	1.15	0.95	0.93	34.9	31.4	24.5	28.3
Indian Tamil	1.77	1.77	1.74	1.61	59.1	48.4	44.8	48.7
Moor and Malay	0.87	0.89	0.77	0.73	28.9	24.4	20.0	22.2
Other[c]	–	0.82	0.90	0.95	–	22.5	23.2	28.7
Total	1.00	1.00	1.00	1.00	33.4	27.4	25.8	30.3

a. Employment data differentiated according to ethnic group are not available in the CFS of 1978/79 and 1986/87.
b   1953 data represent sample figures extrapolated to national totals.
c. 'Other' includes Burgher, Eurasian, European, Veddah and other small ethnic groups. For 1953, these groups are not classified in a separate 'other' category, but are included in total.

Source: CBSL (*CFSs*).

Sampled Population by Education and Ethnicity, CFS Years 1953–1981/82

8.1 Communities by education as a percentage of community totals

Year	Community[a]	No schooling[b]	Primary education	Secondary education	SSC or GCE (OL)	HSC or GCE (AL), & higher	Sample population Sample
'53	Sinhala	38.7	48.0	11.3	1.2	0.8	3587
	Sri Lanka Tamil	38.3	50.8	8.3	0.8	1.8	653
	Indian Tamil	60.4	35.9	3.6	0.0	0.0	579
	Moor and Malay	49.8	43.1	5.5	0.3	1.3	311
	Other	24.5-	57.1	14.3	2.0	2.0	49
	Total	41.6	46.8	9.8	1.0	0.9	5179
'63c	Sinhala	33.5	40.4	21.7	3.5	1.0	21028
	Sri Lanka Tamil	36.1	39.1	18.4	4.3	2.1	2960
	Indian Tamil	60.8	31.8	6.6	0.6	0.0	2471
	Moor and Malay	42.2	39.2	15.3	2.8	0.4	2010
	Other	18.9	21.2	39.4	15.9	4.5	132
	Total	36.6	39.2	19.5	3.3	1.0	28601
'73	Sinhala	29.1	36.8	27.0	6.3	0.8	20424
	Sri Lanka Tamil	33.5	41.3	20.8	3.8	0.5	3310
	Indian Tamil	51.5	42.1	5.6	0.8	0.0	2555
	Moor and Malay	36.9	39.6	19.6	3.5	0.4	2143
	Other	17.4	20.6	46.5	12.3	3.2	155
	Total	32.2	37.8	23.6	5.3	0.7	28587
'78/79	Sinhala	21.9	37.9	29.1	9.5	1.6	30821
	Sri Lanka Tamil	23.5	36.1	26.3	12.4	1.6	4022
	Indian Tamil	45.0	47.6	6.2	1.1	0.1	3533
	Moor and Malay	27.1	43.2	22.7	6.3	0.7	3096
	Other	6.5	35.9	43.5	9.8	4.3	92
	Total	24.4	38.8	26.3	8.8	1.4	41564
'81/82	Sinhala	22.5	37.5	28.0	10.0	2.0	30839
	Sri Lanka Tamil	26.6	34.6	23.6	11.9	3.2	4626
	Indian Tamil	44.6	44.9	8.6	1.6	0.2	2802
	Moor and Malay	30.2	41.1	22.1	5.6	0.9	3062
	Other	8.2	27.0	41.0	22.1	1.6	122
	Total	25.0	37.8	25.6	9.3	1.9	41451

a. 'Other' includes Burgher, Eurasian, European, Veddah and others.
b. 'No schooling' category includes children under 4 years of age.
c. The 1963 CFS of 1963 includes separate categories for 'no reply' to ethnicity, and 'not stated' for the education level. These categories are excluded from estimates.
Source: CBSL (*CFSs*).

8.2   Communities by education as a percentage of total population in each of the education levels

Year	Community[a]	No schooling[b]	Primary education	Secondary education	SSC or GCE (OL)	HSC or GCE (AL), & higher	Sample population Sample
'53	Sinhala	64.4	71.0	80.4	86.0	62.2	69.3
	Sri Lanka Tamil	11.6	13.7	10.7	10.0	26.7	12.6
	Indian Tamil	16.2	8.6	4.2	0.0	0.0	11.2
	Moor and Malay	7.2	5.5	3.4	2.0	8.9	6.0
	Other	0.6	1.2	1.4	2.0	2.2	0.9
	Total	2156	2423	505	50	45	5179
'63[c]	Sinhala	67.1	75.6	81.8	78.8	73.0	73.5
	Sri Lanka Tamil	10.2	10.3	9.8	13.5	21.3	10.3
	Indian Tamil	14.3	7.0	2.9	1.7	0.7	8.6
	Moor and Malay	8.1	7.0	5.5	6.0	3.0	7.0
	Other	0.2	0.2	0.9	2.3	2.0	0.5
	Total	10480	11219	5573	932	296	28601
'73	Sinhala	64.7	69.5	81.5	85.3	84.7	71.4
	Sri Lanka Tamil	12.1	12.7	10.2	8.4	8.7	11.6
	Indian Tamil	14.3	10.0	2.1	1.3	0.0	8.9
	Moor and Malay	8.6	7.9	6.2	5.0	4.1	7.5
	Other	0.3	0.3	1.1	1.3	2.6	0.5
	Total	9196	10812	6758	1502	196	28587
'78/79	Sinhala	66.6	72.3	81.9	80.0	84.1	74.2
	Sri Lanka Tamil	9.3	9.0	9.7	13.6	11.1	9.7
	Indian Tamil	15.7	10.4	2.0	1.1	0.7	8.5
	Moor and Malay	8.3	8.3	6.4	5.3	3.5	7.4
	Other	0.0	0.2	0.4	0.2	0.7	0.2
	Total	10131	16146	10944	3664	597	41564
'81/82	Sinhala	67.0	73.7	81.1	80.1	76.7	74.4
	Sri Lanka Tamil	11.9	10.2	10.3	14.3	18.7	11.2
	Indian Tamil	12.1	8.0	2.3	1.2	0.7	6.8
	Moor and Malay	8.9	8.0	6.4	4.5	3.6	7.4
	Other	0.0	0.2	0.5	0.7	0.2	0.3
	Total	10369	15677	10632	3859	804	41451

a.   'Other' includes Burgher, Eurasian, European, Veddah and others.
b.   'No schooling' category includes children under 4 years of age.
c.   The 1963 CFS of 1963 includes separate categories for 'no reply' to ethnicity, and 'not stated' for the education level. These categories are excluded from estimates.
Source: CBSL (*CFSs*).

ශ්‍රී ලංකාව කෙරෙහි විශේෂ අවධානය සහිතව සංවර්ධනය වන රටවල ආර්ථික පරිවර්තනය සහ දේශපාලන ගැටුම්

සිරිමල් අබේරත්න

සාරාංශය

මෙම කෘතියෙහි මූලික අරමුණු දෙකකි. පළමුවැන්න, සංවර්ධනය වන රටවල පවතින දේශපාලන ගැටුම් වලට හේතු වූ ආර්ථිකමය සාධක තේරුම් ගැනීම සඳහා ආර්ථික විද්‍යාත්මක ආකෘතියක් ඉදිරිපත් කිරීමයි. දෙවැන්න, එම ආකෘතිය ඇසුරු කරගෙන ශ්‍රී ලංකාවේ අත්දැකීම් විග්‍රහ කිරීමයි.

දේශපාලන ගැටුම් වල සංවිධානය ඓතිහාසික ක්‍රියාවලියකි. එය කිසියම් විශේෂිත දේශපාලනික අරමුණු ලඟාකර ගැනීම සඳහා සාමූහිකව සාහසික ක්‍රියා භාවිත කරන හෝ ඒ සඳහා නැඹුරුවක් පවතින ක්‍රියාවලියකි. දෙවනි ලෝක යුද්ධයෙන් පසුව ලෝකයේ ඇති වූ දේශපාලන ගැටුම්, එක් අතකින්, *රාජ්‍යයන් අතර හටගන්නා* ජාත්‍යන්තර අරගල වලට වඩා *රාජ්‍යයන් තුළ ඇති වන* සිවිල් අරගල බවට පත් වී ඇත. මේ දේශපාලන ගැටුම්, *අභ්‍යන්තරව* ද, *ලෝකයේ* ආර්ථික ප්‍රදේශවලට වඩා සංවර්ධනය වන ප්‍රදේශ වලට සංකේන්ද්‍රණය වී තිබේ. නූතන දේශපාලන ගැටුම් වල දැකිය හැකි මේ විශේෂ ලක්ෂණ මගින් වැදගත් කරුණු දෙකක් පැහැදිලි වේ. පළමුව, දේශපාලන ගැටුම් විග්‍රහ කිරීම සඳහා උවමනාවට වඩා සාමාන්‍යකරණයට ලක් වූ න්‍යායයන්හි වලංගුභාවය පිළිබඳ සැකයක් ඒ තුළින් ඉස්මතු වේ. දෙවනුව, සංවර්ධනය වෙමින් පවතින ආර්ථිකයන් පිළිබඳ තත්ත්වයන් පදනම් කරගත් විග්‍රහාත්මක ආකෘතියක අවශ්‍යතාව එයින් අනාවරණය වේ.

සංවර්ධනය වන රටවල පවතින දේශපාලන ගැටුම් කෙරෙහි අවධානය යොමු කිරීම සඳහා දැනට පවතින ආර්ථික සම්ප්‍රදායයන්හි අදාළත්වය අධ්‍යයනය කිරීමෙන් අනතුරුව, සංවර්ධන ආර්ථික විද්‍යාව පදනම් කරගත් විග්‍රහාත්මක ආකෘතියක් මෙම කෘතියෙහි දියුණු කෙරේ. මෙම ආකෘතිය තුළ, සංවර්ධනය වන රටවල දේශපාලන ගැටුම් සංවර්ධන ප්‍රශ්නය හා දැඩි ලෙස සම්බන්ධ වූ ප්‍රපංචයක් වශයෙන් සැලකේ. සංවර්ධනය වන රටවල් විසින් මුහුණ පා ඇති වැදගත්ම 'සංවර්ධන ප්‍රශ්නය' වන්නේ, කලින් තීරණය කරන ලද 'මූලික අවශ්‍යතා' සමූහයක් සැපයීම නොව, වර්ධනය වන සමාජ අපේක්ෂා සැපිරීම සඳහා අවශ්‍ය කරන ආර්ථිකමය සම්පත් හා අවස්ථා වැඩි දියුණු කිරීමයි. මෙම සංවර්ධන ප්‍රශ්නය සම්බන්ධයෙන්, සංවර්ධනය වන රටවල ආර්ථික පරිවර්තනය සිදු වන සන්දර්භය කුමක් ද යන්න ඉතා වැදගත් වේ. සංවර්ධනය වන රටවල ආර්ථික පරිවර්තනය සිදු වන්නේ, එක් අතකින්, යටගිය යුරෝපීය රටවල එය සිදු වීමෙන් පසුවය. අනෙක් අතට, මෙම ආර්ථික පරිවර්තනය විශ්වකරණයට භාජනය වූ ආර්ථික පරිසරයක් තුළ ඇති වන ක්‍රියාවලියකි. ඊට අමතරව එය, ආර්ථික සංවර්ධනය වේගවත් කිරීම සඳහා සංවර්ධනය වන රටවල්

විසින් අනුගමනය කරන සංවර්ධන ප්‍රතිපත්ති තුළින් බලපෑම් ලබයි. මේ අනුව එක් අතකින් ආර්ථික පරිවර්තන රටාව ද, අනෙක් අතින් සමාජයීය සංවර්ධන අපේක්ෂාවන් ද තීරණය විම කෙරෙහි අභ්‍යන්තර හා බාහිර බලවේග වල බලපෑම ඉතා වැදගත් වේ.

ආර්ථික කාර්යක්ෂමතාව හා සමානාත්මතාව පදනම් කරගෙන, සංවර්ධනය හා සම්බන්ධ වූ විවිධ අරමුණු කරා ළඟා විම, ඇත්ත වශයෙන්ම, සංවර්ධන වින්තනයෙහි සාධාරණීකරණය කෙරේ. එපමණක් නොව, සංවර්ධන ක්‍රියාවලියට හිතකර වූ ආර්ථික හා දේශපාලනික තත්ත්වයන් වශයෙන් සුභ සාධන කටයුතු සඳහා ප්‍රතිපත්තිමය කැප විම සහ බහු පාර්ශවීය ප්‍රජාතන්ත්‍රවාදි දේශපාලන ක්‍රම වැදගත් පූර්ව කොන්දේසි බවත් සංවර්ධන වින්තනය තුළ පිළිගනු ලැබේ. එසේ නමුත්, සංවර්ධන ක්‍රියාවලිය තුළ ප්‍රතිවිරෝධතා පවතින අතර, එම ප්‍රතිවිරෝධතා තුළින් සංවර්ධන ද්වේවිධියයක් හටගනි. මෙම සංවර්ධන ප්‍රතිවිරෝධතා ඇති විමට හේතුව, එක් අතකට, 'සංවර්ධනය' යන යෙදුමෙන්ම හැඟවෙන පරිදි එය 'සුලභතාව' මැවීමේ ක්‍රියාවලියක් වන තමුත්, අනෙක් අතට, 'හිගකම' මැවීමේ ක්‍රියාවලියක් ද විමයි. සුලභතාව මැවීම නිසා ජනතාවට ලැබී ඇති තෝරා ගැනීමේ පරාසය පුළුල් වේ යැයි කියනු ලැබේ. නමුත් ඊට ප්‍රතිවිරුද්ධව, හිගකම මැවීම නිසා, ඇත්තෙන්ම, ජනතාවට ලැබී ඇති තෝරා ගැනීමේ පරාසය කුඩා වේ.

'සංවර්ධනය යනු තෝරා ගැනීමේ පරාසය පුළුල් විමකි' යන ජනප්‍රිය විශ්වාසය පිළිබඳව සලකා බලන විට, ආර්ථික වර්ධනයේ මූලාශ්‍රය වන හාණ්ඩකරණය විසින් ද්වයාත්මක සුලභතාව ඇති කරයි. ප්‍රතිව්‍යාප්තිය, එසේ නැතහොත්, මූලික අවශ්‍යතා සැපිරීම මගින් ඌණ සංවර්ධනයේ ඇතැම් මූලික ගති ලක්ෂණ පහ කරයි. එහෙත් සමාජය විසින් 'අපේක්ෂා කරන ආකාරයේ තෝරා ගැනීම්' සම්බන්ධව සලකන කල, සංවර්ධනය විසින් තෝරා ගැනීමේ පරාසය කුඩා කෙරේ. හාණ්ඩකරණය, එහි නිර්වවනයෙන්ම හැඟවෙන පරිදි, ජනතාවට ද්වයාත්මක හිගකම මැවීමේ ක්‍රියාවලියකි. ඒ අනුව හාණ්ඩකරණ ක්‍රියාවලිය ජාත්‍යන්තර හා දේශිය ආදායම් හා පරිභෝජන අසමානතාවට හේතු වේ. මූලික අවශ්‍යතා ලැබීම නිසා මිනිසුන්ට ඔවුන් ගේ පැවති සමාජ හා ආර්ථික දුෂ්කරතාවයෙන් මිදීමට හැකි වේ. ඒ නිසා ඔවුන් තම සමාජ හා ආර්ථික තත්ත්වය උසස් කර ගැනීමට උවමනා කරන ද සඳහා තරග කිරීමට අවශ්‍ය නිදහස හා සුදුසුකම් ලබති. නමුත් ඔවුන් ගේ අපේක්ෂාවන් ඉටුකිරීමට තරම් ප්‍රමාණවත් වූ ආර්ථික සම්පත් හා අවස්ථාවන් මෙම තොදියණු ආර්ථිකයන්හි ඒ වන විටත් වැඩි දියුණු වී නොතිබිය හැකිය.

සුලභතාව හා හිගකම යන ප්‍රපංචයන් දෙකම බිහි කිරීම අනුව, සංවර්ධනය ප්‍රතිවිරෝධතා වලින් යුක්ත ක්‍රියාවලියක් විමට වැදගත් හේතුවක් වන්නේ, සමාජ අපේක්ෂාවන් ද ක්‍රියාවලියක් වශයෙන් වැඩි දියුණු වෙමින් පැවතිමයි. දේශිය හා විශ්වීය බලවේගයන්හි බලපෑම ද, සංවර්ධනය තුළින්ම ඇති වන සංවර්ධන අරමුණු වල ළඟා කර ගැනීම ද අනුව සංවර්ධනය වන රටවල සමාජ සන්දර්භය තීරණය වේ. මෙම සමාජ සන්දර්භය තුළ, සමාජ හා ආර්ථික අපේක්ෂාවන් ඉහළ නැගීම කාලානුරූප ක්‍රියාවලියකි. ඒ අනුව සාපේක්ෂ දුෂ්කරතාවේ විවිධ මට්ටම් වලට අනුව, සංවර්ධනය විසින් ඇතැම් ප්‍රශ්න නිරාකරණය කරන අතරම, සංවර්ධනය තුළින්ම විසදිය යුතු තවත් ප්‍රශ්න වැඩි වැඩියෙන් ඇති කෙරේ.

පුද්ගලයන් ගේ හා සමාජ කාණ්ඩ වල අපේක්ෂිත සමාජ ආර්ථික උසස් වීමට අවශ්‍ය කරන ආර්ථික සම්පත් හා අවස්ථා ලබා ගැනීමට ඇති අයිතිය හා හැකියාව හීන වී යාමට සංවර්ධන ද්වේවිධ්‍යය හේතු වේ. මේ තත්ත්වය සමාජීය බැහැර කිරීම වශයෙන් හැඳින්වේ. සමාජීය බැහැර කිරීමට පුතිවිරුද්ධ සංකල්පය වන්නේ සමාජීය ඇතුළත් කිරීමයි. සමාජීය බැහැර කිරීමත්, ඊට පුතිවිරුද්ධව සමාජීය ඇතුළත් කිරීමත් සඳහා විධිමත් හා අවිධිමත් යන දෙආකාරයෙන්ම භාවිත කෙරෙන විවිධ ආර්ථික, සමාජීය, සංස්කෘතික, දේශපාලනික හා නෛතික නිර්ණායකයන් පවතී. පුසාරණාත්මක තරගකාරී සමාජයක් තුළ ඉහළ තැනෙන සමාජ අපේක්ෂාවන්ට සාපේක්ෂව ආර්ථික සම්පත් හා අවස්ථා වල හිඟකම වර්ධනය වීම හේතුවෙන් සමාජීය බැහැර කිරීමේ කියාවලිය තියුණු වේ.

දේශපාලන ගැටුම් වල බිහි වීමට හා පැවැත්මට අවශ්‍ය කරන සාරවත් පසුබිමක් සමාජීය බැහැර කිරීමේ කියාවලියෙන් සැපයේ. සමාජීය බැහැර කිරීමට ලක් වූ පුද්ගලයින් හා සමාජ කාණ්ඩ විසින් තමන් ගේ සමාජීය බැහැර කිරීම පිළිබඳ තත්ත්වයත්, සමාජීය ඇතුළත් වීම සඳහා තමන්ට ඇති අයිතියන් පිළිබඳ අවබෝධය ද මේ සම්බන්ධයෙන් ඉතා වැදගත් වේ. එයට හේතුව, විශ්වකරණයට හසු වූ සමාජයක් තුළ, තමන් ගේ හා අනුන් ගේ තත්ත්වයන් පිළිබඳව අවබෝධය පුළුල් වීම හේතුවෙන් සමාජීය බැහැර කිරීමට ලක් වූ පුද්ගලයින් විසින් තම සමාජ කණ්ඩායම් පිළිබඳ අනන්‍යතාවන් අවධාරණය කිරීමට පටන් ගැනීමයි. සමාජීය ඇතුළත් වීමේ අරමුණු ළඟා කර ගැනීම සඳහා සාහසික නොවන කියාමාර්ග එළඳායි නොවන විට, සාහසික කියාමාර්ග ගැනීම සඳහා ඇති ඉඩකඩ පුළුල් වේ. දේශපාලන ගැටුම් තැඩ නැගීමේ කියාවලිය සාමූහික සාහසික කියාවන්ට පරිවර්තනය වීම සඳහා නායකත්වයක කාර්යහාරය ද අවශ්‍ය කෙරේ. දේශපාලන ගැටුම් තත්ත්වයක් තම අරමුණු සඳහා පුයෝජනයට ගැනීමත්, සාමූහික සාහසික කියා සඳහා සම්පත් ඒකරාශි කිරීමත් නායකත්වයක් බිහිවිය යුතුය.

ශ්‍රී ලංකාව, දේශපාලන නිදහස ලැබීමෙන් පසු සංවර්ධන ඉතිහාසය තුළ, කුමානුකූලව වර්ධනය වූ දේශපාලන ගැටුමක් හා සම්බන්ධ අත්දැකීම් ලැබුවේය. අවසානයේ දී, මෙම දේශපාලන ගැටුම් තුළින්, පවත්නා දේශපාලන කුමයට එරෙහි වූ ද්විත්ව සිවිල් යුද්ධයක් 1980 ගණන් මුල් කාලයේ සිට ආරම්භ විය. මෙයින් එකක් දකුණේ සිංහල තරුණ කොටස් අතරිනුත්, අනෙක උතුරේ දෙමළ තරුණ කොටස් අතරිනුත් පැන නැගුණි. දේශපාලන ගැටුමේ ද්විත්ව ස්වරූපය, තාර්කිකව එකිනෙකින් වෙනස් නමුත්, ඓතිහාසිකව එකිනෙක හා සම්බන්ධ බව පෙනේ. රටේ දේශපාලන ගැටුම, යටත් විජිත වාදයෙන් පසු කාලය තුළ, එහි වැඩි දියුණු වීමේ විවිධ අදියරයන් පසු කරමින් විකාශනය වූවකි. මෙම ඓතිහාසික අදියරයන් පිළිවෙළින් සමාජයේ සංස්කෘතිකමය විෂමතා, ඔනෑ ඡපාකම පිළිබඳ විෂමතා, කැළඹීම්, ගැටුම්, අකුමවත් ලෙස ඇති වූ කෝලාහල හා අවසාන වශයෙන් සිවිල් යුද්ධ වශයෙන් දැක්විය හැකිය. ශ්‍රී ලංකාවේ දේශපාලන ගැටුමේ ඓතිහාසික වර්ධන කියාවලිය තුළින් එහි වැදගත් ලක්ෂණ දෙකක් අනාවරණය විය. එක් අතකින්, සිංහල හා දෙමළ ජාතීන් අතර මෙන්ම, එම ජාතීන් තුළ ද දේශපාලන ගැටුම දක්නට ලැබුණ. අනෙක් අතට, සම්පුදායික හා ස්ථාපිත වූ ද, රැඩිකල් හා ස්ථාපිත නොවූ ද දේශපාලන කණ්ඩායම් දෙවර්ගය අතර දේශපාලන බල අරගලය දියුණු වෙමින් පවතී බව, විශේෂයෙන් 1970 ගණන් මුල් කාලය වන විට පැහැදිලි විය.

ශ්‍රී ලංකාවේ දේශපාලන ගැටුම. එහි ආර්ථික සංවර්ධන ක්‍රියාවලියේ ප්‍රතිවිරෝධතා තුළින් හටගත් සංවර්ධන ද්වෛවිධ්‍යයක උත්සන්න විම හා සමාන්තරව විකාශනය වුවකි. තරගකාරී ප්‍රසාරණාත්මක සමාජයක් තුළ, සමාජ අපේක්ෂාවන් ඉහළ තැගීමත්. ඊට අනුරූපව ආර්ථික සම්පත් හා අවස්ථා වැඩි දියුණු කිරීමට ඇති ආර්ථික හා දේශපාලනික හැකියාව දුර්වල විමත්, ශ්‍රී ලංකාවේ ඓතිහාසික අත්දැකීම විය. මෙම ප්‍රසාරණාත්මක තරගකාරී සමාජය, දේශපාලනික හා ආර්ථික වශයෙන් එක්සත් කරන ලද තනි ඒකකයකි. ප්‍රමාණාත්මක හා ගුණාත්මක වශයෙන් ඒ තුළ තරගය ගිසුයෙන් ඉහළ තැගුණි.

සංවර්ධන ද්වෛවිධ්‍යය පිළිබඳ ප්‍රශ්නයට පදනම් වූ මූලික සාධක කිපයක් තිබිණි. (i) 1950 ගණන් අවසානය දක්වා පැවති ආරම්භක ආර්ථික සෞභාග්‍යය. (ii) ඉහළ මට්ටමේ සුභ සාධනය. (iii) බහු පාර්ශ්වීය හා තරගකාරී දේශපාලන ක්‍රමයක් තුළ 'දේශපාලනික විනය' නොපැවතිම හා (iv) අතාත්වික ආර්ථික කළමනාකරණය යන කරුණු මේ අතර ප්‍රධාන වේ. මෙම තත්ත්වය පදනම් කරගෙන සමාජ අපේක්ෂා ඉහළ තැගුණු නමුත්, එම අපේක්ෂා සැපිරීමට අවශ්‍ය කළ ආර්ථික හැකියාව පිරිහුණ. පුද්ගලයින්, සමාජ කණ්ඩායම්, ජාතින් සහ ප්‍රදේශ වශයෙන් පැන තැගුණු තරගකාරී පාර්ශ්වයන්ට ආර්ථික සම්පත් හා අවස්ථා ලබා ගැනීම සම්බන්ධයෙන් වර්ධනය වෙමින් තිබුණු සමාජයිය බැහැර කිරීමේ ප්‍රශ්නයට මුහුණ පැමට සිදු විය. මෙම ආර්ථික සම්පත් හා අවස්ථාවන් අතර වැදගත් වන්නේ, පෞද්ගලික සමාජ ආර්ථික උසස් විමට අවශ්‍ය කරන ආදායම, පරිභෝජනය, වෘත්තිය සහ අධ්‍යාපනය යන මේවාය.

පුළුල් ලෙස පැතිරී ගිය තරුණ පරපුරේ සමාජයිය බැහැර කිරීම දේශපාලන ගැටුම් වල බිහි විමට හා පැවැත්මට උචිත වූ සමාජ පසුබිමක් බිහි විමට හේතු විය. මෙම අවස්ථාව ප්‍රයෝජනයට ගැනීම සඳහා නායකත්වය ද බිහි විය. එම නායකත්වය විසින් රටේ පැතිරී ගිය තරුණ අසහනය ද්විත්ව සන්නද්ධ අරගලයක් සඳහා සංවිධානය කෙරුණි. සංවර්ධනය වන රටවල්, සංවර්ධිත රටවලට වඩා දේශපාලන ගැටුම් වලට මුහුණ දී ඇත්තේ, ශ්‍රී ලංකාවේ අත්දැකීම් වලින් පැහැදිලි වන පරිදි, එම රටවල සංවර්ධන ක්‍රියාවලියේ ප්‍රතිවිරෝධතා තුළින් දේශපාලනික ගැටුම් සඳහා අවශ්‍ය පසුබිම නිර්මාණය කරන බැවින් යැයි මෙම අධ්‍යයනයෙන් නිගමනය කෙරේ.

அபிவிருத்தியடைந்துவரும் நாடுகளில்
பொருளாதார மாற்றமும், அரசியல் முரண்பாடுகளும்
இலங்கையின் அனுபவத்திற்கான ஒரு விசேட கண்ணோட்டம்

சிறிமால் அபேரத்ன

பொழிப்பு

அபிவிருத்தியடைந்துவரும் நாடுகளில் நிலவுகின்ற அரசியல் முரண்பாடுகளுக்கான பொருளாதார மூலங்களை விளங்கிக் கொள்வதற்கேதுவாக, ஒரு பொருளாதாரக் கட்டமைப்பினை முன்வைப்பதும், இலங்கையின் அனுபவத்தினை ஆராய்வதற்காக அக்கட்டமைப்பினைப் பயன்படுத்துவதுமே இவ்வாய்வின் நோக்கமாகும். அரசியல் முரண்பாடுகள், வரலாற்று ரீதியான உருவாக்கமுறைமைக்கு உட்பட்டிருப்பதுடன், குறிப்பிட்ட அரசியல் குறிக்கோள்களை அடைவதற்கான வழிமுறையாக, கூட்டுவன்முறையின் பயன்பாட்டினை அல்லது பயன்பாட்டுச் சாத்தியத்தினை கொண்டுள்ளன. போருக்குப் பிற்பட்ட காலகட்டத்திலே, உலகில் நிலவும் அரசியல் முரண்பாடுகள், 'அரசுகளிற்கிடையிலான' முரண்பாடுகள் என்பதனை விட, 'அரசிற்குள்ளேயே' இடம்பெறுகின்ற முரண்பாடுகளாக பெரும்பாலும் மாறியிருப்பதுடன், அபிவிருத்தியடைந்த பிராந்தியங்களை விட, அபிவிருத்தியடைந்து வரும் பிராந்தியங்களிலேயே இவை கூடுதலாக மையங்கொண்டுள்ளன. நவீன அரசியல் முரண்பாடுகளின் இந்தனைய அம்சங்கள், முருவாலவுநாக மிகவும் பொதுவாய்ப் படுத்தப்பட்ட கோட்பாடுகளின் ஸ்திரத்தன்மை மீது ஐயப்பட வைப்பதுடன், இரண்டாவதாக, அபிவிருத்தியடைந்து வரும் பொருளாதாரங்களைப் பொறுத்தவரையில் ஒரு விபரமான கட்டமைப்பினையும் வேண்டி நிற்கின்றன.

அபிவிருத்தியடைந்துவரும் நாடுகளில் நிலவும் அரசியல் முரண்பாடுகள் மீது கவனம் செலுத்துவதற்காக, கிடைக்கக்கூடியதாகவுள்ள பொருளாதார மரபுகளின் பொருத்தப்பாட்டினை ஆராய்ந்த பின்னர், அபிவிருத்திப் பொருளியல் என்ற நிலைக்குட்பட்ட ரீதியில் ஒரு ஆய்வுக் கட்டமைப்பானது இவ்வாய்வில் விருத்தி செய்யப்படுகிறது. அபிவிருத்தியடைந்துவரும் நாடுகளில் நிலவும் அரசியல் முரண்பாடுகள், 'அபிவிருத்தியின் பிரச்சனை' என்பதுடன் குறிப்பிடக்கூடியவிற்கு இணைந்துள்ள ஒரு தோற்றப்பாடாகவே இக்கட்டமைப்பினுள் கையாளப்படுகிறது. அபிவிருத்தியடைந்துவரும் நாடுகளிலுள்ள அரசுகளினால் எதிர்கொள்ளப்படும் முக்கிய அபிவிருத்திப் பிரச்சனையென்பது, படிப்படியாக அதிகரித்துவரும் சமூக நாட்டங்களை நிறைவு செய்வதற்கான பொருளாதார வளங்களையும், சந்தர்ப்பங்களையும் உருவாக்குவதேயொழிய, முன்கூட்டியே வரையறுக்கப்பட்ட ஒரு தொகுதி 'அடிப்படைத்தேவைகளை' வழங்குவதல்ல. அபிவிருத்தியடைந்துவரும் நாடுகளின் அபிவிருத்திப் பிரச்சனையைப் பொறுத்தவரையில், பொருளாதார மாற்றம் இடம் பெறுகின்ற சூழ்நிலை முக்கியமானது. அபிவிருத்தியடைந்துவரும் நாடுகளில் நிகழும் பொருளாதார மாற்றமானது, மேற்கைரோப்பிய நாடுகளில் இம்மாற்றம் இடம்பெற்ற பின்னரும், பூகோளமயப்படுத்தப்பட்ட ஒரு பொருளாதாரச் சூழ்நிலையிலுமேயே இடம் பெறுகிறது. அத்துடன், இம்மாற்றமானது அபிவிருத்தியடைந்துவரும் நாடுகள் பொருளாதார அபிவிருத்தியினைத் துரிதப்படுத்துவதற்காக ஏற்றுக்கொண்ட அபிவிருத்திக் கொள்கைகளின் செல்வாக்கிற்கும் உட்பட்டுள்ளது. எனவே, உள்நாட்டு, வெளிநாட்டுக் காரணிகள் இரண்டும், ஒரு புறத்தில், பொருளாதார மாற்றத்தினையும், மறுபுறத்தில், சமூகத்தின் அபிவிருத்தி எதிர்பார்ப்புக்களையும் வரையறுப்பதில் வேறுபட்ட அளவுகளில் முக்கியம் பெறுகின்றன.

நலன்பேணும்வாதத்துடன் தொடர்புடைய அபிவிருத்திச் சாதனைகள், அதற்கான கொள்கைப் பிரயோகம், இவற்றுடன், அச்சாதனைகள் இடம்பெறுவதனை இலகுபடுத்துகின்ற தாராள ஜனநாயக முறைமைகள் என்பன, அபிவிருத்திச் சிந்தனைகளில், செயற்றிறன் மற்றும் சமத்துவம் ஆகியவற்றின் அடிப்படைகளில் உண்மையில் நியாயப்படுத்தப்படுகின்றன. எவ்வாறெனினும், அபிவிருத்திச் செய்முறையில் பல முரண்பாடுகளுமுள்ளனவென்பதுடன், இவை 'அபிவிருத்தி பற்றிய முரண்வாதமாக' பிரதிபலிக்கப்படுகின்றன. இம்முரண்பாடுகள் எழுவதற்கான காரணம், ஒரு புறத்தில், அபிவிருத்தி என்ற பதம் கருதுவது போல, தெரிவுகளின் வீச்சினை அதிகரிக்கின்ற வகையில் 'மிகையினை' உருவாக்கும் முறைமையேயாகும். மறுபுறத்தில், அதற்கு முரணாக, தெரிவுகளின் வீச்சினை சுருக்குவதன் மூலம் அபிவிருத்தியானது அருமைத்தன்மையினை உருவாக்கும் முறைமையாகிறது.

அபிவிருத்தியானது தெரிவுகளின் வீச்சினை விரிவாக்குகிறது என்ற பரவலான நம்பிக்கையுடன் தொடர்புபடுத்தி நோக்கும் போது, பொருளாதார வளர்ச்சிக்கு மூலதாரமான பண்டமயப்படுத்தலானது பொருள் மிகையினை உருவாக்குகிறது. அடிப்படைத்தேவைகளின் வழங்கல் அல்லது அவற்றின் மீள்பங்கீடு, குறைந்த மட்ட அபிவிருத்திக்குரிய குணாம்சங்களைத் தனிக்கின்றன. இவ்வாறான அபிவிருத்திச்சாதனைகள், சமூகத்தினால் நாடப்படும் 'தெரிவுகளின் வகைகள்' என்பதைப் பொறுத்தவரையில், தெரிவுகளின் வீச்சினைச் சுருக்கவும் முடியும். வரைவிலக்கணப்படி, பண்டமயப்படுத்தும் செய்முறையானது, பொருள் அருமைத்தன்மையின் உருவாக்கத்தினைக் கருதுவதுடன், அது சர்வதேச, உள்நாட்டு வருமான மற்றும் நுகர்வுச் சமனின்மைக்கு இட்டுச்செல்கின்றது. அடிப்படைத் தேவைகளை வழங்குகின்றமையானது, மக்களை அவர்களது சமூக மற்றும் பொருளாதார பின்னடைவுகளிலிருந்து விடுவிக்கிறது. குறைந்தமட்ட அபிவிருத்தியடைந்த பொருளாதாரங்களில் அடையப்பட சாத்தியமற்ற சமூக பொருளாதார முன்னேற்றத்திற்கான வழிவகைகளிற்காக போட்டியிட அவர்கள் தகுதியுள்ளவர்களாகின்றனர். சமூக நாட்டங்கள் ஒரு செய்முறையாக படிப்படியாக அதிகரிப்பதனாலேயே, மிகை மற்றும் அருமைத்தன்மை இரண்டனதும் உருவாக்கத்துடன் தொடர்புடையதாக அபிவிருத்திச் செய்முறையிலுள்ள முரண்பாடுகள் எழுகின்றன. உள்நாட்டு மற்றும் சர்வதேச சக்திகளினாலும், அதேபோன்று, அபிவிருத்திச் சாதனைகளினாலும் நிபந்தனைப்படுத்தப்படும் சமூக சூழ்நிலை தொடர்பாக நோக்கும் போது, சமூக பொருளாதார முன்னேற்றத்திற்கான சமூக நாட்டங்கள் காலப்போக்கில் அதிகரிக்கின்றன. இந்தவகையில், வேறுபட்ட சார்புப் பின்னடைவு மட்டங்களில், அபிவிருத்தியானது சில பிரச்சனைகளை தீர்ப்பதுடன், அதே அபிவிருத்தியினாலேயே தீர்க்கப்பட வேண்டிய மேலதிகமான பிரச்சனைகளையும் உருவாக்குகிறது.

அபிவிருத்தி முரண்வாதமானது, தனிநபர்கள் மற்றும் சமூகக்குழுக்கள், சமூக – பொருளாதார முன்னேற்றத்திற்குத் தேவையான பொருளாதார வளங்களையும், வாய்ப்புக்களையும் அடைவதிலிருந்து புறக்கணிப்பு நிலைக்கு இட்டுச்செல்கிறது. சமூகப் புறக்கணிப்பிற்கும் அதற்கு முரணாக சமூக உட்படுத்தலுக்குமென, முறைமையாகவும் முறைமையற்ற ரீதியிலும் கையாளப்படுகின்ற பொருளாதார, சமூக, கலாச்சார, அரசியல் மற்றும் சட்டரீதியான காரணிகளின் வேறுபட்ட வடிவங்கள் உள்ளன. விரிவடைந்து செல்லும் போட்டி நிறைந்த சமுதாயத்திலே, அதிகரித்துச் செல்லும் சமூக எதிர்பார்க்கைகளுடன் சார்பு ரீதியாக நோக்கும் போது, பொருளாதார வளங்கள் மற்றும் வாய்ப்புக்களின் அருமைத்தன்மை அதிகரித்துச் செல்லும் சூழ்நிலையில், சமூகப் புறக்கணிப்பு செய்முறை துரிதமடைகிறது. இது, அரசியல் முரண்பாடுகளின் எழுச்சிக்கான வளமான அடித்தளத்தினையும், ஆதரவினையும் வழங்குகிறது. சமூக புறக்கணிப்பிற்குள்ளாக்கப்பட்டோர், தமது சமூகப்புறக்கணிப்பு நிலையினையும், பூகோளமயப்படுத்தப்படும் சமுதாயத்திலே சமூக உட்படுத்தலத்தலிற்கான தமது உரிமையினையும் உணர்கின்ற வேளையில் தமது குழு அடையாளங்களை வலியுறுத்தத் தொடங்குகின்றனர். சமூக உட்படுத்தல் நோக்கங்களை அடைவதற்கான வன்முறையற்ற வழிவகைகள் செயற்றிறனற்றதாக இருக்கும்போதே, வன்முறை வழிவகைகளுக்கான நோக்குகள் விரிவடைகின்றன. அரசியல் முரண்பாட்டுச் செய்முறையிலே வெளிப்படும் கூட்டுவன்முறையானது, இந்த முரண்பாட்டு நிலைமையினை பயன்படுத்தி, படித்த வேலையற்ற இளைஞர்கள் போன்ற வளங்களை கூட்டுவன்முறைக்கு நகர்த்தக்கூடிய ஒரு தலைமைத்துவத்தின் பங்கினை வேண்டி நிற்கிறது.

இலங்கை, அதன் காலனித்துவத்திற்கு பின்னைய அபிவிருத்தி வரலாற்றிலே, அரசியல் முரண்பாடுகளின் தொடர்ச்சியான அதிகரிப்புக்களை, படிப்படியாக அனுபவித்து வந்துள்ளது. இறுதியில் இந்த முரண்பாடானது, ஸ்தாபிக்கப்பட்ட அரசியல் ஒழுங்கிற்கெதிராக 1980களின் ஆரம்பத்திலிருந்து இடம்பெறுகின்ற இரட்டை உள்நாட்டு போர்களின் தோற்றத்திற்கு வழியிட்டது; இவற்றில் ஒன்று தெற்கின் சிங்கள சமூகத்திலும், மற்றையது வடக்கின் தமிழ் சமூகத்திலும் தோற்றம் பெற்றது. அரசியல் முரண்பாட்டின் மேற்படி இரு வெளிப்பாடுகளும், தர்க்க ரீதியில் அல்லாமல், வரலாற்று ரீதியாகவே தொடர்புபட்டுள்ளன. காலனித்துவத்திற்கு பின்னையகால அரசியல் முரண்பாடானது, கலாச்சாரம் மற்றும் நலன் வேறுபாடுகள், குழப்பநிலைகள், முரண்பாடுகள், கலகங்களின் ஒழுங்கற்ற வெடிப்பு, இறுதியில், உள்நாட்டு போர்கள் ஆகிய தொடர்ச்சியான அதிகரிப்பு கட்டங்களை கொண்டதாக படிப்படியாகத் தோற்றம் பெற்றது. காலனித்துவத்திற்குப் பின்னைய காலத்தில் படிப்படியாக தீவிரமடையத் தொடங்கிய அரசியல் முரண்பாடானது, இரு வேறுபட்ட அம்சங்களை வெளிப்படுத்தியது. இம்முரண்பாடானது, ஒருபுறத்தில், சிங்கள மற்றும் தமிழ் இனக்குழுக்களிற்கிடையிலும், அதேவேளை அக்குழுக்களுக்குள்ளேயும் தீவிரமடைந்தது. மறுபுறத்தில், குறிப்பாக, 1970களின் ஆரம்பத்திலிருந்து, இம்முரண்பாடானது, 'ஸ்தாபிக்கப்பட்டிருந்த பாரம்பரிய' அரசியல் குழுக்கள், மற்றும் 'ஸ்தாபிக்கப்படாத அடிப்படைவாத' அரசியல் குழுக்கள் ஆகியவற்றிற்கிடையே அதிகரிக்கத்தொடங்கியது.

இலங்கையின் அரசியல் முரண்பாடானது, காலனித்துவத்திற்குப் பிற்கால அதன் அபிவிருத்தி வரலாற்றிலே, அபிவிருத்திச் செய்முறையிலிருந்த முரண்பாடுகளினால் ஏற்பட்ட அபிவிருத்தி முரண்வாத அதிகரிப்புடன் இணைந்த வகையிலேயே தோற்றம் பெற்றது. இலங்கையைப் பொறுத்தவரையில், ஒரு போட்டி நிறை சமூகத்திலே அதிகரித்துச் சென்ற சமூக எதிர்பார்ப்புக்களின் சார்பாக நோக்குமிடத்து, அவற்றை நிறைவு செய்வதற்கான பொருளாதார வளங்கள் மற்றும் வாய்ப்புக்களை உருவாக்கும் இயலளவானது வீழ்ச்சியடைந்து சென்றுள்ளது. பொருளாதார ரீதியிலும், அரசியல் ரீதியிலும் ஒன்றுபட்ட ஒரே அமைப்பான இந்த போட்டி நிறை சமுதாயமானது, அளவுர்தியிலும், பணயுர்தியிலும் துரிதமாக விரிவடைந்தது. அபிவிருத்தி முரண்வாத பிரச்சனைக்குப் பொறுப்பான முக்கிய காரணிகளாக (i) 1950களின் இறுதிவரை நிலவிய ஆரம்ப பொருளாதார செழிப்பு நிலை (ii) அதிகளவு நலன்பேணும் தன்மை (iii) ஒரு தாராண்மை மற்றும் போட்டி அரசியல் முறைமையிருந்த நிலைமைகளில் அரசியல் ஒழுங்குபற்றாக்குறை, இவற்றோடு (iv) தவறான பொருளாதார முகாமைத்துவம் ஆகியவற்றைக் குறிப்பிடலாம். இந்த நிலைமைக்குள்ளே, சமூக நாட்டங்கள் தொடர்ச்சியாக அதிகரித்த அதேவேளை, இந்நாட்டங்களை நிறைவு செய்வதற்கான பொருளாதார இயலளவு குறைந்து சென்றது. இவ்வகையில், தனிநபர்கள், சமூகக் குழுக்கள், இனக்குழுக்கள் மற்றும் பிராந்தியங்கள் என்பதாக எழுச்சியுற்ற போட்டிக்குழுக்கள், அவர்களின் சமூக, பொருளாதார முன்னேற்றத்திற்குத் தேவைப்பட்ட நுகர்வு, வருமானம், வேலைவாய்ப்பு மற்றும் கல்வி போன்ற பொருளாதார வளங்கள் மற்றும் வாய்ப்புக்களை அடைவதிலிருந்து அதிகளவில் சமூகப்புறக்கணிப்பிற்கு உட்பட வேண்டியிருந்தன. இளைஞர்கள் பரவலான ரீதியில் சமூக புறக்கணிப்பிற்கு உட்படுத்தப்பட்டமையானது, அரசியல் முரண்பாடுகளுக்கான வளமான அடிப்படையினை வழங்குகிறது. இக்கால தலைமைத்துவத் தோற்றமானது, இளைஞர்களின் குழப்பநிலையினை ஒழுங்குபடுத்தி, அதனூடு நாட்டின் இரட்டை ஆயுதப்போராட்டம் ஏற்படும் வகையில் இச்சூழ்நிலையினைக் கையாண்டது. அபிவிருத்தியடைந்த நாடுகளை விட, அபிவிருத்தியடைந்துவரும் நாடுகள் அதிகளவில் அரசியல் முரண்பாடுகளுக்கு முகங்கொடுக்க வேண்டியுள்ளன என்பதுடன், இலங்கையின் நிலைமையைப்போன்றே, அரசியல் முரண்பாட்டுச் சூழ்நிலையினைத் தோற்றுவிக்கின்ற இந்நாடுகளின் அபிவிருத்தி செய்முறையிலுள்ள முரண்பாடுகளே இதற்குக் காரணமென்பதே இவ்வாய்வின் முடிவாகும்.

Economische verandering en politieke conflicten in ontwikkelingslanden, in het bijzonder in Sri Lanka

Gedurende de decennia na het einde van de tweede wereldoorlog zijn internationale oorlogen zeldzaam geworden. Op het gebied van politiek geweld is hun plaats ingenomen door burgeroorlogen. En groot deel van die burgeroorlogen vindt plaats in zogenaamde 'ontwikkelingslanden', wat suggereert dat er een verband bestaat is tussen 'ontwikkeling' en het voorkomen van politieke conflicten. Het doel van dit proefschrift is het ontwikkelen van een conceptueel kader dat gebruikt kan worden om de economische wortels van politieke conflicten in ontwikkelingslanden te verklaren, en om dat kader te gebruiken om de gebeurtenissen in Sri Lanka na de onafhankelijkheid in 1948 te begrijpen.

De concentratie van burgeroorlogen in ontwikkelingslanden leidt, in de eerste plaats tot twijfel omtrent de validiteit van algemene economische theorieën omtrent gewelddadige politieke conflicten, en in de tweede plaats tot de behoefte een specifieke verklaring te vinden voor gewelddadige conflicten in ontwikkelingslanden.

Daartoe wordt allereerst een overzicht geboden van de bruikbaarheid van enkele inzichten op het gebied van politieke conflicten, ontleend aan bestaande economische tradities. In aansluiting daarop wordt een analytisch kader ontwikkeld ten behoeve van de verklaring van conflicten in ontwikkelingslanden. Politieke conflicten in ontwikkelingslanden worden in dit verband inderdaad gezien als uitvloeisels van het ontwikkelingsprobleem.

Het strategische ontwikkelingsprobleem van ontwikkelingslanden is het genereren van economische bronnen en mogelijkheden om te kunnen voldoen niet alleen aan de bevrediging van vaststaande, elementaire behoeften, maar ook aan de snel groeiende aspiraties van de bevolking. Voor het ontwikkelingsprobleem is de context waarin economische verandering plaatsvindt van belang. Economische verandering treedt in ontwikkelingslanden veel later op dan in West Europa, en het vindt plaats in een mondiaal economisch milieu. Bovendien wordt ontwikkelingsproces beïnvloed door een beleid in ontwikkelingslanden dat is gericht op het versnellen van economische verandering. Zowel interne en externe krachten die op uiteenlopende manieren economische verandering conditioneren, als de verwachtingen die in een samenleving leven omtrent ontwikkeling zijn daarom belangrijk.

Er schuilt echter een tegenstrijdigheid in het ontwikkelingsprobleem op grond waarvan gesteld kan worden dat er sprake is van een 'ontwikkelingsparadox'. Deze tegenstrijdigheid ontstaat omdat, aan de ene kant, ontwikkeling gezien wordt als een proces dat overvloed brengt (ontwikkeling als groei) en dus het aantal keuzes vergroot. Aan de andere kant leidt economische ontwikkeling, door het economiseren van de samenleving en verwaring ('commoditization'), juist tot schaarste. Overvloed leidt tot hogere aspiraties, verwaring tot ongelijkheid op internationaal en nationaal niveau - en tot uitsluiting. Op deze manier lost ontwikkeling weliswaar sommige problemen op (het aantal armen in de wereld is verminderd over de afgelopen jaren) maar het schept tegelijkertijd nieuwe problemen, onder andere gevoelens van relatieve deprivatie.

De ontwikkelingsparadox leidt dus tot de uitsluiting van individuen en groepen, die geen toegang hebben of krijgen tot economische bronnen en mogelijkheden in aansluiting op de socio-economische vooruitgang van zij die niet uitgesloten worden. Dit uitsluitingsproces is niet puur economisch van aard: het hangt samen met sociaalpolitieke, juridische en culturele factoren in een land. Uitsluiting vormt een vruchtbare bodem voor het ontstaan en voortbestaan van politieke conflicten. De uitgesloten hebben de neiging hun collectieve identiteit te benadrukken vanaf het moment dat zij zich hun uitsluiting, en hun recht op insluiting, gaan realiseren. Ruimte voor het ontstaan van gewelddadige conflicten wordt mede bepaald door de (on)mogelijkheden belangenverschillen op vreedzame wijze op te lossen. Het daadwerkelijk uitbreken van collectief geweld in een politiek conflict vereist een leider die het conflict van benutten en die de betrokken kan mobiliseren.

De geschiedenis van Sri Lanka na de onafhankelijkheid in 1948 laat een geleidelijke escalatie van politiek conflict zien. Dit conflict leidde in de jaren tachtig tot een dubbele burgeroorlog, één tussen vertegenwoordigers van Sinhala bevolking in het zuiden van het eiland en van de Tamil bevolking in het noorden, de ander tussen de post-koloniale establishment en degenen die uitgesloten dreigden te worden. De twee kanten van het politieke conflict zijn logisch geheel onafhankelijk van elkaar maar raakten synergetisch verbonden in de strijd tussen de door Sinhala gedomineerde regering (de Sinhala establishment) en de Liberation Tigers of Tamil Eelam (de uitgesloten Tamils). Het politieke conflict escaleerde in de post-koloniale oorlog in verschillende stadia: van kleine socioculturele verschillen naar verschillen in belangen, van belangenverschillen naar spanning, van spanning naar erupties van geweld - en mondde tenslotte uit in permanente burgeroorlog vanaf 1983. In het conflict het dubbele gezicht waarneembaar: het omvatte ook strijd binnen de twee etnische groepen, namelijk tussen de traditionele establishment en de radicale non-establishment: de eerste slachtoffers van de Liberation Tigers waren Tamil establishment politici.

Het politieke conflict in Sri Lanka ontwikkelde zich parallel aan de ontwikkelings paradox en uit de contradicties van het ontwikkelingsproces zelf gedurende de vijf decennia na de onafhankelijkheid. Er was gedurende die decennia een afnemende mogelijkheid om aan de stijgende verwachtingen te voldoen. De in toenemende mate competitieve samenleving, die in de koloniale tijd tot één geheel was gemaakt, expandeerde snel zowel in kwalitatieve als in kwantitatieve zin. De sleutelfactoren in de ontwikkelingsparadox zijn: (1) de aanvankelijke welvaart die tot het einde van de jaren vijftig duurde, (2) de conceptie van de Sri Lankaanse staat als 'welvaartsstaat', (3) het gebrek aan poli-

tieke discipline in de context van een pluralistisch en competitief politiek sys-
teem, en (4) economisch wanbeheer. Mede dankzij de groeiende invloed van
mondiale processen reikten de aspiraties steeds hoger, maar de economische
mogelijkheden om aan die aspiraties te voldoen namen af. Individuen en so-
ciale, etnische en regionale groepen werden in toenemende uitgesloten van
hulpbronnen en mogelijkheden zoals werk, inkomen, en onderwijs en con-
sumptiegoederen die aansloten bij hun verwachtingen. Die uitsluiting werd gebruikt door opkomende leiders om agitatie onder jongeren om te vormen tot
opstandige bewegingen – daaruit kwam de burgeroorlog voort.

De conclusie van het proefschrift is dat ontwikkelingslanden meer kans
lopen op gewelddadige politieke conflicten dan ontwikkelde landen vanwege
de contradicties in het ontwikkelingsproces zelf.